REAL
ESTATE
INVESTMENT

William R. Beaton
Florida International University, Miami

REAL

ESTATE

INVESTMENT

Prentice-Hall, Inc., Englewood Cliffs, New Jersey

PRENTICE-HALL SERIES IN REAL ESTATE

Library of Congress Catalog Card Number: 71-151510

Printed in the United States of America

13–762955–9

Current Printing (last digit):

10   9   8

PRENTICE-HALL INTERNATIONAL, INC., *London*
PRENTICE-HALL OF AUSTRALIA, PTY. LTD., *Sydney*
PRENTICE-HALL OF CANADA, LTD., *Toronto*
PRENTICE-HALL OF INDIA PRIVATE LIMITED, *New Delhi*
PRENTICE-HALL OF JAPAN, INC., *Tokyo*

To
Lillian and Robert

Preface

The purpose of this book is to present some of the basic principles and practices of investing in real estate in both practical and traditional terms. The approach is designed to assist the reader—be he investor, broker, developer, lender, property manager, or student—to become a more knowledgeable and thus a potentially more profitable investor in real estate.

Investing in real estate brings into play many factors. Among the most pertinent covered in this book are basic investment fundamentals (Chapter 1), income tax considerations (Chapters 2, 3, and 4), ownership forms for the investment (Chapter 5), financing the investment (Chapters 6 and 7), and analyzing and projecting investment returns in the traditional manner (Chapter 8).

Consideration is then given, with numerous actual case examples, to several specific types of investment properties. Land is analyzed in Chapter 9. Industrial property—including industrial parks, loft buildings, and warehouses—is studied in Chapter 10. A feasibility study of a shopping center is given in Chapter 11. The rapidly growing demand for office space and its impact on this type of investment property is presented in Chapter 12. Residential property as an investment—including apartments, condominiums, single-family houses, and mobile-home parks—is considered in Chapters 13 and 14. Further readings and references are included at the end of each chapter for readers who wish to delve more deeply into a specific subject.

Real estate is a dynamic field and changes occur quickly. This is especially true with regard to mortgage interest rates and mortgage constants. Also subject to change are income tax regulations as they affect real estate finance and investment. Operating expenses of a property seldom remain static, and investment guidelines for such items as property ad valorem taxes, labor, utilities, and maintenance are subject to continual review and updating. The attractiveness of certain types of property as investment media can and does change. The cases and examples used in this book contain figures which are current as of a given date in a given locality; inevitably, changes occur between the date of the example and the date of publication of this book. Although the figures in some instances—particularly the interest rate and constant—may not reflect market conditions at all times, the principles, techniques, and procedures of the analysis remain essentially the same. The reader need only to "plug in" current figures applicable to his particular situation.

Many persons in several geographic locations contributed to the preparation of this book: brokers, appraisers, property managers, investors, commercial bankers, mortgage bankers, executives of savings and loan associations, developers, accountants, attorneys, and my colleagues and students in the academic field. Their assistance took the form of providing practical examples from their work experience to illustrate various subjects; spending many hours in interviews discussing their respective operations; reviewing parts of the manuscript of this book and offering comments for its improvement; and freely and generously making available their time and wise counsel either in person, by telephone, or by correspondence to help answer my many questions. Sincere appreciation is extended to each of them.

Acknowledgment is made to the following: Clyde Banks, The Banks Companies, Miami, Florida; Ken Keyes, Jr., President, and Thomas J. Dixon, Analyst, Keyes National Investors, Miami; Ted Pappas, President, and Stephen T. Cox, Keyes Realty International, Inc., Miami; Realtor Edward M. Waronker, A.S.A., Miami; Thomas Gates, Amprop, Miami; Jack S. Pyms, Pyms–Suchman Real Estate Company, Kendall, Florida; E. O. Knight, President, International Realty, Inc., Ft. Lauderdale, Florida; the Honorable Phillip Pickens, M.A.I., C.P.M., Phillip Pickens Agency, Lake City, Florida; Bill Gaynier, Bill Gaynier and Associates, Realtors, Dallas, Texas; James E. Gibbons, M.A.I., C.R.E., President, Sackman–

Gilliland Corporation, Brooklyn, New York; Thomas V. Cauble, M.A.I., President, Cauble and Company, Realtors, Atlanta, Georgia; John S. Schneider, M.A.I., C.R.E., Atlanta; James Starnes, M.A.I., President, Phipps–Harrington Corporation, Atlanta; and Fred Harp, Assistant Mortgage Loan Officer, Commercial Loan Department, Citizens and Southern National Bank, Atlanta.

Acknowledgment is also made to persons who aided in the research and contributed material for the section in the book that reprints the article "The Detached-House Condominium" (pp. 255–69). In Sarasota, Florida, Realtors Paul P. Paver and Stanley D. Paver, Paver Construction Company, and Realtor Richard Traugott gave liberally of their time and knowledge in discussing and showing their respective condominium projects. Others assisting in the study were Clyde Deaux, Thomas Dixon, Steven Miller, Robert Snider, and Clayton Zehner. Editorial guidance was provided by Mrs. Warren Menke of the University of Florida, Bureau of Economic and Business Research.

Chapter 6 (Commercial Leasehold Financing) originally appeared as an article in the *Valuation* journal. Assistance in the preparation of the original article was graciously provided by Charles G. Bartenfeld, The Bartenfeld Co., Atlanta, Georgia; Thomas V. Cauble, M.A.I., Cauble and Company, Realtors, Atlanta; and L. Travis Brannon, Jr., of the law firm of Hansell, Post, Brandon, and Dorsey, Atlanta.

Professor William H. Hippaka of San Diego State College and Professor Karl G. Pearson of the University of Michigan reviewed the final manuscript for the book. Their constructive comments were of considerable assistance and appreciation is extended to each of these gentlemen. Any errors and shortcomings in the book are, of course, the sole responsibility of the author.

It is hoped that the many other persons and firms who assisted me in some manner will understand and pardon my inability to name all of them specifically in this acknowledgment. The list of contributors is long and, inevitably, in an extensive listing someone would be overlooked despite my best efforts to keep complete notes of all visits and telephone conversations during the several years this book was in preparation. So to each of them I extend my thanks and hope the finished product will justify their time given to its preparation.

Motivation and inspiration to complete this book was provided by my wife, Lillian, and my four-year-old son, Robert. The former was determined that, once the project was near completion, she was not going to let "all that work to date be wasted" by my not finishing it. The latter contributed his part by playing hard outside while Daddy worked at the typewriter. To them—my family—this book is dedicated.

William R. Beaton

Contents

Table of Cases and Examples

Chapter 4

Chapter 8

Chapter 9

Chapter 10

Chapter 11

Chapter 12

Chapter 13

Chapter 14

REAL
ESTATE
INVESTMENT

1

Real Estate Investment Fundamentals

The purpose of this chapter is to give the person who considers making an investment in real estate certain fundamentals about the field. The basis of successful investing is a knowledge of the fundamentals; everything else takes off from that point. The chapter—indeed the entire book—is based on the concept that the "investor" is a person who investigates before he invests; his decisions are made on the basis of a careful study of the facts in a given situation, backed up by a broad knowledge and understanding of the fundamentals about the commodity and its market. Some concepts and subjects appear more than once in the chapter as well as in the succeeding chapters because of their importance and application to the particular subject under consideration.

ECONOMIC SOUNDNESS

Investment in any given project or venture should be considered first and foremost from the viewpoint of the economic soundness of the project itself. Look beyond the paper figures of the proposal; all the unique financing techniques and planned income tax shelters will be of little avail for a project that is unsatisfactory and unsound at its inception. Does the project make sense—is there a market demand for the space, services, and amenities offered by it? Are its costs and values realistic and have all contingencies been considered and provided for? A "good product" is a basic essential for a successful investment.

CHANGE AND TRENDS

Investment in real estate is not made in a static environment or economy. Social, economic, physical, and political forces and influences are constantly at work, creating a climate of ever-present change and transition. Locations—region, city, neighborhood—as well as specific properties are constantly changing, often very slowly, at times rapidly. Property values are modified with change, and the investor must remember that he is looking at change—and the future—when considering a given property.

In considering change and its effect on investment decisions, the investor will be aware of various trends in the economy. Each investor will have his own ideas of what trends he watches, but all investors should consider a trend from certain common elements: the speed of the trend, its direction (up, down, sidewise), its strength, its duration, and its probable limit.

INCOME TAX CONSIDERATIONS

Federal and state (where applicable) income tax laws and regulations must be considered in *advance* of acquisition of any real estate investment. Income taxes affect nearly all real estate investments and ventures; and acquisitions, operations, and dispositions must be planned so as to obtain maximum benefits from the tax laws consistent with the objectives of the investor.

TYPICAL INCOME TAX BENEFITS

Real estate offers the investor many income tax benefits through its ownership, financing, operation, and disposition. While many of these benefits are discussed in more detail elsewhere in this book, the selected examples below provide an introductory indication of some of the wide range of possibilities open to the investor. They are certainly fundamental items to consider in a real estate investment decision.

1. *Tax-free exchange.* Real estate can be exchanged for other real estate, and tax on any gain may be postponed. This process may be repeated with many properties.

2. *Installment sale.* Gain on the sale of real estate on the installment plan may be spread out over a period of time, and the tax is also spread over each installment.

3. *Deductible loss.* Losses on the sale of real estate may be deducted from taxable income, within specified limitations.

4. *Capital gain.* Favorable tax treatment is available on real estate sold at a gain, provided certain requirements are met.

5. *Depreciation.* Deductions are permitted for depreciation of real estate improvements; these deductions are among the most important tax benefits to the investor in real estate.

6. *Ownership forms.* Real estate may be held in a variety of ownership forms and different kinds of legal interests. Each can be fitted to the individual investor's particular tax needs.

7. *Mortgage interest.* Interest on a mortgage on real estate is a deductible expense.

8. *Property taxes.* Ad valorem taxes on real estate are deductible as an expense of the property.

9. *Lease rental.* The rental on leased property is deductible by the tenant as a business expense.

10. *Improvements by tenant.* The value of improvements made by tenants is not taxed under certain conditions. When the investor sells the property he may realize the increased value because of the improvements at capital gain rates.

11. *Sale–leaseback.* The sale–leaseback permits the investor to have a current deduction for the rent paid for the ground. This in effect enables him to convert nondeductible land value into a deductible item.

12. *Involuntary conversions.* When a property is involuntarily converted, as through condemnation, there is no tax on the proceeds if the investor places them in another property with a value equal to or more than that realized on the conversion.

13. *Mortgage cash.* The investor may realize liquid funds on an increase in the value of a property by mortgaging it. The receipt of the cash is not taxed at the time, but the tax is computed when the property is ultimately sold.

14. *Repairs.* The cost of repairs, including labor, supplies, and certain other items, is a deductible expense.

15. *Investment expenses.* The investor may deduct expenditures which are ordinary and necessary for the production or collection of invest-

ment income or for the management of property held for the production of income.

GROWTH OF REAL ESTATE VALUES

It is reasonable to assume that over the long run the trend of real
estate values in general will be upward. Historically this has been true for
many years. It is also reasonable to assume that this growth will not occur
in every region or community nor will it continue at a regular pace; in fact,
there will be a decline in values in some areas and the rate of growth may
be rapid in one area but slow in another location. There are a number
of general factors which tend to support real estate values over the long
run, and the investor will consider the trends of these factors in his investment decisions.

Population Growth

The growth of population is a basic force underlying all real estate
markets. While there will be continual change in population numbers
and composition, and while growth may be slower at times than at others,
with composition changing the form of demand at times, the growth of
population pressing against a fixed supply of land will always over the
the long run be a major factor creating an upward pressure on land values.

Increased Incomes

The typical American family will undoubtedly continue to increase its
income, improve its standard of living, and have some surplus money left
over for discretionary spending. The upgrading of the living standard will
include better housing and continue existing pressures on the housing
segment of the real estate market. Further, a portion of the disposal or
surplus income should find its way into real estate investment as more
people become aware of the advantages of this form of investment and
as more opportunities are opened for the small investor, such as through
real estate investment trusts.

Leisure Time and Recreation

Increased leisure time and increased incomes mean more travel and
recreational activities for many families. These factors will accelerate the

demand for new land uses: second homes, golf courses, resorts, marinas, and a host of other real estate forms to accommodate the new leisure.

Highway Growth

New highways, particularly the interstate highway system, are opening up new land areas for development. Further, older existing highways are being modernized and widened in many locations. Highways tend to generate traffic; and where the people go land values should rise, since people make value. The traveling public also generates a demand for numerous types of roadside facilities, such as quick-food drive-in stands, gasoline service stations, and motels.

Retirement and Better Income

Many retired persons as a result of improved Social Security benefits, private pensions, and personal investments, have money to spend for real estate and are buying retirement homes. Whole communities have been developed in some parts of the country to accommodate this market. Also, medical coverage plans, both private and public, give older persons the ability to use nursing and medical services to a greater extent than previously, thus creating a demand for nursing homes and other forms of professional health services requiring investment in real estate. Older persons, too, place some of their surplus funds in real estate investment and thereby help to provide capital to sustain the demand.

Urban Renewal

The clearing of blighted sections of a community, especially in the downtown area, has opened land for new and more profitable uses. Persons and business firms displaced by urban renewal need to be relocated, thus generating a demand for land in other locations.

Historical Restoration and Scenic Preservation

In many cities the restoration of historical sections of the community has revived land values in the area and created a demand for houses, shops, and facilities catering to visitors to the area as well as to permanent residents. Closely akin to historical restoration has been the trend toward preservation of scenic areas, such as seashore, natural wildlife, and wet-lands areas. These endeavors frequently preserve and increase land values in their vicinity, particularly in light of the increased demand for recreational activity.

Suburban Trend of Industry

Industry will undoubtedly continue its trend toward locating away from the center of the city. In outlying areas larger tracts of land are available, there is less congestion, transportation facilities are readily available (especially trucking), industrial parks can be built at the metropolitan fringe, and the location is attractive to labor which frequently lives in the surrounding suburban neighborhoods. Also, the new interstate highways, expressways, and belt roads around cities are opening up new land areas for suburban industrial growth.

Education

A greater portion of the public is learning about real estate in some if not all of its ramifications: home ownership, investment benefits, land uses, and the like. This new awareness is coming about as a result of an increase in the number of articles about real estate in the news media as well as by the fact that the average person cannot help but notice the development of land uses everywhere he looks: new apartment buildings, subdivisions, office structures, shopping centers, recreational projects, and a host of other developments. These factors combined with his increased disposable income can certainly be counted as an important element increasing the demand for real estate.

VALUE PRINCIPLES AND CONCEPTS

The investor should as a part of his background knowledge of the product—real estate—and its market acquire an understanding and appreciation of certain basic principles and concepts of real estate value. This will enable him to make more intelligent investment decisions as well as better communicate with his professional counsel. The prudent investor will undoubtedly retain professional counsel for the application of these principles and concepts to a specific investment project; in fact, when a mortgage is involved, the institutional lender will normally require the use of professional real estate appraisal counsel to determine project feasibility and estimated market value.

Balance

Maximum value is found where there is a balance between the supply of a given land use and the economic demand for that use. Too many facilities of the same type—office buildings, apartments, shopping centers, and the like—in relation to demand for such facilities can mean a loss in property value to all parties. The investor should be familiar with the land use pattern in the market area in which he is considering an investment and the trend of the demand for certain land uses in that market.

Conformity

Maximum value and maximum returns tend to be created when there is a reasonable degree of homogeneity about a property—physical land use, economic, and sociological. The emphasis here is on *reasonable*, since monotonous similarity would tend to depress values.

Contribution

In spending money for the modernization or remodeling of a property the investor must be certain that the added investment is justified. The principle of contribution holds that the improvement investment should contribute an added income flow from the property large enough to cover operational costs of the improvement as well as amortization and interest costs over its economic life. The value of the project is measured by its contribution to the net return of the property.

Highest and Best Use

An investor is usually interested in seeing that land is utilized to its most profitable use. The concept of highest and best use may be defined as that legal and possible use which is most likely to produce the greatest net return to the land or to the land and building over a given period of time. A site can have only one highest and best use at a given time, and the determination of this use is an assignment for professional real estate counsel. Analysis must be made of various alternative possible uses of a given site and a study made of the influence of economic, social, and political trends on these uses over their estimated economic life.

Competition

When the net profit generated by a property—not the business profit, but that portion of the property's net income after customary expenses (labor, coordination, capital, and land)—becomes "excessive," the "excess" profit will generate ruinous competition. Competition will cause the excess profit to disappear as creation of the services exceed their demand.

Substitution

Assuming no undue and costly time delay, the upper limit of value tends to be set by the cost of acquiring an equally desirable comparable substitute property. The substitution may be made by an existing property available in the market or by the acquisition of a site and the construction of a new structure.

Change and Anticipation

As pointed out earlier in this chapter, the investor must be aware when analyzing a property that he is viewing change. Further, value is the present worth of future benefits to be derived from a property. It is the anticipation of the future benefits that is of interest to the investor and it is these benefits which make a property attractive in the market. The past is of importance to the extent that it is useful in analyzing trends.

Economic and Contract Rent

Income attributable to land under its highest and best use—when land is utilized at its most productive use—is referred to as economic rent. It is the market rent—the rent that the property will bring in the open market. Contract rent is any other amount agreed upon between tenant and owner; it is the actual rent being paid by the tenant. Economic and contract rent are the same if the property is rented at its fair market rental value. If contract rent is less than economic rent, the owner in effect transfers some of the land value to the tenant. If contract rent is greater than economic rent, the owner in effect acquires a portion of the tenant's interest (his leasehold) in the property in addition to the owner's normal interest in the land.

Bundle of Rights

The investor in real estate should remember that he is investing in more than simply physical things. His investment is really in a bundle of legal rights and interests, and the value of a property is affected by the extent to which these rights are present and whether there are any contractual limitations on them. Basic rights of ownership include possession, control, enjoyment, and disposition. Basic governmental limitations on these rights are eminent domain, police power, escheat, and taxation.

Market Value

Useful to the investor is the concept of market value, which is the starting point—or certainly one of the important criteria—for the analysis of a proposed investment. While definitions of market value vary somewhat and are under constant modification, the concept may reasonably be defined as follows: market value is the highest price estimated in terms of money which a property will bring if exposed for sale in the open market, allowing a reasonable time to find a buyer who buys with knowledge of all the uses to which it is adapted and for which it is capable of being used; also, the seller is fully informed and neither party is under undue pressure to sell or buy and both parties are willing to sell or buy.

SOURCES OF INCOME AND GAIN

A real estate investment has the potential of generating a yield from a number of sources. The total profit from the investment depends in part on its financial structure and the degree of leverage possible; in part on the investor's handling of certain income tax alternatives, such as selection of depreciation methods; and in part on the ownership form in which the investment is held, such as individual, partnership, or corporate, and the variations of these forms.

Traditional Yield

When an investor speaks of the "yield" from an income-producing property, he is traditionally referring to its net income after meeting vacancy and collection loss allowances, all operating expenses of the property, and a deduction for debt service (principal and interest payments on the mortgage). The resulting "cash flow" is usually expressed as a percentage of the investor's equity in the property. Some investors also deduct the income tax on the property income from the cash flow before computing the property yield.

Appreciation Gain

An increase in the value of the property over and above the investor's initial investment is a further source of gain. This gain is not realized until ultimate disposition of the property by the investor.

Income Tax Saving

An additional return or gain is possible through certain income tax deductions. Depreciation deductions, for example, can "shelter" the traditional yield from income tax as well as generate a tax-loss deduction to apply against other income of the investor, thereby reducing his taxes.

Mortgage Amortization

As the investor pays off the mortgage on the property, the principal portion of the payments increases his equity in the property. This periodic reduction of the mortgage and the resulting build-up of equity may be considered as an additional return on the investment. The cumulative equity build-up is realized upon the ultimate disposition of the property, such as by its sale. Or, the existing mortgage may be refinanced for a larger amount and the investor may realize some of his accumulated equity in this manner. It is assumed that the property will maintain its value.

CHARACTERISTICS OF THE ASSET AND ITS MARKET

In dealing with any investment, the better the knowledge the investor has of its features and the market in which it is bought and sold, the greater should be his ability to make a sound analysis and decision in a given situation. Real estate as a capital asset has certain attributes of any investment; it also has its own unique features. The real estate market operates within the framework of the general financial market and is subject to its influences; it also has market characteristics of its own. Consideration is given below to certain physical, legal, and economic characteristics of real estate and its market.

1. Real estate is geographically fixed in location; the land is immobile and improvements usually cannot be moved economically. This fixity of location tends to restrict the scope of the real estate market, making it more or less local in character. Real estate must attract income and a market to its particular location; it is not able to move about to the most desirable market as can other goods and services. Detailed information about individual properties must usually be acquired from local sources, such as real estate brokers. The quantity and quality of the data can vary considerably, and it is reasonable to assume that data weaknesses and limitations narrow participation in the real estate market as compared with markets for other goods and services for which reliable and comprehensive data is readily available on a national basis. Fixity of location also means that real estate is directly subject to its immediate environment. Factors affecting the area in which a property is located will affect investment decisions, either favorably or adversely. The value of a property is greatly influenced by factors outside the property itself, indeed more so than by factors originating within the property. Fixity of location also makes real estate easily subject to taxation and various forms of local regulation.

2. Each parcel of real estate is different from all others; there are no two pieces of real estate exactly alike. This individuality or nonhomogeneity means that investment decisions must be related to a specific location and the property must be analyzed in terms of its specific features in that location. It is hazardous to be "general" or to rely too heavily on "rules of thumb" or to make decisions on what others have done with "similar" properties. Study the individual property before investing! Uniqueness of properties also makes comparison difficult and limits the development of a standardized trade vocabulary.

3. Real estate is usually considered to be a long-term or long-life asset. The land is physically permanent; it is durable and indestructible. Buildings and other improvements on the land have a longer physical life than most other assets. Once land, particularly urban land, is committed to a given use, it is seldom feasible to change that use for a number of years.

4. Real estate typically involves units of large size, both physically and financially. Individual parcels have a high dollar value and transactions can involve financing arrangements which are complex and expensive. Such a characteristic is one factor accounting for the existence of the real estate business—a business needed to bring these large physical and economic units together with buyers and sellers in the marketplace; also, a

business needed to provide professional management and valuation services for the units. The large size of the units can be a limitation upon participation by investors in the market. However, the large dollar value along with fixity of location does make real estate an attractive asset for the mortgage lender and at the same time gives the investor a desirable medium for creating financial leverage.

5. The real estate market is seldom in balance as to demand and supply and is slow to make adjustment to changes in the marketplace. The supply of real estate is relatively fixed and inflexible. Properties have a long life, and the additions to the total supply each year are few. Many properties are annually removed from the supply through deterioration, demolitions, and destruction by hazards such as fire. Supply cannot be adjusted quickly when demand decreases or increases. It takes time to construct new properties; existing properties constitute part of the total supply, even if they are not used.

Predicting demand is surrounded with uncertainty. Demand for real estate is based upon a wide variety of factors: incomes, credit, population, governmental actions, tastes and preferences, costs savings, taxation, and the like. Some of these factors can cause a sudden change in the demand for certain types of real estate, such as a change in consumer tastes for recreation; other factors can have a long-range depressing effect on the market, such as a change in the pattern of savings flow or a change in government monetary policy. The significance to the investor of this imbalance of supply and demand lies in the fact that such a condition makes a real estate investment a higher risk venture than one in a field where the market is more predictable. This greater risk factor must be compensated for in computing the rate of return necessary to attract an investor to a given project.

6. There is no centrally organized and controlled real estate market. The "market" is in reality simply a combination of local markets; there is no national market as is found in the securities market. Not only are markets geographically local, but there are markets for each type of property, such as the market for apartment houses, for shopping centers, or for warehouses.

Further disorganization is created by the lack of a standardized commodity and the usual confidential climate in which transactions in the commodity are conducted. The uniqueness of real estate requires an analysis by the investor of each parcel before committing his capital. It also means that there can be no substitution of one parcel for another; that is, legally there must be "specific performance"—delivery by the seller of one specific commodity at a given location. As pointed out earlier, uniqueness also makes a standardized trade vocabulary difficult to develop; terms and descriptions may not be applicable to all properties or have the same meaning to all parties. A smoothly functioning market demands a commonly used and recognized vocabulary.

The confidential climate in which most real estate transactions are conducted tends to limit the amount of information available on which investment decisions can be based. Seldom is complete and comprehensive data readily available on all transactions in a given area at a given time. Courthouse recordings are of some help, as are data available from credit reporting services and real estate brokers, but these are for the most part limited and sketchy. There is no comprehensive central data bank for all real estate transactions.

Adding to the disorganization of the market is the fact that the supply of properties is delivered by a wide variety of suppliers acting for the most part on intuition and "experience" rather than any intensive research of the market. Single-family housing supply is provided largely by small independent contractors with little or no formal research activity into the market supply-and-demand situation. Commercial and industrial properties are created more by larger organizations which, particularly with large projects, retain professional consultants for market studies. But even here, much of the supply is provided by small builders either speculatively or on contract without much thought to the ability of the market to absorb the space over the long run.

7. Real estate and the real estate market are greatly influenced by government at all levels—federal, state, and local. The ad valorem property tax is a major consideration in investment decisions; the tax burden on real estate has a direct effect on its value. Governmental financial regulations and programs have a heavy influence, particularly in the field of real estate finance. Government continues to be the largest real estate owner through its ownership of such assets as national and state parks, highways, public buildings, reservations, and military facilities. Government subsidies in various forms can influence real estate values and decisions: urban renewal projects; tax exemptions to some classes of property, such as churches, educational institutions, and foundations; and governmental housing and finance programs which offer terms more favorable than available in the private sector of the market.

OBJECTIVE AND CAPABILITIES

Before embarking upon any investment, it is fundamental that the investor decide: (1) What are his objectives or goals—what does he want to accomplish by making an investment? and (2) Does he have the capabilities, both economic and noneconomic, to carry through with the chosen objectives? Once a decision has been made as to these two basic factors, he is then ready to seek a property to match them.

Investment incentives and motives vary with the individual investor and his needs and desires, and one investor may have several objectives at the same time. Objectives may vary over time and the investment portfolio must be reviewed and revised periodically in accordance with any changed objectives or conditions. Objectives generally find their origin in the widely recognized merits of real estate as an investment; it is to these factors that attention is given below.

Investment Advantages

Pride of Ownership

The ownership and possession of a unique visual asset can be a strong motive for acquisition of real estate. People like to own real estate because of the status such ownership confers to the holder. This goal may be primary or, as is probably more often the case, it may be an attraction along with economic benefits derived from a real estate investment.

Personal Control

Real estate can give the investor an opportunity to exercise a degree of direct personal control over his investment, a control usually not available in other investment forms, such as securities. He can be the boss—direct personal decision maker—over his asset rather than having the decision making function delegated to a board of directors or a group of trustees.

Investment for Use

An investor may acquire a parcel of real estate for his own use and consumption, such as for conducting a business. Such an investor–user would probably have different expectations concerning the property than a person acquiring primarily for investment yield and profit.

Estate-building

Real estate offers an attractive way to build an estate. As the mortgage is reduced, the amortization of the principal builds up the investor's equity in the property. The property may then be clear of any indebtedness when the investor retires, and he will also enjoy a good cash flow at a time when he is also probably in a lower tax bracket. During the early years of the property ownership the tax shelter would have been of benefit to the investor.

In addition to a free and clear income from his estate upon retirement, any appreciation or enhancement in the capital value of the property during the years of ownership may receive favorable tax treatment in the event that the property is disposed of either through sale, exchange, or inheritance. A sale of the property may be eligible for capital gain benefits. An exchange may be tax-free. Or, if the property is passed on to heirs, they may receive the property at its then-current market value and there is no tax on the appreciation in value. The estate is subject to the appropriate federal estate tax and any state inheritance tax.

The tax-free exchange is the basis of the technique known as "pyramiding." This is an estate-building technique by which an investor's equity in a small parcel of property is used to acquire a larger property. When a person pyramids his investment in the smaller property by exchanging it for a larger property, there is no capital gains tax imposed on the transaction at that time.

High Yield

The before-tax yields on real estate investments are generally higher than for other investment outlets. Prime real estate will yield a before-tax return on total investment, including equity and debt, of from 8 to 15 percent. Speculative real estate will show yields of up to 25 percent or more. Also, through leases the investor is able to obtain a reasonably certain return with a minimum of risk. To the "investment" yield may also be added the profit from the mortgage amortization as well as any tax savings.

While such yields are attractive and constitute a major objective of investment in real estate, some investors consider the true measure and objective of the investment the ability to "leverage" the yield to an unusually high degree and then shelter the return from income taxes. The effect is to increase the after-tax yield.

Leverage

Real estate is probably the most desirable kind of leverage investment, which is possibly its major attraction. Leverage refers to a situation whereby property is acquired with as little of the buyer's own cash as possible and as much as possible of the purchase price is borrowed. The objective is to increase the rate of return on the cash invested. Through the use of other people's money, a large investment may be controlled with only a small amount of equity capital, and a small cash outlay can return a substantial profit. Leverage and financing are key factors in most real estate investments. Most if not all of the large fortunes in real estate have been created through the interplay of these two factors operating within the framework of federal income tax laws and a growing economy. A detailed discussion of leverage, including its limitations, is found in Chapter 8.

Depreciation

Depreciation is the magic word in real estate investing and is a major—indeed, often a decisive—factor in investment decisions. Depreciation deductions can provide a tax-free return of the investment. It provides a tax shelter unavailable to the investor in securities. It covers the usually taxable principal payments on a mortgage in that there is a tax-free cash flow to the extent that depreciation exceeds the principal or amortization payments.

Capital Gain

Capital gain is often the prime objective of an investor in real estate; indeed, the ability to sell a property at a gain is a sufficient objective in itself, and the yield from the property may be of little or no interest. Long-term appreciation in value, when realized upon disposition, may receive favorable tax treatment: the tax rate on the capital gain is a maximum of 25 percent of the gain. Also, the investor may exchange the property for another tax-free and save the capital gains tax for investment in additional real estate.

Inflation Hedge

Real estate may provide a degree of hedge against the effects of inflation—that is, protection against loss in the purchasing power of the dollar. Undoubtedly, government efforts to control inflation will continue, but investors generally anticipate that some degree of inflation has become a permanent way of life. Real estate incomes and values tend to rise with inflationary trends. But it must be remembered that each parcel of real estate is a unit in itself and at a specific location. The degree to which a given parcel will be affected by inflation and provide the investor with a hedge will depend upon numerous factors as to that particular property.

Tax Shelter

As pointed out earlier, tax considerations enter into all real estate investment decisions. Tax shelter is a major attraction of real estate and is frequently the major objective of the investor, particularly those in a high-income tax bracket. In fact, the tax shelter created by depreciation is considered by some investors to rank second only to financial leverage as an attraction of real estate. The large profits realized through high leverage can now be shielded from the payment of income tax. The shelter is created because, under the Internal Revenue Code, the depreciation allowances are deductible expenses even though the allowances do not require an actual outlay of cash. Further, the depreciation allowance is based upon the total cost (or other "basis") of the improvements (land is not depreciable). It includes not only the investor's equity in the improvements, which is usually small, but any mortgage debt as well, which is usually heavy. The amount of down payment invested in the property has no effect upon the allowance for depreciation.

The payment on the mortgage principal, which is not deductible for income tax purposes, does require a cash outlay. Therefore, to the extent that the depreciation deduction exceeds nondeductible mortgage amortization payments in a given year, taxable income is less than cash income from the project and the excess income is a tax-free return on the property.

Another way to view the concept of tax shelter is to consider it as the tax savings possibly made possible by the depreciation deduction allowed by the Internal Revenue Code. Accelerated depreciation methods will during the first 5 to 7 years of ownership not only shelter or offset the net operating income from the property but will usually exceed this income. The excess is a paper loss for tax purposes.

Investment Disadvantages

The investor must also keep in mind the fact that real estate may have some limitations as an investment medium. The degree to which each is important will depend upon the individual investor. Generally, the advantages of real estate as an investment heavily outweigh the few claimed disadvantages. Among the latter are the following:

1. Real estate as a physical asset *does* incur depreciation of a real nature —that is, other than the income tax allowance deduction which is an accounting write-off rather than an actual decline in value. Actual loss in value can occur from three sources of depreciation: physical deterioration, functional obsolescence, and economic or locational obsolescence. Appropriate reserves should be created and maintained out of the income from the property to provide for normal maintenance and replacements.
2. Adequate allowance must be made for possible loss of income due

to vacancies in the building. Property seldom remains 100 percent rented over long periods of time, except possibly commercial and industrial properties under long-term net leases.

3. Real estate must be managed if it is to yield maximum benefits and maintain or improve its capital value over a given period of time. It is not an investment for the lazy man. The management function can be performed by either the investor himself or by a professional management service retained for the purpose. But the property must be managed and proper allowance for "management" made in the expense statement for the property. Further, the investor will want an appropriate rate included for management of the investment portfolio in developing or building up the capitalization rate necessary to attract his capital to the investment.

4. Real estate may not be as quickly or easily converted into cash (liquidity) without undue loss of capital value as, say, securities. There is, however, always a market for good real estate—provided the seller recognizes the fair market value of the property and is willing to accept it. Too frequently the claimed disadvantage of nonliquidity is based upon the inability of an investor to dispose of a property at an unrealistic price.

CAPABILITIES

Once the objectives of the investor are determined, it is then necessary to ascertain his ability to realize them. The objectives must be realistic and the investor must accept a realistic evaluation of his capacity to achieve them. Too frequently, particularly in the case of the small or nonprofessional investor, emotions can become the controlling influence over an investment decision, with sound financial judgment laid aside. Financial overcommitment to a project or venture can lead to bankruptcy. The investor should consider his capabilities from several points of view:

1. Is he capable, both psychologically and financially, of living with the commitment of large sums of money—debt and equity—to a project over an extended period of time, in an uncertain future? (Remember that while real estate yields are now trending upward and appreciation in values is expected to continue, there is no guarantee that they will continue to do so.)

2. Does the investor have sufficient cash reserves on hand to provide for contingencies requiring a future need for cash?

3. Is the investor willing to seek out and utilize professional advice in handling his investments?

4. Has the investor previously owned real estate? What types? Was the experience successful? (Investors seldom cover the entire spectrum of properties but usually concentrate their attention in relatively narrow areas. Apartment house investors, for example, seldom invest in industrial properties, although their interests may include a few commercial projects, such as small office buildings.) ·

KINDS OF INVESTMENT PROPERTIES

Real estate offers a wide range of properties for investment outlets. No one classification or listing can encompass the total diversity because of the numerous possible variations of ownership and the uniqueness of each property. The classification which follows will give an idea of the broad spectrum of property types open to the investor. Individual consideration is given to several of the property types in later chapters.

Industrial	*Recreational*
Industrial parks	Golf driving ranges
Warehouses	Miniature golf courses
Factories	Camp sites
	Marinas
Franchise	Hunting preserves
Auto laundries	Travel trailer parks
Short-order restaurants	Theaters
	Bowling alleys
Commercial	Drive-in theaters
	Golf courses
Gas service stations	Target practice ranges
Truck stops	Baseball batting ranges
Shopping centers	
Parking lots and garages	*Residential Income-Producing*
Airport concessions	
	Hotels and motels
Office	Resort lodges
	Low- and high-rise apartments
Office parks	Nursing homes
Professional buildings	Mobile home parks
High-rise office buildings	College dormitories
	Cooperatives
Land	Condominiums
Raw acreage	
Scattered lots	
Farms, ranches, and groves	
Recreational acreage	

RATING FACTORS FOR INVESTMENTS IN GENERAL

The investor in real estate should be familiar with the factors used to rate any investment. Such knowledge will enable him to compare investment mediums while aiding him to make a sound analysis of a specific proposed real estate investment.

There are four commonly recognized basic features to weigh in any investment: risk, appreciation, liquidity, and management. Also to be considered is the impact of inflation and taxation.

Risk

Every investment involves a degree of risk; there is no such thing as a completely riskless investment. Risk refers to the possibility that the investor will lose his capital sum invested in the property. Investors also tend to think of it as including the quantity, quality, and durability of the income stream from the property. What is the amount of the income? What is the reliability of its source? How long is it expected to continue? The return from an investment will vary directly with the degree of risk.

Liquidity

Liquidity refers to the degree to which an investor can readily and quickly obtain cash for his investment, either through a sale in the open market or by obtaining a loan with the property as security. To what extent can the market value of the investment be obtained without undue loss?

Appreciation

To what extent does the investment have potential for growth or appreciation in value? The return on an investment can be in the form of the income stream as well as the profit or gain to be realized at the time of its disposition.

Management

Any investment requires management. This function may be performed by the investor himself, or he may retain professional management. Management of the investment portfolio must be compensated regardless of who performs it. An allowance must be made for this cost in weighing an investment decision.

Also certain to have an influence upon any investment medium are the factors of inflation and taxation. The income stream from an investment and its potential appreciation in value must be viewed in terms of their true purchasing power in the future. As for taxes, investors in all categories recognize that government is a silent partner in every transaction and that the income stream and appreciation gains are both subject to taxation, though in various ways and with different consequences.

OWNERSHIP FORMS

The real estate investor must decide in advance of any acquisition what is the best form of ownership—the legal entity—for his investment consistent with his objectives and capabilities. There are a variety of types of ownership and each can have different legal and tax consequences. Listed below are the more commonly utilized ownership forms; several will be considered separately in Chapter 5.

Individual
Joint tenancy
Tenancy in common
Partnership—general and limited
Corporation
Joint venture
Syndicate
Real estate investment trust

DISPOSITION

Advance planning is necessary if a real estate investment is to be disposed of with the maximum benefit to the investor consistent with his objectives and overall investment program. Planning for disposition should begin prior to acquisition, since the form of ownership can affect the disposition results, particularly the tax consequences.

FUNDAMENTALS AND ADVANCE PLANNING

Two basic ingredients make up the successful investor: first, a learning—and a relearning—of the fundamentals of the field in which the investor is involved. In this instance it is the basics of real estate economics, real estate finance, principles of real property value, financial analysis, and fundamental economic trends. As pointed out at the beginning of this chapter, everything springs from the fundamentals—the tax plans, the get-rich-quick angles, and the unusual financing techniques.

The second ingredient, which is really a fundamental also, is investigation and advance planning—with professional counsel. A real estate investment should not be a "do-it-yourself" project. The complexity of real estate as a commodity—its physical, economic, and legal characteristics—along with the unique features of its market should make obvious the need for advance planning and competent guidance. Professional counsel is available: legal, tax, accounting, financial, architectural, market analysis, engineering, real estate, and economic. Use it—both before and after you invest and when you are ready to dispose of your investment.

Further Readings and References

Beaton, William R. "Corporate Investment in Real Estate," *Economic Leaflets*, February, 1969. Gainesville, Florida: Bureau of Economic and Business Research, College of Business Administration, University of Florida, 1969.

Brown, Robert Kevin. *Real Estate Economics*. Boston: Houghton Mifflin Company, 1965.

Casey, William J. *Real Estate Investment Planning*. Looseleaf. New York: Institute for Business Planning, Inc., 1965.

Hanford, Lloyd D. *Development and Management of Investment Property*. Second Edition. Chicago: Institute of Real Estate Management of the National Association of Real Estate Boards, 1968.

Kahn, Sanders A., and Frederick E. Case, and Alfred Schimmel. *Real Estate Appraisal and Investment*. New York: The Ronald Press Company, 1963.

Ratcliff, Richard U. *Real Estate Analysis*. New York: McGraw-Hill Book Company, Inc., 1961.

Schraub, Edgar D. *What You Must Know Before You Invest*. Englewood Cliffs, N. J.: Prentice-Hall, Inc., 1968.

Weimer, Arthur M., and Homer Hoyt. *Real Estate*. Fifth Edition. New York: The Ronald Press Company, 1966.

Wendt, Paul F., and Alan R. Cerf. *Real Estate Investment Analysis and Taxation*. New York: McGraw-Hill Book Company, Inc., 1969.

2

Depreciation

Depreciation is a major and often decisive factor in real estate investment decisions. Indeed, obtaining the "tax shelter" provided by the depreciation deduction is frequently the sole objective of some investors. It is not the purpose of this chapter (or of any of the chapters of this book dealing with accounting and tax matters) to present a comprehensive treatise on the many complex accounting and tax ramifications of a subject. Rather, the purpose is to survey the highlights of its features and its "workings" rather than the "mechanics," so that the investor may understand and appreciate the significance of the subject to his investment planning and the need to consult competent professional counsel before he acts in a given situation.

THE CONCEPT—ECONOMIC DEPRECIATION
VS. TAX DEPRECIATION

This chapter is concerned with depreciation in a tax or accounting sense as contrasted with depreciation in an economic sense; the distinction between the two is important for a proper understanding of each. Economic depreciation is actual loss in value of an asset. This loss in value may be caused by several factors: physical deterioration through normal use and exposure to the elements; functional obsolescence; or changes in the environment of the property due to forces outside of it, such as a decline of the neighborhood.

Tax depreciation is a statutory concept which permits the recovery of the cost or other basis of an asset over its useful life to the individual taxpayer. It is an accounting procedure concept which may not have any relation to the actual depreciation of the property. It is a cost recovery provision for tax purposes, and the amount recovered in any one year may bear no relation to any true depreciation for that year.

WHO MAY DEDUCT

Generally, the depreciation deduction allowance may be claimed by any individual or taxable entity, such as a corporation, that has a legal or equitable proprietary interest in the property, that has a capital investment in it, and that will bear any economic loss. A real capital investment in the property is essential; bare legal title alone does not in itself permit a depreciation deduction. Where ownership of the property is divided, such as in a trust or estate or by tenancy in common or joint tenancy, the depreciation deduction must be apportioned or allocated among the parties.

DEPRECIABLE PROPERTY

Not all property is subject to depreciation allowance for tax purposes. Property must meet certain qualifications if it is to be eligible for the depreciation deduction: (1) it must have a definitely limited and determinable useful life, and (2) it must be used in the taxpayer's trade or business or held for the production of income. Real estate excluded from depreciation deductions would be land, residential property, and property held for sale to customers in the regular course of business. Therefore, no depreciation is permitted on a taxpayer's residence or on property making up his business inventory. Since land does not have a limited useful life but is considered to be indestructible and exist in perpetuity, no depreciation is allowed on it.

ANNUAL ALLOWANCE

The depreciation allowance is an annual "allowable" deduction and must be taken as such; an omission in the year allowed cannot be made up in later years. Also, the basis of property must be reduced for the depreciation allowable regardless of whether or not it was actually taken when allowed or whether there was any tax benefit to be derived from the allowance or deduction. Failure to take the deduction allowable in a prior year will not prevent the taxpayer from taking the proper depreciation deduction allowable in a later year. But the taxpayer is not permitted to omit taking allowable depreciation in prior years and then claim an accumulated deduction in a later year. Failure to claim depreciation for a given year results in a loss of that amount which should have been claimed; no deferment is permitted.

ALLOCATION OF LUMP SUM PURCHASE PRICE

As stated earlier in this chapter, land is not depreciable for tax purposes, while improvements generally are subject to the depreciation allowance. Therefore, when a parcel of property is acquired which contains both land and building, the acquisition cost must be allocated between the land and the building or improvements. The depreciation allowance is limited to an amount bearing the same proportion to the lump sum price that the fair market value of the depreciable property at the time of acquisition bears to the fair market value of the entire property at that time. It is necessary, therefore, to determine the market value of the entire property as a whole and then the market value of the depreciable part of the whole.

An allocation may be set forth in the contract of sale between buyer and seller in a real estate transaction. The allocation, however, must be reasonable and made as a matter of objective and arm's-length negotiations between the parties. Otherwise, it may not be acceptable if questioned by the tax authorities.

SALVAGE VALUE

Salvage value is the amount estimated to be received from the property when it is sold or otherwise disposed of at the end of its useful life. It is not necessarily junk or scrap value; it is an estimate of the future value of the property after the taxpayer has ceased using it—that is, an estimate of the proceeds the property would bring at the conclusion of its useful life to the taxpayer.

Salvage value is estimated at the time of acquisition of the property by the taxpayer and must be taken into consideration in determining the annual depreciation deduction, except for the declining balance method of computation. Generally, property cannot be depreciated below its salvage value. The estimated salvage value cannot be changed to reflect fluctuations in price levels. If the useful life of the asset is redetermined, however, the salvage value may also be appropriately changed to conform to conditions existing at the time of the change. Also, if there is a substantial difference between the estimated salvage value and actual salvage value at the end of the useful life of the property, an appropriate adjustment may be made in the computation.

Salvage value is deducted from the cost basis (usually the purchase price) of the property before computing the annual depreciation allowance. There is no deduction from basis when the declining balance method of depreciation is used, because this method will leave an undepreciated balance at the end of the useful life of the property. This amount is considered to be the salvage value, assuming it is reasonable.

USEFUL LIFE

The period of time over which an asset can be depreciated for tax purposes is referred to as its "useful life" and is an essential element in the determination of the amount of the annual depreciation deduction. Useful life is not necessarily the actual physical life of the asset, and the concept does not measure actual physical deterioration. Useful life is the period of time over which the asset can be expected to be useful to a particular taxpayer in his trade or business or in the production of income.

Useful life is a matter of judgment for each individual taxpayer; there is no fixed average useful life that can apply to all property. Each case is one of fact for that particular situation. Factors to consider include the age of the property when acquired; the amount of use given the property; climatic and other local conditions; the taxpayer's policy as to repair, renewals, and replacement; his past experience with similar property; wear and tear or decay and decline from natural causes; the normal rate of economic change in the industry; and current developments.

A guideline of useful lives for many commercial and industrial properties has been published by the U. S. Treasury Department to aid the taxpayer in determining a useful life. These depreciation guidelines, unfortunately, are not really suitable for a real estate situation, and their use for buildings has been limited.

Also, a written agreement may be entered into with the Treasury Department covering the useful life, depreciation rate, and handling of any salvage. The agreement is binding on both parties and is useful to avoid later questioning concerning these aspects of the property. Any later changes must be supported by new facts not considered when the original agreement was made.

METHODS OF DEPRECIATION

There are three commonly used methods of depreciation: straight-line, declining balance, and sum-of-the-years-digits. Each has its merits and limitations and must be used by the taxpayer according to his particular objectives and situation. A brief coverage of the workings of each is given here, followed by a comparison of the methods and their results.

STRAIGHT-LINE. The cost or other basis of the property, less any estimated salvage value, is deducted in equal annual installments over the estimated useful life of the property. The rate of depreciation is a constant annual figure. The method may be used on any depreciable tangible property, new or used, regardless of its useful life and its date of acquisition.

DECLINING BALANCE. A constant or uniform annual rate, which may be up to double the straight-line rate, is applied to the remaining (or unrecovered or undepreciated) cost basis of the property each year. Salvage value is not deducted from the cost basis in making the computation. A balance representing salvage value will remain when the property is fully depreciated.

The declining balance method is commonly referred to as the "double declining balance" method, or the "200 percent rate" method, because the maximum rate permitted (double the straight-line rate) is usually used. Application of this method is as follows: determine the straight-line rate that would be used; double this rate; apply it against the remaining cost basis of the property each year. The depreciation amount decreases each year; the largest deduction is taken in the first year, when the rate is applied to the full cost basis of the property. It then declines each year thereafter until it eventually becomes very small.

The property is not written off over its estimated useful life under the declining balance method. It is not permissible to write off the unde-preciated balance in the last year of the original life expectancy, but this balance can be written off upon the sale of the property. Also, the property may be depreciated until it is exhausted if the taxpayer continues to use it. It is possible to change from the double declining balance method to the straight-line method so as to avoid this inequity. The year of change should be carefully determined so that it is made in the proper year; otherwise, property might not be exhausted over its estimated useful life.

SUM-OF-THE-YEARS-DIGITS. The cost of the property, less its estimated salvage value, is computed. A fraction is then determined. The numerator of the fraction (the top number) for each year is the number of remaining years of the useful life of the property. The denominator (bottom number) is the sum of the digits of all the years in the useful life. The numerator changes each year while the denominator remains constant. This changing fraction is applied each year to the same original basis—that is, cost less estimated salvage value.

OTHER METHODS. There are other methods of depreciation. Any method recognized in accounting practice is satisfactory for tax purposes. Once a method is elected, however, it must be used consistently.

TAX REFORM ACT OF 1969

The Federal Tax Reform Act of 1969 includes provisions directly affect-ing depreciation on real property. New real property subject to depreciation, except for new residential rental property, is no longer eligible for the double declining balance method or the sum-of-the-years-digits method unless, before July 5, 1969, either of two situations existed: (1) construc-tion of the property had physically started, or (2) a binding written commit-ment was in effect for the permanent financing of the property or a similar contract existed for the construction of the building. The 150 percent de-clining balance method is applicable to real property, except for residential.

The double declining balance method and the sum-of-the-years-digits method are still available to new residential rental real property. The 125 percent declining balance method is available for used residential rental real property acquired after July 24, 1969, provided the remaining life of the building is 20 years or more. Only the straight-line method may be used if the remaining life of the building is less than 20 years.

The straight-line method is applicable to all other used real property acquired after July 24, 1969, and *only* the straight-line method may be used with such property. The 150 percent declining balance method, formerly available to used property, may be applied to any used real property acquired after July 24, 1969, if it was subject to a binding written contract for acquisition or permanent financing as of that date.

Residential rental property is a property in which at least 80 percent of the gross rents are obtained from residential units, such as an apartment building designed to provide living accommodations. The building must not be a motel or hotel or such an establishment where more than one-half of the units are occupied on a transient basis.

The following table illustrates the basic methods of computing depreciation. The table assumes a parcel of depreciable real property costing the investor $10,000.00 and a useful life of 10 years. Salvage value is not considered in order to simplify the illustration, although it must be remembered that salvage value must be taken into consideration in the straight-line method and sum-of-the-years-digits method.

Year	Straight-Line	Double Declining Balance	150% Declining Balance	Sum-of-Years-Digits
1	$ 1,000.00	$2,000.00	$1,500.00	$ 1,818.18
2	1,000.00	1,600.00	1,275.00	1,636.36
3	1,000.00	1,280.00	1,084.00	1,454.55
4	1,000.00	1,024.00	921.00	1,272.73
5	1,000.00	819.00	783.00	1,090.94
6	1,000.00	655.00	666.00	909.09
7	1,000.00	524.00	566.00	727.27
8	1,000.00	420.00	481.00	545.45
9	1,000.00	336.00	409.00	363.64
10	1,000.00	268.00	347.00	181.82
	$10,000.00	$8,926.00	$8,632.00	$10,000.00

COMPARISON OF DEPRECIATION METHODS

The declining balance and sum-of-the-years-digits methods of depreciation are commonly referred to as "accelerated" or "rapid" depreciation. Neither method permits any larger total recovery than the investment in the property, but both methods provide for greater annual deductions in the earlier years of the life of a property and smaller deductions in the later years than does the straight-line method.

As between the double-declining balance method and the sum-of-the-years-digits method, the former gives the greater amount of depreciation in the first year but the lesser amount starting with the second year and thereafter. The sum-of-the-years-digits method gives the greater annual deduction starting with the second year. The declining balance method does not permit full recovery of cost (without a change to the straight-line method) over the useful life of the property, whereas the sum-of-the-years-digits method does result in such full recovery.

The amount of unrecovered cost under the declining balance method may be reduced by changing to the straight-line method. The switch could be made when the straight-line method would give a larger depreciation deduction over the remaining useful life of the property than would a continuance of the declining balance method. The coordination between the two methods should be carefully considered and planned if maximum advantage is to be obtained from the change. Salvage value, for instance, is a major consideration which affects the decision as to the year to make the change. It is necessary to estimate the salvage value at the time of the change, taking into consideration current conditions, and then to deduct this salvage value from the remaining undepreciated basis of the property. Therefore, a change might be made earlier if the salvage value is minimal, or later if the amount is large.

The accelerated or rapid depreciation methods permit the investor to take increased deductions in the early life of the property, resulting in a reduced taxable income and reduced tax payments. Whether such a result is of benefit to a taxpayer depends upon his individual situation. The increased income (due to the larger depreciation deductions) can mean additional working capital, which might be an immediate need or desire. A growing business could use this additional money for expansion; or the funds could be used for investment in other income-producing property; or the funds could be applied to any mortgage on the property and increase the equity build-up if this is desirable. It may be that the investor has no other substantial income to offset at present, and large deductions would not be of much use to him; the straight-line method, with its constant deduction, may be the one to use in this situation.

Depreciation deductions reduce the basis of the property and, when the property is sold, the gain on the sale is the difference between the reduced basis and the sales price. If the property is sold in its early years—say, at the end of 5 years—the accelerated depreciation results in an additional amount of gain realized on the sale. The gain, however, is taxed as a capital gain in the case of real property held for more than 6 months and held for the production of income or used in the taxpayer's trade or business. The taxpayer has in effect converted ordinary income into capital gain. Accelerated depreciation has enabled him to take larger deductions against ordinary income in prior years and then to convert this added income into capital gains when the property is sold.

BONUS OR EXTRA FIRST-YEAR DEPRECIATION

In addition to regular depreciation, a taxpayer may elect to deduct an extra 20 percent of the cost of tangible personal property, such as machinery and equipment, in the year of its acquisition. While the special deduction does not apply to real estate, it may be utilized by real estate investors. A large part of the investment in a building may be made up of items of tangible personal property. A motel or hotel, for example, may contain a considerable amount of equipment not considered as a part of the realty, such as furniture, individual air-conditioning units, and refrigerators. Treasury Department regulations, and not local law, govern whether an item of equipment is a fixture and part of the realty or whether it is personalty.

The tangible personal property must have a remaining useful life of 6 years or more when acquired and have been acquired after December 31, 1957. It may be either new or used property. The allowance is limited to 20 percent of $10,000, or to 20 percent of $20,000 in the case of a joint return. That is, the maximum extra deduction is $2,000 on a separate return and $4,000 on a joint return. The additional write-off must be elected by the taxpayer on his return and is available only in the first year of acquisition of the property. The special deduction is allowed in full even though the property is acquired during the year. It is computed without reference to salvage value, but the basis of the property must be reduced by the amount of the extra allowance taken plus the salvage value (except in the declining balance method) in computing the regular depreciation under the usual method selected by the taxpayer.

The bonus depreciation is not available on property acquired through inheritance from a decedent or as a gift. Also, a trust is not eligible for the deduction, nor are certain transactions between relatives as set forth in the income tax regulations. Certain other transactions between "controlled" groups, such as a stockholder and a corporation under his control, are not eligible. Many technical rules apply and competent counsel is needed as always.

DEPRECIATION RECAPTURE

Accelerated depreciation taken on qualified real estate reduces the investor's taxable income each year. When the real estate is sold, presumably at a profit, the investor pays a lower long-term capital gain tax on the gain from the sale. The investor has in effect converted ordinary income into capital gain. This ability to recover ordinary depreciation deductions as a capital gain when the property is sold is a major feature of real estate as an investment.

There are, however, certain tax law limitations upon the investor's ability to convert ordinary income into capital gain via the depreciation route. The law (Section 1250 of the Internal Revenue Code) provides that a part or all of any capital gain realized on the sale or disposition of a property on which accelerated depreciation has been taken after 1963 will be taxed as ordinary income. "Recapture" means that part or all of the gain is taken back or recaptured from the capital gain classification and put into the ordinary income classification. The impact is to increase the amount of tax the investor must pay on the sale.

The amount of the capital gain that may be recaptured as ordinary income is based on two items: first, the "applicable percentage" must be determined; and, second, the "applicable percentage" must be multiplied by the lower of two figures: (a) the total gain from the sale, or (b) the "additional depreciation."

The "applicable percentage" is determined from the date of acquisition of the property by the investor and is based upon the time the investor has held the property: 100 percent for the first 20 months, then reducing by 1 percent for each full month thereafter the property is held. This is the percentage of depreciation or total gain subject to recapture. For example, for property held for 30 months, the recapture would be 90 percent of the excess of the accelerated depreciation over straight-line, or 90 percent of the total gain from the sale, whichever is less. The following table illustrates these percentages.

Property Held up to:	Applicable Percentage
20 months	100%
24	96
36	84
48	72
60	60
72	48
84	36
96	24
108	12
120 .... (10 years)	0

The "additional depreciation," as previously discussed, is the excess of depreciation taken over the depreciation which would have been taken under the straight-line method. The excess, of course, results from the use of accelerated methods of depreciation. The additional depreciation is applicable only to the depreciation taken after 1963. The examples below illustrate the depreciation recapture provisions and computations.

SALES OF REAL ESTATE
RECAPTURE PROVISIONS OF SECTION 1250, IRC (1954)

The following examples exclude the treatment of the land sold with buildings, since land is not a 1250 asset and, therefore, all gains from land sales are capital gains.

All of the examples are based on the following schedule of depreciation:

Cost of building: $100,000
Estimated life: 25 years
Depreciation Method: Double declining balance (8%)
Note: Straight-line (SL) depreciation would be 4%
($4,000 per year)

Year	Depreciation	Examples 1 & 2	Example 3
		Calendar Year of Depreciation in the Examples	
1	$8,000	1964	1962
2	7,360	1965	1963
3	6,770	1966	1964
4	6,230	1967	1965
5	5,730	1968	1966
6	5,270	1969	1967
Total, 6 years:	$39,360		

EXAMPLE 1

Assume the building was constructed by taxpayer on January 1, 1964, and is sold on January 1, 1970 for $90,000.

1/1/70 selling price		$90,000
1/1/64 cost	$100,000	
(less depreciation taken)	(39,360)	
Adjusted basis	60,640	
Expense of sale	9,000	69,640

(A)	Total gain on sale		20,360
	Depreciation taken	$39,360	
	SL depreciation	24,000	
(B)	Excess depreciation	15,360	
	Applicable percentage:		
(C)	100 − 52 (72 − 20) =	48%	
(D)	Ordinary income:		
	(C × lesser of A or B)		
	$15,360 × 48% =		7,373
Long-term capital gain * (A − D)			$12,987

* Per Section 1231, IRC.

EXAMPLE 2

Assume the building was constructed by taxpayer on January 1, 1964, and is sold on January 1, 1970 for $80,000.

	1/1/70 selling price			$80,000
	1/1/64 cost		$100,000	
	(less depreciation taken)		(39,360)	
	Adjusted basis		60,640	
	Expense of sale		8,000	68,640
(A)	Total gain			11,360
	Depreciation taken		$39,360	
	SL depreciation		24,000	
(B)	Excess depreciation		15,360	
	Applicable percentage:			
(C)	100 − 52 (72 − 20) =		48%	
(D)	Ordinary income:			
	(C × lesser of A or B)			
	$11,360 × 48% =			5,453
Long-term capital gain * (A − D)				$ 5,907

* Per Section 1231, IRC.

EXAMPLE 3

Assume building was constructed by the taxpayer on January 1, 1962, and is sold on January 1, 1968 for $90,000.

1/1/68 selling price		$90,000
1/1/62 cost	$100,000	
(less depreciation taken)		
Prior to 1/1/64	(15,360)	
After 12/31/63	(24,000)	
Adjusted basis	60,640	
Expense of sale	9,000	69,640
(A) Total gain		20,360
Depreciation taken:		
After 12/31/63	$24,000	
SL depreciation after		
12/31/63	16,000	
(B) Excess depreciation	8,000	
Applicable percentage:		
(C) 100 − 52 (72 − 20) =	48%	
(D) Ordinary income:		
(C × lesser of A or B)		
$8,000 × 48% =		3,840
Long-term capital gain * (A − D)		$16,520

* Per Section 1231.

EXAMPLE 4

Assume same facts as in Example 3. In addition, assume that the terms of sale are $10,000 down payment and $10,000 principal plus interest at X% each January 1 until paid. The gain may, at the taxpayer's option, be reported as follows:

The percentage of each payment realized as gain would be 22.62% ($20,360 ÷ $90,000).

Year	Principal Collected	Total Gain	Ordinary Income	Long-Term Capital Gain
1968	$10,000	$2,262	$2,262	$ 0
1969	10,000	2,262	1,578	684
1970	10,000	2,262	0	2,262
1971	10,000	2,262	0	2,262
1972	10,000	2,262	0	2,262
1973	10,000	2,262	0	2,262
1974	10,000	2,262	0	2,262
1975	10,000	2,263	0	2,263
1976	10,000	2,263	0	2,263
Totals:	$90,000	$20,360	$3,840	$16,520

Of course, the interest collections would be ordinary income. Imputed interest, if less than 4%, would be imputed at 5%.

The limitations discussed above, of course, reduce the amount of capital gain possible on the sale of real estate, but the impact is usually not too great in many instances. It is still possible to realize either in whole or in part capital gain on the excess of accelerated depreciation over straight-line, depending upon the holding period of the investor. Further, the portion of the total gain that may be recaptured as ordinary income reduces over time, until after 10 years all of the excess depreciation can be taken as capital gain. Only investors who have a rapid turnover of properties may be seriously affected by these provisions. Also, where a major portion of the total gain is due to enhancement of land value, the gain attributable to this part of the investment will not be subject to the recapture provisions, since land is not depreciable and thus not affected by the provisions. The exact tax cost of the recapture provisions to the investor will, of course, depend upon his tax bracket. The impact can be reduced by careful planning as to the best time to make a disposition of a property, particularly at a profit.

TAX REFORM ACT OF 1969

The recapture rules and illustrations as set forth above will continue in effect as to additional depreciation attributable to periods prior to January 1, 1970, and after December 31, 1963. For example, property acquired on January 1, 1965, and sold at a gain 8 years later on January 1, 1973, would have full recapture of additional or excess depreciation for 1970–72 but no recapture for the excess depreciation taken prior to 1970.

The 1969 Act did, however, make a major change in the depreciation recapture rules. The additional or excess depreciation attributable to periods after December 31, 1969, will henceforth be recaptured totally— that is, 100 percent—with two exceptions as follows:

1. For property constructed prior to 1975 and financed with an FHA 221(d)(3) mortgage or 236 of the National Housing Act, the additional depreciation will be recaptured under the rules in effect before the 1969 Act; that is, there will be no recapture after the tenth year.
2. Where a rehabilitation amortization was allowed on residential or low-income rental housing, the recapture rate is as follows: 100 percent for the first 100 months or $8\frac{1}{3}$ years; the rate then declines at 1 percent per month. There is no recapture after $16\frac{2}{3}$ years.

DEPRECIATION AND TAX SHELTER

At least three key factors need to be kept in mind to fully understand the importance of the depreciation deduction in real estate investment. First, the depreciation allowance is an expense deduction which does not involve an actual outlay of cash by the investor; second, the depreciation allowance is based upon the *total* cost of the improvements (land is not depreciable), which includes not only the investor's equity or own cash but any mortgages on the property as well; the amount of cash down payment has no effect upon the depreciation allowances; and, third, the depreciation allowance may have no relationship to the actual decline in the value of the property and in fact may exceed the true decline, particularly where accelerated methods are used.

The net result of the above factors is that a property can produce a definite cash flow and at the same time the investor reports no taxable income from it—or even a paper tax loss, particularly in the early years of the investment. The example below will clarify this concept.

EXAMPLE 5

Terms of purchase:
  Purchase price—$100,000 (Land, $25,000; building, $75,000)
  Cash paid down (equity)—$20,000
  Mortgage—$80,000 over 27 years, 7 months @ 9% constant
  Net operating income—$10,000 annually
  Useful life of building—25 years
  Depreciation method—150% declining balance

Cash Flow		
Net operating income		$10,000
Less: debt service (mortgage payment)		
interest	$6,400	
principal	800	7,200
Cash flow:		$ 2,800

Taxable Income		
Net operating income		$10,000
Less: mortgage interest	$6,400	
depreciation	4,500	10,900
Taxable income (loss):		$ (900)

The property in the above example produces a cash flow of $2,800. For income tax purposes, however, the investor reports a tax loss of $900 because of the mortgage interest deduction and the depreciation deduction (6 percent of $75,000).

The amortization or principal payments on the mortgage do require an outlay of cash and, furthermore, they are not deductible for tax purposes. The amount by which the deductible depreciation deduction exceeds the nondeductible principal or amortization payment in a given year provides the investor with a tax-free cash flow and is referred to as "tax shelter" or "tax shield." Tax shelter is a tax savings due to the depreciation deduction. The accelerated methods (150 percent declining balance in Example 5) create deductions which not only shelter or offset net operating income but may exceed this income and result in a tax loss. The depreciation deduction reduces the investor's tax by an amount equal to the deduction times his ordinary tax rate, and the higher the tax bracket of the investor, the greater will be the benefit. An investor in the 50 percent bracket with a $900 tax loss receives the equivalent of a $450 cash grant from the government. It is easy to visualize the benefit if the figures were in the thousands of dollars.

Another way to explain the concept is to point out that when taxable income is less than cash flow, the excess by which cash flow exceeds taxable income is tax-free return or tax shelter from the property. It is obvious in the computations in Example 5, for instance, that net operating income and interest expense equally affect both cash flow and taxable income. The difference in the two sets of computations exists because mortgage amortization requires an outlay of cash but is nondeductible, while depreciation is deductible but does not require an outlay of cash. Taxable income is less than cash flow because the depreciation deduction is greater than the mortgage amortization amount.

Tax shelter is the reduction, elimination, or deferral of a tax due. The depreciation tax shelter described above is a reduction or elimination against present income. It has permitted the investor to put a certain amount of income into his pocket without first paying income tax on it. The effect of the depreciation allowance on the investor's tax return is the same as exemptions. Other tax shelter can come from capital gains, which is a reduction of future tax due; from deductible mortgage interest (leverage, too, produces a tax shelter, since interest is payment for use of other people's money), which is a reduction or elimination against present income; and from a tax-deferred exchange, which is a deferral or reduction of tax due. Capital gain and exchanges are discussed in detail in Chapters 3 and 4.

The investor is increasing, along with the cash flow, his equity or ownership interest in the property through the periodic principal payments on the mortgage ($800 in the above example). This "equity buildup" or "equity purchased" assumes that the property will maintain or increase its market value. Further, the tax-free return may be used to purchase additional equity.

As pointed out earlier, depreciation deductions reduce the basis of the property. If the property is later sold at a gain, as is the usual case, the gain will be the difference between the reduced basis and the sale price. The gain, however, will be taxed at the lower capital gain rate, depending upon the length of time the investor has held the property and the method of depreciation used. This factor is discussed fully in the next chapter.

The depreciation and mortgage amortization relationship needs to be projected for at least several years in advance. The depreciation deductions through the use of the accelerated methods are high in the early years of the investment and the mortgage amortization payments are low, which, of course, accounts for the tax-free yield in the early years. However, in later years there will be reduced depreciation deductions and increased amortization, which will create a tax liability for the investor and reduce his yield from the property. The tax shelter is gradually reduced until it is lost and taxable income exceeds cash flow to an extent that may not be acceptable to the investor, depending upon his objective. The investor may then consider some form of disposition of the property (assuming tax shelter in his investment objective), or may refinance the mortgage to reduce amortization, and then balance the new situation against yield and depreciation.

3

Capital Gain, Capital Loss, and Installment Sale

The preferred treatment provided for capital gain under the federal income tax regulations makes this tax benefit one of the most important to the real estate investor. The preferred treatment is a reduced tax (lower than if the gain were taxed in full as ordinary income) on any gain from the sale of the investor's real estate if property has been held for a stipulated period of time. Losses, within certain limits, are permitted to be deducted from the investor's tax return and carried back and forward until used up. The discussion below pertains to capital gain and loss for the individual investor. Treatment of the subject for the corporate investor follows in the succeeding section.

CAPITAL GAIN—INDIVIDUAL INVESTOR

In most instances when an investor speaks of a "capital gain," he is referring to "long-term" gain as contrasted to a "short-term" gain. The distinction between the two is crucial, not only in determining which treatment a sale comes under but in timing a sale in tax planning so as to obtain maximum tax benefits.

A property must be held by the investor for more than 6 months to be classified as "long-term" and to qualify for capital gain treatment. Property held 6 months and under is classified as "short-term" holding and is not eligible for the preferred treatment; the gain is fully taxed as ordinary income tax rates. The holding period is basic in determining whether a sale gain is eligible for long-term capital gain treatment, and an error of 1 day in the computation can make a significant difference in the tax treatment of any gain. The rules for determination of the holding period should be clearly understood and carefully adhered to. Generally, the day on which the property was acquired is excluded and the day on which the property was sold is included in the count.

There is no such thing as a separate and distinct "capital gain tax," although reference is commonly made to such a tax among investors. The investor divides his total yearly capital asset transactions into long-term and short-term transactions and in each classification offsets the gains and losses against each other. Net short-term gain is included in full in other income and is fully taxed as ordinary income. Only one-half (50 percent) of the net long-term gain is included in ordinary income; in other words, one-half of the net long-term gain is excluded from ordinary income. The investor then computes his tax on his total taxable income in the usual manner. This method and computation of the tax is known as the "regular" method.

The maximum tax on capital gain, however, is 25 percent. The investor may compute the tax on a long-term gain under a method known as the "alternative" method, by which an alternative rate of tax is limited to a flat 25 percent of the net long-term gain. In short, the maximum tax is 25 percent of the total net long-term gain. Actually, the inclusion of only one-half of the gain in ordinary income under the "regular" method can result in an effective tax of less than 25 percent of the gain. The "alternative" method will in fact only be used when the investor is in a tax bracket exceeding 50 percent, since the computation may result in a lower tax than the taxation of one-half of the gain at ordinary income rates under the "regular" method. Examples of the two methods of computation will clarify the above descriptions. (*Note:* The Tax Reform Act of 1969 made some changes in these regulations. The changes are discussed later in this chapter.)

EXAMPLE 1 [1]

CAPITAL GAIN DEDUCTION

For the individual investor with a net long-term capital gain exceeding his net short-term capital loss, a deduction equal to 50% of such excess, may be claimed. If there is no net short-term capital loss, the capital gain deduction is 50% of the net long-term capital gain.

Assume that during the year, an individual had the following transactions:

Long-term capital gain	$5,400	
Long-term capital loss	(1,750)	
Net long-term capital gain		$3,650
Short-term capital gain	$2,600	
Short-term capital loss	(3,790)	
Net short-term capital loss		(1,190)
Excess of net long-term capital gain over net short-term capital loss		$2,460

Although there is a net gain of $2,460 from capital transactions, only 50%, or $1,230, is actually taxed. There is a deduction of 50% of the excess of the net long-term capital gain over the net short-term capital loss. This deduction is not available to corporations.

THE REGULAR AND ALTERNATIVE TAX

The alternative tax on the net long-term capital gain is 50% of the Capital Gain Deduction. If the individual investor files a separate return and has taxable income over $26,000, it may be to his advantage to use the alternative computation. This is also true if you are a head of household with taxable income over $38,000; file a joint return with your husband or wife and have a taxable income over $52,000; or are a surviving spouse and have a taxable income over $52,000. The investor may use the alternative computation or the regular computation, whichever produces the lesser tax.

COMPUTATION OF TAX

There are three steps involved:
    1. From taxable income (line 1 of the *Computation of Alternative*

---

[1] Excerpted from U. S. Treasury Department, Internal Revenue Service Document No. 5048 (10/67), *Sales and Exchanges of Assets*, p. 11. This chapter is based largely on Internal Revenue Service documents.

> *Tax* section on page 2, Schedule D) subtract that portion of the excess of the net long-term capital gain over the net short-term capital loss which is included in taxable income.
> 2. Compute a partial tax at the regular rates on the amount of ordinary net income so determined.
> 3. To this partial tax add 50% of the amount of capital gain which was eliminated from taxable income in (1) above.

EXAMPLE 2

Investor has taxable income of $70,000 (exclusive of the excess of net long-term capital gain over net short-term capital loss) and is filing a separate return for the calendar year 1967. During the year he had a net long-term capital gain of $16,000 and a net short-term capital loss of $6,000.

REGULAR TAX

Taxable income (excluding capital gains)		$70,000
Excess of net long-term capital gain over net short-term capital loss	$10,000	
Less: capital gain deduction (50% of excess of net long-term capital gain over net short-term capital loss	5,000	
		5,000
Taxable income		$75,000
Regular tax		$38,490

ALTERNATIVE TAX

Taxable income (for regular tax computation)	$75,000
Less: 50% of excess of net long-term capital gain over net short-term capital loss	5,000
Ordinary income subject to regular tax	$70,000
1. Tax on $70,000	$35,190
2. Add 50% of $5,000	2,500
Alternative tax	$37,690

CAPITAL GAIN—CORPORATE INVESTOR [2]

The alternative tax on capital gains of a corporation is 25 percent of the excess of the net long-term capital gain over the net short-term capital loss. Since a corporation's income tax consists of a normal tax of 22 percent on its taxable income, plus a surtax of 26 percent on its taxable income in excess of $25,000, a corporation with taxable income of $25,000 or less will not benefit from the alternative tax computation. If taxable income is in excess of $25,000, however, the corporation may pay less tax because of the alternative tax computation on capital gains.

Alternative Tax Computation

There are three steps involved:

1. From the corporation's taxable income [line 17, page 2, Schedule D (Form 1120)] subtract the excess of the net long-term capital gain over net short-term capital loss.
2. Compute a partial tax at the regular rates on the amount of ordinary net income so determined.
3. To this partial tax add 25 percent of the amount of capital gain which was eliminated from taxable income in (1) above.

EXAMPLE 3

A corporation had taxable income of $30,000 for 1967, which included the following:

Long-term capital gain	$6,500	
Long-term capital loss	(1,800)	
Net long-term capital gain		$4,700
Short-term capital gain	$1,000	
Short-term capital loss	(2,700)	
Net short-term capital loss		(1,700)

---

[2] U. S. Treasury Department, IRS Document No. 5048 (10/67), op. cit., pp. 11–12.

Excess of net long-term capital gain
over net short-term capital loss $3,000

REGULAR TAX

Normal tax, 22% of $30,000 (taxable income) $6,600
Surtax, 26% of $5,000 (taxable income in
excess of $25,000) $1,300

Regular tax $7,900

ALTERNATIVE TAX

1. Taxable income $30,000
    Less: excess of net long-term capital gain over
    net short-term capital loss (see above)   3,000

                                                                         $27,000

2. Partial tax on (1)
    Normal tax, 22% of $27,000 $ 5,940
    Surtax, 26% of $2,000   520

                                                                         $ 6,460
3. Add 25% of the $3,000 capital gain   750

    Alternative tax $ 7,210

The computation of alternative tax is basically the same for corporations as for individuals. Since taxable income of a corporation includes the entire excess of net long-term capital gain over net short-term capital loss, the corporation's taxable income is reduced by this amount in the alternative tax computation to arrive at the income subject to tax at regular rates. To the tax computed on this amount you add 25% of such excess net long-term capital gain.

CAPITAL LOSS—INDIVIDUAL INVESTOR [3]

An individual must first offset his capital losses against his capital gains. The excess, if any, of his capital losses over capital gains is deductible from

---

[3] Ibid., pp. 12–13.

ordinary income to the extent of his taxable income or $1,000, whichever is less. Taxable income for this purpose is taxable income computed without regard to capital gains and losses or personal exemptions.

EXAMPLE 4

If an individual has the following transactions, the allowable deduction would be computed as follows:

Net short-term capital loss	($4,000)
Net long-term capital gain	2,500
Excess	($1,500)
Taxable income (exclusive of capital transactions and personal exemptions)	$ 780
Amount of loss deductible	$ 780

The deduction is limited to the taxable income of $780, but the balance of the net short-term capital loss of $720 may be carried over to the next year. If the taxable income had been $1,200 instead of $780, the amount of loss deductible would have been $1,000, which is the maximum allowed and the balance of $500 would be carried over.

Capital Loss Carryover

If there is a net capital loss which exceeds the amount the investor is to deduct, the excess may be carried over indefinitely until absorbed. When carried over, such capital loss will retain its original character as long-term or short-term; thus, a long-term capital loss carried over from a prior year will first offset long-term gains of the current years before it will offset short-term gains of the current year. In addition to an unabsorbed carry-over offsetting capital gains in subsequent years, a capital loss deduction may be claimed to the extent such carryover exceeds capital gains but not to exceed taxable income or $1,000, whichever is less, as indicated above. To the extent net capital losses are deducted from ordinary income, a net short-term capital loss must be deducted first without regard to whether it was sustained before or after a net long-term loss.

If there is an unabsorbed capital loss carryover sustained in a tax year beginning before January 1, 1964, it is treated as a short-term capital loss, irrespective of its original character. A loss sustained in the calendar year 1958, or before, could only be carried over for a period of 5 years.

EXAMPLE 5 [4]

A calendar-year taxpayer with one personal exemption had the following transactions: a net capital loss carryover from 1963 in the amount of $800 and long-term capital loss carryovers from 1965 and 1966 in the total amount of $1,900. In 1967 he had a net long-term capital gain of $1,500; no short-term transactions; and taxable income, exclusive of capital transactions and his personal exemptions, in excess of $1,000. He, therefore, has a long-term capital loss carryover to 1968 of $200, computed as follows:

1967 long-term capital gain		$1,500
Less: long-term capital loss carryovers from 1965 and 1966 (retain their original character)		1,900
Net long-term capital loss for 1967		$ 400
Net short-term capital loss (1963 capital loss carryover, which is treated as a short-term capital loss carryover)		800
Net capital loss for 1967		$1,200
Amount deductible in 1967 (limited to $1,000 or taxable income, whichever is less)		
Net short-term capital loss	$ 800	
Net long-term capital loss	200	1,000
Long-term capital loss carryover to 1968		$ 200

CAPITAL LOSS—CORPORATE INVESTOR [5]

Corporations may deduct capital losses only to the extent of capital gains. Any capital loss which is not allowed as a deduction in the current year be-

---

[4] Ibid., pp. 12–13.
[5] Ibid.

cause it exceeds capital gains is a capital loss carryover to succeeding years until exhausted, but for not more than 5 years. The capital loss carryover is treated as a short-term capital loss in succeeding years regardless of whether it was a short-term or a long-term capital loss in the year it was sustained. For example, if a corporation had a net short-term capital gain of $3,000 and a net long-term capital loss of $5,000, it could offset the $3,000 gain, but the remaining capital loss of $2,000 would be a carryover, and treated as a short-term capital loss, to the 5 succeeding years, if not exhausted sooner. If a corporation has two or more carryovers, the capital loss carryover from the earliest year is applied first to reduce current year net capital gains, then the carryover from the next earliest year, etc., until all carryovers are absorbed. In computing the amount of a capital loss to be carried over from the current year, the amount of any net capital loss carryover from prior years may not be taken into account.

TAX REFORM ACT OF 1969

The 6-months holding period required to be eligible for capital gain treatment remains the same. The changes described below are applicable to taxable years starting after December 31, 1969.

The capital gains rate of 25 percent remains in effect for payments received before January 1, 1975, for binding contracts in effect on October 9, 1969. This rule will primarily affect installment sale contracts made prior to October 10, 1969, and contracts to sell where the sale is completed after October 9, 1969. Income from installment contracts will be subject to the new regulations for 1975 and years thereafter.

For the individual investor or taxpayer, the 25 percent rate will remain on the first $50,000 of long-term capital gains. The increased alternative rates are applicable to long-term capital gains which exceed $50,000 in a taxable year. The alternative tax rate is increased in three stages for long-term capital gains ineligible for the 25 percent rate. These stages are as follows: for 1970, the rate is 29½ percent; for 1971, the rate is 32½ percent; and for 1972, the maximum rate becomes 35 percent. Since 35 percent is equal to one-half of the new maximum individual tax rate of 70 percent, there is obviously no alternative tax rate on a long-term capital gain over $50,000 when the rate reaches the 35 percent level in 1972.

The alternative tax rate for corporations is increased in two steps for taxable years 1970 and 1971. In 1970 the rate is 28 percent and in 1971 the rate is 30 percent.

DEALER VS. INVESTOR

An important consideration in determining whether a person is eligible for capital gain treatment on a sale or exchange is whether he is classified as an "investor" or a "dealer." A dealer holds property primarily for sale to customers in the ordinary course of trade or business. The property is his stock in trade and is included in his business inventory. Gains on the sale of this inventory property are taxed in full as ordinary income and losses are deductible in full. Also, a dealer is not eligible for tax-free exchanges of property, as is an investor.

An investor holds property primarily for an investment motive. Such a motive is usually thought of as the holding over a long period of time for income and value appreciation. It is not dealer property. Investor property is defined as a capital asset and is eligible for capital gain treatment.

There is no clear distinction between the classifications. Each transaction must be considered on the facts of that particular situation. There are, however, a number of criteria which may serve as useful guidelines to aid the investor in avoiding "dealer" classification. No one factor is necessarily controlling, and all may be pertinent.

1. The investor should limit real estate buying, selling, and reinvesting to a few transactions during the year; he should not become too active and make numerous and frequent transactions. There are no set rules as to the number of sales or amount of activity that will cause an investor to be classified as a dealer, but it seems clear that frequent, continuous, and regular selling and buying is not indicative of an investment motive.

2. The investor should have a full-time occupation and income other than real estate; that is, he should make the real estate activity and income incidental to his primary occupation and income source. He should be careful that real estate investing activity does not become so great as to overshadow his main occupation and be classified as a business in itself; the investor could then be said to be concurrently conducting two businesses and lose the investor status.

3. The investor should avoid any act which might identify him as being affiliated with the real estate business. Included in such acts might be the holding of a real estate broker's or real estate salesman's license; membership in a real estate dealers' association, such as a local real estate board; having a real estate office; or any activity usually identified with dealers.

4. The primary objective in acquiring and holding a property should be for investment—the holding over a long period of time for income

and appreciation as contrasted with short-term sale and profit. The short-term outlook—the short-term transaction, the intention to sell soon after acquisition—is associated with dealer or business motive.

5. The investor should not actively and aggressively advertise and solicit sales or have a broker, as his agent, do the same; he should remain relatively passive in the transaction and let the purchaser contact him.

6. The investor should hold investment property completely separate from other property and business activity and should maintain complete and accurate accounting records for each transaction. This is particularly pertinent if the investor is also a full-time real estate dealer and owns investment property. The property may be held in a separate investment account. Separate legal entities might be set up, one for investment property and one for other activities, such as regular business operations.

7. The holding period for investment property should be substantial. Longer than 6 months gives the capital gain treatment, but ideally the property should be held much longer to indicate investment motive. Too many sales soon after the minimum 6-month holding period, at a profit, and with reinvestment in other property may be taken as indicative of dealer activity and should be avoided.

8. The investor should avoid subdividing activity. This factor is discussed further in the following section.

SUBDIVIDING ACTIVITY

The subdividing of property will almost certainly classify the developer as a dealer, although a limited amount of such activity may be acceptable without losing investor status. Capital gain treatment may be permitted on subdivided property under certain conditions (Section 1237, IRC):

1. If the lots have been held for at least 5 years, unless they were inherited;

2. If the investor or any organizations related to him did not make any substantial improvements on the tract which increased the value of the lots sold;

3. If the developer did not hold any other real property as a dealer in the year the lots were sold;

4. If the developer had never held the subdivided tract or any part of it primarily for sale to customers; and

5. If the developer was not a real estate dealer in the year in which the lots were sold.

The investor-vs.-dealer problem again, as in all aspects of investing, points out the necessity of advance planning if maximum benefits are to be obtained from an investment. The criteria discussed here should be considered before any action is taken; investment intent must be evident at the time of acquisition of the property, during the holding period, and at the time of disposition or liquidation. Investment activity must be carefully planned and watched, since too much of it can place an investor in the dealer category. A real estate dealer can hold investment property and still get capital gain treatment on its disposition, but he faces more obstacles than the investor who is not a dealer in his regular occupation. Again, professional legal and accounting counsel is advisable in every transaction.

Gain on Sale of Lots [6]

If property meets the tests to qualify it as "investment" property, the gain realized on its sale or exchange will be treated for income tax purposes as described below.

If the sale is for fewer than six lots or parcels from the same tract, the entire gain is a capital gain. In computing the number of lots or parcels sold, two or more contiguous lots sold to a single buyer in a single sale are counted as only one parcel.

With the sale or exchange of the sixth lot or parcel from the same tract, then the amount, if any, by which 5 percent of the selling price exceeds the expenses incurred in connection with its sale, will be treated as ordinary income and the balance of any gain will be treated as capital gain. Five percent of the selling price of all lots sold or exchanged from the tract in the tax year the sixth lot is sold or exchanged and in subsequent years is considered ordinary income. Thus, in a sale of the first six lots of a single tract in one year, to the extent of gain, 5 percent of the selling price of each lot sold will be treated as ordinary income. On the other hand, in a sale of the first three lots in a single tract in 1967 and the next three lots in 1967, only the gain realized from sales made in 1967 will be subject to the 5 percent rule. The selling expenses in connection with the sale must first be deducted from the portion of gain treated as ordinary income and any remaining expenses are to be deducted from the portion of gain treated as capital gain. Deduction of the selling expenses as ordinary business expenses from other income is not permitted.

An exchange is treated the same as a sale. If the lots are exchanged for other property, the selling price is the fair market value of the property received plus any money received. If a lot is exchanged for other property

---

[6] Ibid., p. 10.

in a transaction of the type classified as a "Nontaxable Exchange," the gain is not taxed. However, in counting the number of lots sold, all lots disposed of are counted whether or not the gain or loss is recognized.

If no sales are made for 5 years, the remainder of the tract will be treated as though the investor had acquired it new on the day following the last sale.

EXAMPLE 6 [7]

Five lots from a single tract are sold in 1966. In 1967 the sixth lot is sold for $10,000. The basis for this lot is $5,000 and selling expenses are $750. The gain is $4,250, all of which is capital gain, computed as follows:

Selling price		$10,000
Less: basis	$5,000	
expense of sale	750	5,750
Gain from sale of lot		$ 4,250
5% of selling price	$ 500	
Less: expense of sale	750	
Gain reported as ordinary income		0
Gain reported as capital gain		$ 4,250

EXAMPLE 7 [8]

Assume in Example 6 that the selling expenses are $300. The amount of gain is $4,700, of which amount $200 is ordinary income and $4,500 is capital gain, computed as follows:

---

[7] Ibid.
[8] Ibid.

Selling price		$10,000
Less: basis	$5,000	
expense of sale	300	5,300
Gain from sale of lot		$ 4,700
5% of selling price	$ 500	
Less: expense of sale	300	
Gain reported as ordinary income		200
Gain reported as capital gain		$ 4,500

Loss on Sale of Lots

The 5% rule, explained above, does not apply to losses. A lot sold at a loss will be treated as a capital loss if it was held for investment. If it was used in the investor's trade or business, it may be either a capital loss or an ordinary loss.

OPTIONS TO BUY OR SELL [9]

Gain or loss from the sale or exchange of an option (or privilege) to buy or sell property which is—or would have been, had the property been acquired—a capital asset in the investor's hands is a gain or loss from the sale of exchange of a capital asset. Gain or loss from the sale or exchange of an option (or privilege) to buy or sell property which is not, or would not be, a capital asset in the investor's hands is ordinary gain or loss. Such gain or loss may, under certain circumstances, be treated as a capital gain or loss.

If the holder fails to exercise an option to buy or sell and incurs a loss, the option is deemed to have been sold or exchanged upon the date that it expired. The loss is treated the same as explained in the paragraph above. Any gain to the grantor of the option arising from its holder's failure to exercise it is ordinary income.

If the investor grants an option on property he owns and it is not exercised, he realizes ordinary income on the amount received, even though the option may have been on a capital asset held by him. If the option is exercised, he adds the option payment to other amounts received to com-

---

[9] Ibid., pp. 7–8.

pute the amount realized on the sale of the property. Classification of the gain or loss is then determined by the type of property sold.

The capital asset treatment does not apply (1) if the gain from sale of the property underlying the option would be ordinary income; (2) to a dealer in options, if the option is part of his inventory; or (3) to loss from failure to exercise a fixed-price option acquired on the same day the property identified in the option is acquired. The holding period for property acquired under an option to purchase begins on the day after the property was acquired, and not on the day after the option was acquired.

INSTALLMENT SALE

The installment sale method is an important and commonly used tax benefit in real estate transactions. The method permitted by the Internal Revenue Code grants a seller the option of spreading the reporting of a gain or profit from the sale of realty over a period of time rather than re-porting it all in the year of sale. Losses, both ordinary and capital, may not be reported on the installment method but must be deducted in full in the year of sale, subject to the capital loss limitations. The method is not available to full-time dealers who regularly operate on installment selling.

Computation

The mechanics of the installment method are relatively simple, and an understanding of them should be helpful in investment planning. Compu-tations involve several terms: gross profit, selling price, contract price, and initial payment.

GROSS PROFIT—the gain on the sale as computed in the usual manner, namely, the selling price of the property less its basis and selling expenses.

SELLING PRICE—the total cost of the property to the purchaser, including any existing mortgage balance assumed or paid by the purchaser.

CONTRACT PRICE—generally, the same as the "selling price," except where any existing mortgages are involved (mortgage debt is included in the selling price). If any existing mortgage is greater than the seller's basis of the property, the excess is included in the "contract price" regardless of whether assumed by the purchaser or not. The contract price is generally the actual proceeds or amount to be received by the seller; it is the seller's equity in the property.

INITIAL PAYMENT—payments in the year of sale must not exceed 30 percent of the "selling price." Such payments include all cash and property given by the buyer to the seller during the year of sale. This is the crucial "3 percent test" so often referred to in connection with the installment method. It might be pointed out that the term "initial payment" is not the same thing as "down payment." Some of the items included in the initial payments are:

1. all principal payments on mortgage during the year of sale;
2. payment by purchaser in the year of sale of any existing liens on the property (but not payment of liens in later years), and cancellation of a debt owed by seller to the purchaser;
3. any prior-year option payment that becomes part of the down payment in the year of sale;
4. notes of a third party given seller by the buyer in the year of sale, included at their fair market value; and
5. debt assumed by the purchaser to the extent of the excess of the debt over the seller's basis.

Once the correct items are determined for inclusion in the above concepts, the steps for calculating the installment method of reporting gain are as follows:

Gross profit is divided by contract price, yielding the percentage of each payment that is to be reported by the seller as income. Each payment is then multiplied by this percentage to determine the amount of profit to be reported each year.

Economic and Tax Benefits

The installment sale method has several possible benefits or advantages for the investor. These include the following:

1. It is a relatively easy method to use. There are technical requirements and rules which must be met, but once a determination is made of the classification of items the formula is clear and quite simple.
2. Payment of the total tax liability is deferred by being spread out over the years.
3. The proportionate amount of the gain that is included in the taxable income each year is taxed at rates in effect in each year. It is possible that future rates may be more favorable than the current rates. The opposite effect could occur, too.

4. It is possible that the total tax liability on the sale can be smaller, with a resulting tax saving, than if the entire gain is reported and taxed in one year. This is because of the graduated tax rates and the ability to report long-term capital gain on the "regular" method.

EXAMPLE 8 [10]

Assume that in 1957 you bought a lot for $5,000 and in 1958 you borrowed money to erect a house which you occupied. The loan was secured by a 5% first mortgage on the property. The house cost $16,950, making your total cost $21,950.

In 1967 you sold the house to Jones for a total of $27,500, paying a commission of 3% (or $825) on the sale. Jones paid $5,000 in cash; assumed your mortgage with a balance of $10,000; gave you his 8% 2d mortgage note for $10,000, payable in equal annual installments of $2,000, beginning January 1, 1968; and transferred, by endorsement to you, a short-term $2,500 note of the Apex Company which was valued at par, for the balance of the purchase price.

The transaction qualifies as an installment sale, since the payments of $7,500 (cash $5,000 and Apex Company note valued at $2,500) received in the year of the sale do not exceed 30% of the selling price of $27,500, or $8,250. The two mortgages represent debts of the purchaser and are not considered in determining the amount of the payments received in the year of the sale.

The percentage of each installment payment to be reported as profit is computed as follows:

Sale price of home	$27,500
Less: commission paid on sale	825
Net sale price	$26,675
Basis of property to you	21,950
Gross profit to be realized on sale	$ 4,725
Contract price:	
Sales price	$27,500
Less: mortgage assumed by purchaser	10,000
contract price	$17,500

---

[10] U. S. Treasury Department, IRS Document No. 5108 (10/67), "Installment and Deferred-Payment Sales," p.4.

Gross profit percentage:

$$\frac{\text{Gross profit to be realized} \quad \$ 4{,}725}{\text{Contract price} \quad \$17{,}500} = 27\%$$

Accordingly, the profit realized on the 1967 receipts of $7,500 is 27% thereof, or $2,025, and the profit realized on the 1968 installment of $2,000 will be 27% thereof, or $540. Since the home was a capital asset which you held for more than 6 months, the realized profit is a long-term capital gain. Therefore, in determining your net long-term capital gains (or losses) for 1967, include the $2,025 profit realized in that year, and include in your long-term capital gains for 1968 the $540 profit realized in that year.

If in the above example the purchaser paid off the mortgage on the property at the time of sale instead of assuming it, the sale would not qualify as an installment sale since the payments in the year of sale would be $17,500, which exceeds 30% of the selling price.

Imputed Interest

It is essential in an installment sale over $3,000 that a rate of interest be stated. If no rate is specified or if the rate given is below 4 percent simple interest, the Internal Revenue Service will impute interest at the rate of 5 percent. This means that a part of each installment payment will be considered interest for both seller and buyer. Such a rate imputation could reduce the selling price to an extent that the initial payment exceeds 30 percent of it and thereby disqualify the transaction for installment reporting.

4

Nontaxable Exchange

A real estate "exchange" is a reciprocal transfer of investment property. A real estate "trade" is a reciprocal transfer of homes. Attention is focused in this chapter on the exchange, specifically the tax-free exchange possible under Section 1031 of the Internal Revenue Code.

Real estate held for investment may be exchanged for other investment real estate without an immediate tax recognition of any gain or loss on the transaction. The property acquired is considered to be a continuation of the taxpayer's investment in the first property. Such a transaction is referred to as a "nontaxable exchange" or a "tax-free exchange."

The tax is not really forgiven but is deferred or postponed until the property is ultimately disposed of in a taxable transaction. In other words, there is no tax in the year of the exchange on any gain, nor is any loss deductible. Such exchanging and deferred recognition of gain may continue indefinitely over many properties; the process is known as "pyramiding." But ultimately recognition will have to be given. Only the taxpayer's death will result in a true tax-free exchange when the property of the deceased acquires a new, usually stepped-up basis.

BASIC REQUIREMENTS

To qualify as a nontaxable exchange, a transaction must meet certain strict requirements. These requirements have to do with "like-kind" property, "boot," and the purpose for which the property given and received was held.

Like-kind Property

Properties exchanged in a transaction must be of "like kind." The words have reference to the nature or character of the property and not to its grade or quality. One kind or class of property may not be exchanged for property of a different kind or class. Real estate exchanged for real estate is a like-kind exchange. The fact that any real estate involved is improved or unimproved is not material, for that fact relates only to the grade or quality of the property and not to its kind or class. Examples of like-kind exchanges—and, thus, exchanges nontaxable in the year of the transaction—are the exchange of city real estate for a farm or ranch, an exchange of a 30-year leasehold for fee simple title to another parcel of real estate, the exchange of an apartment house for vacant or unimproved land, and an office building for a hotel. Real estate exchanged for personal property does not qualify as like-kind, since these properties are of a different nature or character.

The above properties are simply examples; other kinds of real estate may qualify as like property. It is essential to determine the character of each property.

Boot

Cash or other unlike property involved in an exchange is referred to as "boot" and can affect the tax treatment of the exchange. The receipt of cash or other property in addition to the "like-kind" property exchanged results in gain being recognized by the receiver of the boot at the time of the exchange, but only to the extent of the sum of the cash and fair market value of the other property. In other words, a partially taxable exchange can result when items of "boot" (or property not in the tax-free classification) are included in an exchange.

If the amount of boot received is greater than the actual or realized gain on the transaction, the tax is limited to the amount of the actual gain. The excess boot received in the exchange is considered to be a tax-free recovery of part of the owner's basis for his former property. In other words, the amount of gain recognized on an exchange is limited to the amount of boot received. If the boot exceeds the gain, the entire gain will be recognized. But if the boot is less than the gain, the gain to be recognized is limited to the amount of the boot. The receipt of boot does not entitle a taxpayer to deduct a loss realized on a tax-free exchange, although the basis will be affected.

The giving of boot does not make a transaction taxable for the giver. Only the receipt of boot may make the transaction partially taxable to the receiver.

Mortgages As Boot

A mortgage on a property is treated as "boot" in a like-kind exchange. Suppose an investor owns a property with a mortgage on it, and exchanges it for another property which has no mortgage on it, but the owner of the latter property assumes the mortgage or takes the mortgaged property subject to the mortgage (it makes no difference taxwise). The owner who has been relieved of the mortgage debt is considered to have received "boot" in the amount of the mortgage released. In other words, the mortgage is treated the same as cash in computing recognized gain when the receiver of the mortgaged property assumes the mortgage or takes it subject to the mortgage.

The investor who gave the unencumbered property in exchange for a mortgaged property does not create a taxable exchange. The assumption of the mortgage liability of another is treated the same as the giving of "boot."

If both properties in an exchange are mortgaged and each party to the transaction assumes the other's mortgage or takes the property subject to the mortgage of the other party, the amounts of the respective mortgages offset each other and only the net debt is treated as the receipt or payment of "boot." That is, the net liability assumed by the other party to the exchange is the amount of "boot" recognized to the party giving the property. Or, stated another way, the difference between the mortgages is treated as "boot" to the owner whose original property was encumbered by the larger mortgage.

If there is cash involved in an exchange such as may be needed to balance the exchange, in addition to mortgages on both properties, it would be best to use the cash to reduce the larger mortgage. That is, increase the equity in the property with the smaller equity rather than pay the cash to the other party. Consideration received in the form of cash is not offset by consideration given in the form of an assumption of a mortgage debt, and a gain is recognized to the extent of the amount of the cash received. However, consideration given in the form of cash is offset against consideration received in the form of an assumption of a mortgage. That is, if one of the investors secures a reduction in debt through the exchange, and pays cash in addition, the cash offsets the amount of debt from which he is released. Gain is recognized only to the extent of any excess of reduction of debt over the cash payment.

Purpose

Both the property given and the property received must be held by the investor for business or investment purposes. Neither property can be property owned for personal purposes, such as a residence. (There are, however, special rules in the case of trading residences, and a tax deferment is possible here, too, under certain conditions.) Also, neither property can be property that the taxpayer sells to customers in the ordinary course of business. Further, property held for productive use in trade or business or for investment does not include stocks, bonds, notes, choses in action, certificates of trust or beneficial interest, or other securities or evidences of indebtedness or interest.

Careful attention must be given to situations where a property is exchanged for another one and the latter is immediately resold. The transaction may be considered a taxable one because at the time the new property was acquired there was an intent to resell it. The new property must be held for business or investment purposes and not for immediate resale if the transaction is to qualify as a nontaxable exchange.

HOLDING PERIOD

The holding period of the old property, assuming it was held as a capital asset or qualified as trade or business property before the exchange, is added on to the new property acquired in the exchange. This is in accord with the theory that the new property acquired in the exchange is essentially a continuation of the holding of the property given up.

BASIC COMPUTATIONS

There are four basic computations in an exchange transaction: (1) balance the equities, (2) compute the realized gain, (3) compute the recognized gain, and (4) compute the new basis of the property received in the exchange. The new basis must be allocated between land and improvements and between like and unlike property.

Balancing The Equities

Two properties exactly alike in value and mortgage balance are seldom found. There is usually a difference to be made up by an adjustment in the form of cash or the transfer of other property. Balancing the equities is the making up of this difference.

REALIZED GAIN VS. RECOGNIZED GAIN

A distinction is made between "realized" gain and "recognized" gain. A realized gain is the maximum gain that would be treated as income if the transaction were a sale instead of an exchange. It is the same thing as actual gain or indicated gain. It is computed by deducting the consideration given from the consideration received. Or it may be computed by deducting the adjusted cost basis of the property given from its fair market value.

Recognized gain is the same as taxable gain. It is the part of realized gain that is taxable and its amount depends upon the amount of "boot" received in the exchange. The amount of recognized gain may be less than the amount of realized gain, but never greater than the amount of realized gain.

LOSS

A loss on a tax-free exchange may not be deducted from the investor's gross income in computing his taxes. The loss not deducted is an adjustment to the basis of the property received. A potential loss could occur when the cash received plus the fair market value of the property received is less than the basis of the property given up. The loss is not deductible irrespective of whether cash is received or paid in the exchange, or whether the property received is mortgaged or free and clear.

Allocation Of Basis

The basis of property received in a nontaxable like-kind exchange is generally the same as the basis of the property given up. Suppose an investment property with an adjusted basis of $5,000 is exchanged for another like-kind investment property with a fair market value of $7,500. Then the basis of the property received is $5,000, the same basis as the former property.

In a partially taxable exchange (one in which "unlike" property or money is received in addition to "like" property), the basis of the property acquired is the same as the basis of the property given up, decreased in the amount of any money received, and increased in the amount of gain recognized on the transaction. The basis so determined must be allocated to the basis of the properties (other than money) received on the exchange. The "unlike" property is assigned an amount equivalent to its fair market value on the date of the exchange.

For example, assume that real estate held for investment purposes and with an adjusted basis of $5,000 is exchanged for other real estate also to be held for investment purposes, a truck, and $1,000 in cash. The fair market value of the other real estate at the time of the exchange is $2,500 and the fair market value of the truck is $1,800. There is a recognized gain on the transaction of $300 and the basis of the respective properties received is as follows:

Adjusted basis of real estate transferred	$5,000
Less: cash received	1,000
	$4,000
Plus: gain recognized	300
Total basis of property received (to be allocated):	$4,300

The basis of $4,300 is allocated between the truck and the real estate. The basis of the truck is its fair market value, $1,800, and the basis of the real estate is the remainder, $2,500.[1]

---

[1] U. S. Treasury Department, Internal Revenue Service, Document No. 5516 (10/67), *Cost or Other Basis of Assets*, p. 3.

There are also certain types of exchanges of property for property of a like kind in which a loss may not be recognized, although, in addition, the investor receives unlike property or money. The basis of the property or properties received, other than money, is the same as the basis (adjusted to the date of the exchange) of the property transferred, decreased by the amount of money received. This basis must be allocated with the unlike property receiving an amount of the basis equivalent to the fair market value of the unlike property on the date of the exchange.

For example, assume that you exchanged a boat, used in your business and having an adjusted basis of $8,000, for another boat to be used in your business, land to be held for investment, and $500 cash. The fair market value of the boat received is $5,000 and of the land received $1,500. There is a nonrecognized loss of $1,000 on the transaction and the basis of the respective properties received is as follows:

Adjusted basis of boat transferred	$8,000
Less: cash received	500
Total basis of the properties received (to be allocated):	$7,500

The basis of $7,500 is allocated to the land received at its FMV (fair market value) of $1,500. The remainder of $6,000 is the basis of the boat acquired.[2]

NONTAXABLE EXCHANGE FORMULA

Computation of Realized Gain

FMV of property received
Plus: release of mortgage on old property transferred
      Cash and other boot received
Total consideration received
Less: consideration given
      Adjusted basis of old property transferred
      Cash given
      Mortgage assumed on new property received
(A) *Realized gain*

---

[2] Ibid.

Computation of Recognized Gain

Boot received:
    Mortgage transferred
    Less: mortgage assumed
    Net Mortgage Relief
Less: cash or boot paid
Recognized net loan relief
Plus: other cash or boot received
    Total net
(B)   *Net boot received*
Recognized gain = (A) or (B), whichever is lower

New Basis of Property Acquired

Basis of old or transferred property
Plus: cash paid and other boot given
      New loans or liability assumed
      Gain recognized
(A) *Total*
    Less: cash and other boot received
      release of mortgage on old property transferred (old loan)
(B) *Total*
    New adjusted basis = (A) *minus* (B)

EXAMPLE 1

APPLICATION OF NONTAXABLE EXCHANGE FORMULA
EXCHANGE OF TWO APARTMENT HOUSES

Realized gain	D	E
FMV	$250,000	$220,000
Plus: release of mtg.	80,000	150,000
cash	40,000	
Total consd. recd.:	370,000	370,000
Less: consd. given		
adj. basis of old	100,000	175,000
cash given		40,000
mtg. assumed	150,000	80,000
	250,000	295,000
(A) *Realized gain:*	120,000	75,000

Recognized gain

Boot received:		
Mortgage transferred	80,000	150,000
Less: mtg. assumed	150,000	80,000
Net mtg. relief	0	70,000
Less: cash or boot paid		40,000
Recognized net mtg. relief		30,000
Plus: other cash or boot recd.	40,000	
(B) *Total net boot received:*	40,000	30,000
Recognized gain is lower of (A) or (B)		

New basis

	D	E
Basis of old property	100,000	175,000
Plus: cash paid & other boot given		40,000
new loans or liability assumed	150,000	80,000
gain recognized	40,000	30,000
(A) *Total:*	290,000	325,000
Less: cash & other boot received	40,000	0
release of mtg. on old property	80,000	150,000
(B) *Total:*	120,000	150,000
New adjusted basis = (A) *minus* (B):	170,000	175,000

Realized and Recognized Gain to D

The amount of boot received by D is $40,000 cash. The consideration received by D in the form of a transfer subject to a liability of $80,000 is offset by consideration given in the form of a receipt of property subject to a $150,000 liability. Therefore, only the $40,000 is treated as boot, and of the $120,000 realized gain only the $40,000 is recognized.

Realized and Recognized Gain to E

The realized gain to E is $75,000. The recognized gain is only $30,000, the net amount of the boot received by E. Consideration received by E in the form of a transfer subject to a liability of $150,000 is offset by consideration given in the form of a receipt of property subject to an $80,000 liability and by the $40,000 cash paid by E. Although consideration *received* in the form of cash or other property *is not* offset by consideration *given* in the form of an assumption of liabilities or a receipt of property subject to a liability, consideration *given* in the form of cash or other property *is* offset against consideration *received* in the form of an assumption of liabilities or a transfer of property subject to a liability. Accordingly, $30,000 of the $75,000 gain is recognized.

Basis of Apartment House Acquired by D

The basis of the apartment house acquired by D is $170,000. To the adjusted basis of the property transferred ($100,000) is added the liability to which the new property is subject ($150,000), and the amount of gain recognized upon the exchange ($40,000), or a total of $290,000. Deducted from the $290,000 is the cash received ($40,000) and the liability subject to which property was transferred ($80,000), or a total of $120,000. The new adjusted basis is the difference between $290,000 and $120,000, or $170,000.

Basis of Apartment House Acquired by E

The basis of the apartment house acquired by E is $175,000. To the adjusted basis of the property transferred ($175,000) is added the cash given ($40,000), the liability to which the new property is subject ($80,000), and the amount of gain recognized upon the exchange ($30,-000), or a total of $325,000. Deducted from the $325,000 is the amount of liability subject to which property was transferred ($150,000), or a total of $175,000, the new adjusted basis.

Taxable Exchanges

Exchanges of unlike property and exchanges of properties held by a dealer are considered sales of property. Each party to the exchange is deemed to be a seller of his property and the amount realized on the sale is the fair market value of the property received in exchange. Any gain or loss realized in the exchange is recognized for tax purposes just as if the property had been sold for cash equal to the value of the property received.

The recognized gain is the difference between the fair market value of the property received and the adjusted basis at the date of the exchange of the property transferred. The owner's basis for the newly acquired property will be the price he paid, measured by the cash plus any fair market value of property transferred.

EXCHANGES AND EXCESS DEPRECIATION RECAPTURE
(SECTION 1250)

Section 1250 of the Internal Revenue Code is concerned with the recapture as ordinary income of all or a part of the gain on the sale of real property. The effect of Section 1250 upon like-kind exchanges must be considered in planning the disposition of property.

A like-kind exchange does not result in ordinary income when Section 1250 property is disposed of unless "boot" is received. The Section 1250 gain cannot exceed the greater of two limitations: (1) the total amount of the "boot," or (2) the amount of Section 1250 gain that would be recognized if the exchange was fully taxable, less the fair market value of the Section 1250 property received.[3]

When Section 1250 property is received in exchange, the unrecognized Section 1250 gain of property disposed of in a like-kind exchange is carried over to the Section 1250 property received in the exchange. This carryover is added to the "excess" depreciation taken after the exchange when ultimate disposition is made of the property. The holding period begins when the Section 1250 like-kind property is acquired. The recognized gain on the resale is computed by adding together the carryover gain and the "excess" depreciation taken on the new property and then multiplying this total by the applicable percentage.[4]

The impact of Section 1250 upon like-kind exchanges of Section 1250 property for Section 1250 property is given below. Two situations are presented: column (1), in which no gain is recognized; and column (2), in which there is partial recognition of gain because of the receipt of boot.[5]

---

[3] Prentice-Hall 1969 *Federal Tax Course*, Students Edition (Englewood Cliffs, N.J.: Prentice-Hall, Inc., 1969), p. 1621.

[4] Ibid.

[5] Reprinted by permission from Martin Atlas: *Tax Aspects of Real Estate Transactions*, Fourth Edition, copyright 1966 by The Bureau of National Affairs, Inc., Washington, D. C., pp. 178–179.

EXAMPLE 2

	(1) No Gain Recognized	(2) Partial Recognition of Gain
Amount realized—fair market value of property received in (1) and (2), plus $100 cash received "to boot" in (2)	$3,000	$3,100
Less: adjusted basis of property transferred	2,500	2,500
Gain realized:	500	600
Gain recognized (limited to "boot"):	$ 0	$ 100
In the Sec. 1250 property transferred there was $300 "excess" depreciation. Such property was held 36 months; the applicable percentage is 84%, or	$ 252	$ 252
Less: gain recognized taxable as ordinary income	0	100
Sec. 1250 potential—i.e., the nonrecognized Sec. 1250 gain transferred to the new property	$ 252	$ 152
Basis of new property	$2,500	$2,500
It is used 4 years, taxpayer deducting double declining depreciation, 5-year life, or a total of	2,176	2,176
It is then sold, the then-adjusted basis being	324	324
Amount realized from sale	1,800	1,800
Gain recognized:	$1,476	$1,476

The "excess" depreciation attributable
to the new property is:

Carryover from old	$ 252	$ 152
Double-declining depreciation on new property ($2176) in excess of straightline ($2000)	176	176
Total:	$ 428	$ 328

The new property being used 4
years (48 months), 72% of
"excess" depreciation is taxed
as ordinary income $ 308.16 $ 236.16

ADVANCE PLANNING

Advance planning is necessary to determine whether a nontaxable exchange is desirable for a particular investor in a given situation, or whether there should be an outright sale of the present property for cash and the purchase of another one, namely, a taxable exchange.

The factors of basis and depreciation may be crucial considerations in reaching a decision on whether to exchange or sell. In a like-kind exchange with no boot, the new property takes the same basis as the old property given up. In an outright sale, the basis of the new property is its fair market value. If the investor wants a high basis for depreciation and resulting higher depreciation deductions, it may be desirable to sell his old property outright, pay the capital gains tax on any gain, and reinvest the net proceeds of the sale in another property.

On the other hand, if an investor exchanged his property on which there was a large difference between the basis and its present fair market value, he would be able to accomplish at least two interrelated benefits. First, the investor could use the entire value of the present property (which includes any appreciation) to acquire a new property instead of using only net proceeds after tax on the gain. Secondly, by deferring the tax on the gain he in effect has the use of this tax saving in his business for the length of time he holds the new property.

The advantage of an increased basis and larger depreciation deductions possible from an outright sale and purchase of another property must be weighed against the savings in tax on a nontaxable exchange and the value of this cash saved to the investor's objectives and needs.

A loss is not recognized in a nontaxable exchange. It may be desirable, therefore, for the investor to sell rather than exchange if he wants to benefit from a tax loss deduction. On the other hand, it may be to the investor's advantage to exchange and forfeit the loss deduction if he wants to preserve a high-depreciation basis now available on his existing property. Such a situation could occur if the basis of the existing property exceeded the value of the new property. Also, the investor may not be able to take full advantage of the loss deduction due to the limitations on capital loss deductions. So planning is necessary to maximize the tax advantage of a potential loss.

It is also possible that the investor may not need increased depreciation deductions, as in the case where he has no taxable income to offset. Allowable depreciation must be taken from the basis of the property, yet would serve no useful purpose to the investor. He would only be reducing his basis, thus increasing his gain when disposition was made of the property at a later date. It does seem clear that a nontaxable exchange is attractive to an investor with a low-basis–high-value property desiring long-term appreciation rather than current income if he can make little or no use of the depreciation deduction against current income.

An exchange may also be utilized where an investor wants to sell, or where he needs cash but his present property is difficult to sell or refinance for some reason. An exchange may permit him to acquire a property which can then be more easily sold than the former one. Or, in the case of a need for cash while still maintaining an investment, the investor may exchange for a property which can be more attractively financed.

FORMS

The National Institute of Real Estate Brokers of the National Association of Real Estate Boards publishes a number of forms which may be used in a real estate exchange transaction. Two of these forms are reproduced below for illustration purposes. They are, of course, typically used in conjunction with other forms available from the Institute, such as a Confidential Client Personal Data Worksheet, a Property Analysis, an Individual Tax Analysis, and a Comparative Investment Analysis form. Also available from the Institute is an excellent book which among other things explains with examples the proper use of all of these forms.[6]

---

[6] National Institute of Real Estate Brokers of the National Association of Real Estate Boards, Commercial and Investment Division, *How to Use Taxation and Exchange*

EXCHANGE MOTIVES

The exchange market may be measured in a number of ways, one of which is to know the reasons prompting people to want to give up one property for another. People either want new property or do not want their present property. A checklist of wants may include the following: [7]

1. Immediate income rather than future income
2. Future income rather than immediate income
3. Capital appreciation rather than current income
4. Combining several properties into one, for easier management
5. Dividing one property into several, for diversification of risk
6. Reducing overall holdings
7. Building a larger equity in the property
8. Eliminating management problems
9. Assuming management functions, since this presumably will yield more than a passive investment
10. Owning newer property because it involves less risk or creates more depreciation
11. Owning older property because its potential (by modernizing it) is greater
12. Eliminating borrowing
13. Increasing leverage
14. Expanding commercial premises
15. Sale and leaseback of commercial premises, which frees the equity for new investment
16. Reducing commercial premises, or abandoning expansion plans after land acquired
17. More conservative property
18. More speculative property
19. City residence for country house
20. Farm for city house
21. Residence in older district for one in newer

Techniques in Marketing Investment Real Estate (Chicago: National Institute of Real Estate Brokers of the National Association of Real Estate Boards, 1969). See particularly pp. 159–191 on the subjects of "Exchange of Investment Property" and "The Multiple Exchange."

[7] William J. Casey, Frank J. Curry, J. W. Levine, James M. McMichael, and Carl F. Venter, *Real Estate Exchanges and How to Make Them* (New York: Institute for Business Planning, Inc., 1963), p. 5. Reprinted with permission of the publisher, Institute for Business Planning, Inc., 2 West Thirteenth Street, New York, New York 10011.

EXCHANGE BASIS ADJUSTMENT

PROPERTY BASIS	
CAPITALIZED TRANSACTION COSTS	
ADJUSTED COST BASIS	

NAME _____ DATE ___/___/___

PROPERTY CONVEYED _____

	LINE NO.		(1) PROPERTY		(2) PROPERTY		(3) PROPERTY		(4) PROPERTY		(5) PROPERTY		(6) PROPERTY		
INDICATED GAIN	1	Market Value of Property Conveyed													1
	2	Less: Adjusted Cost Basis													2
	3	INDICATED GAIN													3
BALANCE EQUITIES	4	Equity Conveyed													4
	5	Equity Acquired													5
	6	Difference													6
	7	Cash or Boot Received													7
	8	Cash or Boot Paid													8
DETERMINE RECOGNIZED GAIN	9	Old Loans													9
	10	Less: New Loans													10
	11	NET LOAN RELIEF													11
	12	Less: Cash or Boot Paid (L8)													12
	13	Recognized Net Loan Relief													13
	14	Plus: Cash or Boot Received (L7)													14
	15	TOTAL UNLIKE PROPERTY RECEIVED													15
	16	RECOGNIZED GAIN (LESSER OF L3 OR L15)													16

TRANSFER OF BASIS

	LINE NO.		(1)		(2)		(3)		(4)		(5)		(6)		
TRANSFER OF BASIS	17	Adjusted Cost Basis (L2)													17
	18	Plus: New Loans (L10)													18
	19	Plus: Cash or Boot Paid (L8)													19
	20	Plus: Recognized Gain (L16)													20
	21	Total Additions													21
	22	Less: Old Loans (L9)													22
	23	Less: Cash or Boot Received (L7)													23
	24	NEW ADJUSTED COST BASIS													24

NEW ALLOCATION AND DEPRECIATION

	LINE NO.		(1)		(2)		(3)		(4)		(5)		(6)		
ALLOCATION	25	Land Allocation													25
	26	Improvement Allocation													26
	27	Personal Property Allocation													27
	28	NEW ADJUSTED COST BASIS (L24)													28

	LINE NO.		PP	IMP	PP	IMP	PP	IMP	PP	IMP	PP	IMP	PP	IMP	
DEPRECIATION	29	Estimated Life Term													29
	30	Depreciation Method													30
	31	ANNUAL DEPRECIATION IMPROVEMENTS													31
	32	ANNUAL DEPRECIATION PERSONAL PROPERTY													32

Forms:　NIREB—CID, 155 E. Superior St.
Chicago, Illinois 60611

The statements and figures presented herein, while not guaranteed, are secured from sources we believe authoritative.　**FORM E**

---

* Reprinted with permission of the National Institute of Real Estate Brokers of the National Association of Real Estate Boards, 155 East Superior Street, Chicago, Illinois.

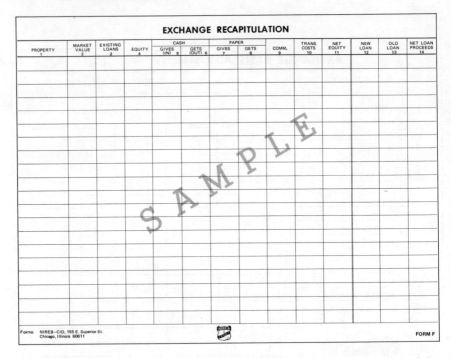

PROPERTY 1	MARKET VALUE 2	EXISTING LOANS 3	EQUITY 4	CASH		PAPER		COMM. 9	TRANS. COSTS 10	NET EQUITY 11	NEW LOAN 12	OLD LOAN 13	NET LOAN PROCEEDS 14
				GIVES (IN) 5	GETS (OUT) 6	GIVES 7	GETS 8						

EXCHANGE RECAPITULATION

Forms: NIREB–CID, 155 E. Superior St.
Chicago, Illinois 60611

FORM F

* Reprinted with permission of the National Institute of Real Estate Brokers of the National Association of Real Estate Boards, 155 East Superior Street, Chicago, Illinois.

LISTING PROPERTY FOR EXCHANGE

The Exchange Division of the National Institute of Real Estate Brokers of the National Association of Real Estate Boards suggests twelve reasons why "exchanging pays." Listed below, they are a good concise statement of some of the principal advantages of exchanging: [8]

1. Exchanging can be the more convenient way of selling your property. It is much simpler at times to exchange, rather than to sell for cash and then look around for a new property.
2. Properties difficult to sell are often easier to exchange.
3. Properties with large equities, or free and clear, adapt themselves to exchanging.

---

[8] "Exchanging or Selling—Our Services Can Help You," leaflet published by the National Institute of Real Estate Brokers of the National Association of Real Estate Boards, 1967. Reprinted with the permission of the National Institute of Real Estate Brokers of the National Association of Real Estate Boards, 155 East Superior Street, Chicago, Illinois.

4. You as owner can pyramid your equity by using the exchange method.
5. Investment properties can be exchanged to defer capital gains tax, until the property taken in exchange is sold.
6. Many buyers have frozen equities in other properties, which you can take in exchange for cash out by your Realtor.
7. Offering your property for exchange can lead to a cash sale.
8. A property offered for either an exchange or a straight sale widens the field for the seller. This attracts many more potential buyers.
9. Exchanging develops more logical transactions for the seller because of current tax regulations on investment properties.
10. Exchanging helps secure for the buyer properties that might not be otherwise obtainable. Because of tax considerations, many owners will not sell for cash.
11. Exchanging may help you obtain a depreciation advantage. If you now own property which has been substantially depreciated, you may acquire a new depreciation level by exchanging.
12. The Membership Roster of the National Institute of Real Estate Brokers, which includes members of its Exchange Division and soon the Commercial and Investment Division, makes possible intercity and interstate exchanges. This cooperation by Realtors affords sellers an unlimited choice of properties.

Further Readings and References

Anderson, Paul E. *Tax Factors in Real Estate Operations*. Second Edition. Englewood Cliffs, N. J.: Prentice-Hall, Inc., 1965.
Brown, Robert Kevin. "Tax Considerations in Sale–Leaseback Transactions," *The Appraisal Journal*, October, 1969, 562–568.
Cerf, Alan R. *Real Estate and the Federal Income Tax*. Englewood Cliffs, N. J.: Prentice-Hall, Inc., 1965.
Considine, Charles R. "Just What Is 'Tax Shelter'?," *Real Estate Today*, July, 1970, 7–10. Chicago: National Institute of Real Estate Brokers, 1970.
Dickerson, William E., and Leo D. Stone. *Federal Income Tax Fundamentals*. Second Edition. Belmont, California: Wadsworth Publishing Company, 1966.
Holzman, Robert S. *Tax Basis for Managerial Decisions*. New York: Holt, Rinehart and Winston, Inc., 1965.
Sandison, Robert W., and Carlyle O. Livingston. "The Tax Reform Act of 1969 As It Affects Real Estate," *The Real Estate Appraiser*, March, 1970, 5–14.
Smith, Dan Throop, *Tax Factors in Business Decisions*. Englewood Cliffs, N. J.: Prentice-Hall, Inc., 1968.
Soelberg, Peer, and Norbert J. Stefaniak. "Impact of the Proposed Tax Reform Bill on Real Estate Investments," *The Appraisal Journal*, April, 1970, 188–211.

5

Ownership Forms

A promoter or a group of individuals as investors must decide in advance of the acquisition of a property which is the best form of business organization or best legal entity in which to take and hold title. This chapter will discuss certain basic ownership forms and considerations pertinent to each. Two factors need to be emphasized at the outset: first, the form of organization for a real estate investment or venture may be decided solely on nontax features; and, second, tax differences between certain organizational forms can be very significant however, and in the great majority of situations where there is an opportunity to choose between several forms, tax factors will heavily influence the ultimate decision, if not be the controlling element. A careful analysis and comparison of all factors—tax, economic, noneconomic—must be made in light of the objectives and capabilities of the promoter as well as of the investor. Ownership forms discussed in this chapter are as follows:

> Individual
> Joint tenancy

Tenancy in common
Limited partnership
Corporation
Joint venture
Syndicate
Real estate investment trust (REIT)

INDIVIDUAL OWNERSHIP

Individual ownership as used here means the ownership of property by a person entirely in his own name as contrasted with, say, corporate ownership. Individual ownership may be desirable in certain instances.

Advantages

1. If a property is expected to show a tax loss, it may be desirable to own it in individual form. The tax loss may be used by the individual to shelter or offset a portion of his income from other sources.
2. Any situation where the corporate form may cause problems taxwise should be considered carefully. Many situations—collapsible corporation, unreasonable accumulated earnings, personal holding company, multiple corporations—could cause the corporate form to suffer penalties as well as lose many of the tax benefits sought.
3. The individual form is desirable if the individual's tax rate is lower than it would be if the corporate form was used.
4. Individual ownership gives the sole owner the absolute control over the investment. There is no reliance upon trustees, managers, and boards of directors. This may be important to some individuals or groups who fear or distrust the corporate form.
5. May be easier to liquidate an entire unit rather than a fractional share.
6. Secrecy; confidential.

Disadvantages

1. Possible interruption of ownership; continuity.
2. Unlimited liability

JOINT TENANCY

Advantage

1. If one of the owners dies this interest goes to the remaining owners.

Disadvantages

1. Limited market ability and/or transferability.
2. Personal liability for all expenses.

TENANTS IN COMMON

A group such as a syndicate may hold title to real estate as tenants in common, whereby each owns an undivided fractional interest in the property. The individuals (1) do not have to own equal interests, or (2) have acquired their interests at the same time, or (3) have to hold their interests under one deed. Each individual may transfer his interest as he sees fit, and the person receiving the interest becomes a cotenant with the other tenants in common. In effect and for all practical purposes, each tenant in common generally owns and controls his share of the property. A tenancy in common is not considered to be a corporation for tax purposes when the property is operated by a managing agent for the owners. Each cotenant reports on his personal income tax his respective share of the income or loss from the operation or sale of the property. The tenant in common is personally liable for only his proportionate share of the expense of the property.

Advantages and Use

1. The tenancy in common is usually used to acquire title to property by a very small number of individual investors, say, three to nine persons. The ownership form may be particularly useful among family members who do not want the survivorship feature of a joint tenancy and yet want to be able to dispose of their respective interests as they see fit.

2. The tenancy in common may be used to avoid the corporate income tax. Other ownership forms, such as the partnership, can accomplish the

same purpose, but there may be other features of these forms which preclude them from being the most desirable for a particular investor's situation.

3. The tenancy in common may be used simply to hold title to property for long-term purposes. Raw land, for instance, may be held in this ownership form for long-term appreciation in value and possible future development.

4. Limited investment.

Georgia Example

In Georgia, for example, the best method of real estate syndication is through tenants in common. A brochure offering investment in such a syndicate points out that tenants in common are not partners and are not liable for the actions of other tenants in common. A judgment, suit, or tax lien against any one tenant in common affects only his interest in the property and the interest of the others is not affected.

It is further pointed out that tenancy in common gives the investor a better return on his money by eliminating corporate taxes on the earned profits. Depreciation accrues pro rata directly to the tenant in common.

Death of one of the tenants in common does not affect the interest of the others. The interest of the deceased tenant in common passes directly to his heirs or devisees.

Limitations

1. The tenancy in common is probably not a practical ownership form, especially if there are a goodly number of co-owners involved, for active operations in real estate dealing, such as buying, operating, and selling of multiple properties. Problems of title transfer can arise and it may not be possible quickly and easily to transfer title.

2. Limited market.

LIMITED PARTNERSHIP

The limited partnership form is commonly used in real estate syndication. There are several reasons for its use:

1. The avoidance of corporate income taxes; the limited partnership

entity itself is a conduit and does not pay a tax but the partners are taxed on their respective shares of the partnership income.

2. Any taxable loss may be used to offset other income.

3. A partner can benefit from depreciation deductions to the extent of his interest in the partnership.

4. The limited partners have the corporate benefit of limited liability; only the general partners have unlimited liability.

The limited partnership form enables an individual to contribute capital to a venture and participate in the profits. At the same time he limits his liability to the extent of his capital contribution and does not have to participate actively in the management of the venture, leaving that to the general partner.

Possible disadvantages of the limited partnership form include the following:

1. The transferability of individual investor's interests is more restricted than in a corporation.

2. There may not be as wide a market for a limited partnership interest as there would be for corporate stock.

3. Lack of continuity of life of the organization.

4. The danger that the limited partnership will be taxed as a corporation if it has too many corporate characteristics; in such a case it might have been better initially to organize a corporation and have all of its benefits.

Avoiding Corporate Characteristics

The limited partnership must be organized carefully so as to avoid being treated as a corporation for income tax purposes yet have some of the powers and characteristics of a corporation to facilitate its operation. If the limited partnership is classified as a corporation, it stands to be taxed under corporate rates and rules and the distributions to the members are also taxable a second time in their hands. To avoid corporate treatment, the limited partnership agreement must be drafted so as to avoid including all of the characteristics of a corporation. Four major corporate characteristics must be considered, and if only two are present in the limited partnership entity, the latter will probably be classified as a limited partnership. If more than two of the corporate characteristics are present, the entity will probably more nearly resemble a corporation and be classified as one. The four major corporate characteristics to consider are as follows:

1. Continuity of life
2. Centralized management
3. Limited liability
4. Free transferability of interests

CORPORATION

A corporation is a legal entity in itself, with an identity independent of its stockholders. As an ownership form in real estate, it is sometimes called by several names: real estate corporation, public real estate corporation, public corporation, or real estate investment corporation.

Advantages

1. The corporate form provides a relatively simple and flexible means of ownership. There are no individual deeds to show each stockholder's interest. The size of the individual investment is flexible and may be in smaller units than in other forms of ownership. Transferability of interests can be accomplished with relative ease. Estate planning may be easier since the shares of a corporation can usually be valued more easily than partnership interests.

2. In a relatively small corporate group the members can be selected for their professional talents—accountant, lawyer, surveyor, and the like. These people can then be given an opportunity to perform services for the corporation. Not only does this give the corporation the advantage of professional services at nominal costs but it also enables the group to keep better informed on the investments of the corporation.

3. Diversification of investments is one of the strongest points in favor of the corporate form of real estate ownership. While other forms may own several properties, this is generally not the case because of restrictions and problems of financing and management. The combining of several individual properties into one corporation and the creation of diversification also gives the investor an added degree of safety. There are generally no legal restrictions on the kinds of properties a corporation may invest in except for any limitation imposed in the by-laws and charter.

4. The corporation is a means of keeping "investment" property separate from "dealer" property. Such distinction is a major consideration under income tax laws since each classification is given different treatment.

5. A corporation can provide fringe benefits for its members which may not be possible under a partnership. The promoter, being a shareholder and employee of the corporation, may enjoy these benefits.

6. A corporate share generally has the attribute of liquidity, particularly in contrast to a relatively nonliquid interest in a partnership syndicate. Liquidity can be of considerable significance to the small investor and indeed to any person needing cash immediately. It must be remembered, however, that the degree of liquidity depends upon the market at any given

time. Also, the extent to which a corporation is known and has an established market for its stock is an important element in liquidity.

It is possible that the corporate form may actually widen the market for the real estate under its ownership since the stock of the corporation is more easily transferable than the real estate. Partial ownership may be transferred to others through shares of stock and yet control of the property may be retained by majority ownership of the corporate stock.

7. The limited liability feature of corporations is also available to the limited partners in a partnership. The promoters in a partnership, however, are usually general partners and have unlimited liability. In a corporation the promoters have limited liability along with other members of the group. Insurance can be obtained to cover the liability hazard and the importance of the limited liability feature should not be overemphasized in any of the organizational forms where it is available.

8. The corporation provides for centralization of management. Also, the larger corporations may have the ability to attract and recruit high-caliber management because of its size and resources. The stockholders exercise a voice in management through their votes for directors and officers. Promoters can maintain control of the corporation by retaining a substantial share of its stock.

9. A corporation can raise additional capital by issuing shares of stock up to the maximum number permitted in its charter. Such a feature enables it to meet relatively quickly a need for capital to acquire additional investments or for use in connection with current investments.

10. A corporation can acquire large investments which would be impossible for the typical small investor to acquire alone. Syndicates also have this ability but to a smaller degree. The corporation usually has many more participants and acquires a larger amount of capital with which to acquire very large properties.

11. A corporation is relatively easy to organize and can begin operations with little cash. A small group can incorporate, contribute capital, acquire a property, and then sell or refinance it and reinvest the proceeds in another property. The members of the group may also contribute additional funds to the organization and sell shares to additional members. The corporation can in this manner begin on a modest basis but eventually achieve substantial growth.

12. A corporation has a perpetual life. This means that its existence, its continuity, is not affected by the death or withdrawal of a member.

13. An owner of real estate may transfer it and any mortgages on it to a corporation in exchange for corporation stock. If the group is in control of the corporation immediately after the transfer, the incorporation of the real estate is held to be tax-free. Control means ownership of 80 percent of the outstanding stock of the corporation. The tax basis of the property to the corporation is the same basis as it was in the hands of the owners.

14. A corporation may acquire property with its stock and at the market value of that stock, which may be more than its par value. For example, stock having a par value of $5 may have a current market value of $30, so that 300 shares would acquire a $9,000 property. The $9,000 would become the basis of the property to the corporation.

15. The present tax on an ordinary business corporation is composed of a normal tax and a surtax, both of which are imposed on the taxable (gross less deductions) income of the corporation. The normal tax rate of 22 percent is applied as a percentage of the taxable income of the corporation. The surtax rate of 26 percent is a percentage of the amount by which the taxable income of the corporation exceeds a surtax exemption of $25,000.

The corporate rate is, therefore, constant at 22 percent until the taxable income of the corporation reaches $25,000. If an investor has a large income, it may be advisable to use the corporate form for a property. If the investor's income from a property, when combined with his income from other sources, puts him in a tax bracket higher than the corporate tax, then he should consider incorporating the investment.

16. There is no tax on any gain in the initial sale of an issue of the corporation's stock. For example, stock with a par value of $20 sells for $25; the total amount of the sale is considered to be a contribution to capital and is not taxable income.

17. A corporation is an excellent entity in which to accumulate earnings. Earnings must not accumulate beyond the reasonable needs of the business; $100,000 or less has been considered to meet this requirement.

18. Certain kinds of corporations, called "Subchapter S" corporations, may be taxed as partnerships if specified requirements are met. Such treatment avoids the double-taxation disadvantage of the corporate form of ownership. This kind of corporation is discussed later in the chapter.

Disadvantages

1. A corporation may not be advantageous if its tax bracket is higher than that of the stockholders. There, of course, may be considerations other than taxes which would outweigh this disadvantage.

2. A corporation may be more closely regulated than other ownership forms. This may be particularly true of real estate corporations offering shares to the public. The close regulation could also be considered an advantage to the investors.

3. While a corporation may be relatively easy to form, organizational costs may be considered by some investors and promoters to be a disadvantage of this form of ownership.

4. The double-taxation feature is a major disadvantage of the corporation. Income is taxed at the corporate level and again at the individual

stockholder level. The corporation form may not be advantageous if a substantial part of its income is distributed to stockholders and is subject to the double taxation.

5. The corporate form does not permit the depreciation allowance to be passed through to the individual investor or shareholder. The depreciation allowance is, however, an advantage to the corporation.

6. Losses may not be passed through a corporation to the individual investor or shareholder and be deducted by him on his personal tax return. In other ownership forms, taxable losses may be used to offset other income of the individual. No immediate tax advantage will be available to the investor if the real estate generates losses in its early stages. The losses may, however, accumulate in the corporation and be used to offset corporate income in the future.

7. The investor has no direct control over the management of his investment in a corporation. His control is through his vote for corporate directors and officers.

8. The yield on corporate investments in real estate as well as on corporate stock may be lower than in the case of real estate and shares in a partnership syndicate. Corporate real estate investments may not be as speculative as in the case of partnership syndicates with resulting lower yields. The diversification, safety, and liquidity factors in a corporation are better. Lower yields were in fact instrumental in prompting the conversion of multiproperty syndicates into one corporation. Prices and costs on properties were increasing so rapidly that the high yields promised by many syndicates could not be maintained.

Other Factors in Corporate Form Analysis

In addition to a consideration of the general features of the corporate form, both pro and con, there are several other points to consider, particularly if the corporation is already in existence. A multiproperty public real estate corporation is difficult to analyze. The points enumerated below are some of the more basic considerations which a prospective investor might check prior to investing and which a group contemplating incorporating a property might keep in mind.

1. What about the management of the corporation? Should it consist of one man, a small group, or a large group? Who controls the corporation and what happens to the interests of this controlling group in the future? Are the salaries of management excessive? Is there any depth in the management ranks?

2. What is the source of the income, as to types of properties and tenants, from which the shareholders are to receive a distribution? Is the

income sufficient to cover distributions? Is it a recurring income or a non-recurring profit? What is the current ratio or working capital position of the corporation? A deficit in working capital may be normal for a real estate corporation since cash is usually invested in real estate as promptly as possible after receipt. However, is the corporation in a position to meet any emergency need for cash without a quick sale at possible distress prices of any of its holdings? How does the corporation measure and report "profit" and "earnings"?

3. If the corporation holds purchase-money mortgages taken back in the sale of properties, how are these mortgages valued on the books of the corporation? Such mortgages are usually salable only at a heavy discount and should not be valued at full face, although the corporate books may show them at such a figure.

4. Have adequate reserves been established for replacements and obsolescence of equipment and other such items? What about reserves for repairs?

5. How is the promoter of the group to be compensated? Does this compensation cause a dilution of the interests of the cash investors or the equity of the public? For example, a common practice is for promoters to accept subordinated shares of stock in exchange for their services; or they may take warrants to buy stock later at below market prices. Such practices are not illegal but they can dilute the interests of the cash investors.

6. The debt–equity ratio in a public real estate corporation is usually higher than is typical for most business corporations; that is, the amount of debt normally exceeds the amount of equity in the corporation because of the heavy use of mortgages. Such a situation is not unusual but there are several items that might be checked. What is the liability of the corporation on the mortgages? Is the corporation personally liable or is liability limited to only the property securing the mortgage? Are there any mortgages with large balloon payments in which substantial sums may become due at one time? How much of the corporate debt is unsecured, thus indicating a possible thin capitalization of the corporation? How much of the debt is on old properties or properties which are marginal in nature?

JOINT VENTURE

Usually a joint venture is created to carry out a single business venture—one specific venture or project. Once this purpose has been accomplished the joint venture will be terminated. It is a special combination of two or more persons who jointly seek a profit in a specific venture without any actual partnership or corporate designation. There is no intent to create a permanent continuing relationship between the parties or to create the usual full range of legal liabilities and obligations of a general partnership or corporation.

The joint venture is commonly used in the real estate finance and investment field, particularly in large-scale land development and building construction where large sums of capital are needed, such as industrial parks, shopping centers, and multitenant office buildings. A developer with construction experience will join with an institutional lender, such as a life insurance company, which provides the capital in return for a participation in the ownership profits of the project.

In addition to the ownership profits of the usual income yield and tax benefits, the developer is frequently able to handle a project he might not otherwise be able to do, and at the same time the lender has a better-than-average investment outlet.

Institutional lenders have many proposals presented to them for joint venture participations, but not all of the proposals will qualify. A major consideration of the lender in joint ventures is the ability and integrity of the developer. A lender will insist that a partner or coventurer have proven development and construction ability, an unquestioned business and moral reputation, and financial strength. In addition to a superb partner, a lender will want a return commensurate with the risk of the high-ratio financing extended in the venture. Further, the property should be one on which the lender would normally make a mortgage loan and which might be expected to generate an increasing income stream.

Further, a proposed project should generally be in some respect better than the average real estate project in order to attract a lender to a joint venture arrangement. The developer should offer something beyond the ordinary—something better than the lender could arrange himself, something better than the average typical transaction which could be financed in other ways. The developer or coventurer should offer significant or distinguishing contributions to the venture. Examples of such distinguishing characteristics are a superior location for the project, major anchor tenants guaranteed, expertise and cost savings in management and leasing, and cost savings in development and construction.

The joint venture, of course, benefits the developer. He is able to obtain funds needed to supplement his cash resources, create large projects, and at the same time minimize his own risks. The joint venture in effect permits the developer a larger-than-normal loan in exchange for sharing an ownership position with outsiders in the form of a partnership agreement with an institutional lender.

The institutional lender, usually an insurance company, is a passive financial partner in the venture. It is not experienced in development, construction, leasing, or management; indeed, this is what the lender expects from the developer partner. The joint venture does require a written agreement between developer and lender specifically setting out the details of the joint arrangement. It might be pointed out that the interests of the lender and the developer may not always be the same (there may be differences such as short-term vs. long-term outlook and different tax positions), and these matters must be mutually settled.

The joint venture does not necessarily have to be on a large scale. It may consist of only a few individuals who jointly take title to property with little formal organization. This will enable an investor to spread his capital over several projects, thereby achieving diversification as well as acquiring new development and management talent with each venture.

A joint venture is not created by simply owning property under a joint tenancy or tenancy in common. For instance, if joint tenants or tenants in common own rental property and share the profits, this does not in itself create a joint venture form of organization. There must be a definite agreement with the express purpose of the joint venture set forth, a clear intent of the parties to establish a joint venture relationship, a setting forth of the interests of the parties, and provisions for the treatment and accounting for funds.

The joint venture may be organized in several forms. It may be an association of individuals, a partnership, a corporation, or a combination of these forms. All forms should be considered in relation to the objectives of the investors before making a decision. Several examples of joint venture proposals are shown in the chapters of this book dealing with specific types of properties.

SYNDICATE

The syndicate is a major method for raising equity capital for real estate investment. The term "syndicate" has no unique meaning or independent significance legally or taxwise; these aspects of it are determined by the underlying form adopted by its participants. A syndicate is a group or association or combination of individuals who join together to pool funds and conduct a common venture, usually a financial business transaction. It is essentially a business arrangement for the accomplishment of some objective; when this objective has been achieved, the group is dissolved. This discussion will consider a syndicate as a group of investors brought together for the particular purpose of investing in one or more parcels of real estate. The underlying form of ownership for the group's real estate—that is, the method by which it holds title to its property—may be of several kinds, and the distinction between them is not always clear: partnership, limited partnership, joint venture, trust, real estate investment trust, and the corporation. Participants may also hold title as tenants in common. (See the section, "Tenants in Common," in this chapter, pp. 78–79.

A syndicate investment may be limited to one property, which is most common, or there may be acquisition of several properties. The syndicate may be private or public. The private offering is a small one with a few investors, perhaps four to ten or maybe twenty participants, and usually with little or no promotional effort. The public offering may involve several hundred or more participants, with considerable promotional effort in soliciting investors on a large scale. A private investor might promote a private syndicate with several of his friends to acquire a small apartment building or small office building; or he could purchase shares in a larger public offering.

The syndicator or promoter—and there may be one or more syndicator partners—is the key factor in the creation of a successful syndicate. It is the syndicator who brings together the capital of several participating investors, selects the property for acquisition by the syndicate members, operates and manages the business affairs of the syndicate, and handles the ultimate disposition of the syndicate real estate and the distribution of financial gains.

There are two commonly used ways of organizing a syndicate:

1. The syndicator or promoter first acquires a property, either by option or by a contract of sale, and then seeks to organize a group to which he assigns or transfers his contractual right to purchase the property in exchange for a share interest in the syndicate; or
2. The syndicate is organized first and then an attempt is made to locate a property for it to acquire.

Irrespective of whether the purchase of property or the syndicate comes first, there are usually several general steps that are followed by the syndicator. These may be enumerated as follows, although they do not necessarily have to follow this sequence:

1. Prospective investors must be solicited and a determination made of their objectives and expected capital investment in this syndicate. This involves the preparation of a brochure or prospectus setting forth factual information about the venture and the property if it has been selected.

2. The property to be acquired must be analyzed as to its physical condition, its location and market factors, and its economic soundness. Also, its yield and present and available financing must be considered. Will the property give the yield desired by the syndicate? What kind of private and institutional financing is available?

3. How will professional management for the syndicate real estate be provided?

4. State and federal laws and regulations governing the issuance of securities must be complied with before any shares or interests in the syndicate are offered. Although certain offerings may be exempt from registration, legal counsel is absolutely advisable in the matter of securities registration.

5. The form of ownership must be determined. The form chosen will depend upon many factors, such as tax considerations, legal aspects, objectives of the group, and type of property.

6. Determination must be made of the respective shares of the syndicator and of the investors. These facts should then be included in the agreement setting up the syndicate.

Investors' Benefits

The individual passive or inactive investor who contributes his capital for a participation in the syndicate expects to share in the benefits of a sound real estate investment with minimum risk and trouble to himself. Most investors in syndicates are private, individual, nonprofessional investors who are willing to combine their capital with the knowledge, experiences, and management of the professional—the syndicator—to share in an active investment opportunity. The benefits which may accrue to them from their participation may be summarized as follows:

1. No management problems.
2. A share in the ownership of a large property for a relatively small investment.
3. Limited liability.
4. A share in the benefits of certain financial and tax features, such as leverage, equity build-up through mortgage amortization, depreciation, interest deductions, and capital gains.
5. Good return—usually higher than on other investments of similar nature and risk.
6. Spreading of risk as well as costs through the pooling of capital.
7. Usually a single large-size property is safer and more profitable than is an investment in a single small-size property. Syndicates give the investor an opportunity to invest in the larger property with resulting benefits.

Growth of Syndication

Syndicates, for both the large investor and the small investor, have experienced substantial growth in recent years. Factors accounting for this growth include the following:

1. The general increase in the prosperity of the economy and the growth in personal incomes. There is more surplus capital available for investment, especially small amounts from individual private investors.
2. The size and costs of real estate projects have increased tremendously and created a demand for vast amounts of capital. Syndication brings together equity capital from many investors.
3. The public generally has acquired a broader knowledge of real estate investments and the advantages of real estate as an investment. Major real estate projects have received widespread publicity. Articles on real estate have occurred with increasing frequency in mass media, such as magazines and newspapers.
4. There are expanded investment opportunities open to everyone, both professional and nonprofessional. The unprecedented demand for real estate of all types has created a real estate boom, and the public is aware of it.

Kinds of Properties

Limitations

The syndicate arrangement does have some potential disadvantages, although, of course, these will vary as to importance with the individual investor. Some of the points to keep in mind include the following:

1. A syndicate share has limited liquidity; there is no organized market for these shares as in the securities field for stocks and bonds.
2. The full benefits from a syndicate may not be realized until the alternate disposition of the property.
3. Financial analysis of a large public offering syndicate can be difficult. Details about the financial and legal makeup of the syndicate may be hard to obtain even though the prospectus is a fine one.
4. Remember that the promised high yields must come from the income generated by the property. Attention must be given to the soundness of this income source as well as to proper protection for its continued distribution.

REAL ESTATE INVESTMENT TRUST

The "real estate investment trust" (REIT), along with the limited partnership syndicate, regular trust, and corporation, is designed to provide an opportunity for large-scale public participation in real estate investment. The REIT, if it meets certain qualifications, is given special status or benefits under federal income tax laws. These qualifications are essentially as follows:

1. Management of the trust must be by one or more trustees.
2. It must be a type of organization that would be taxed as an ordinary domestic corporation except for the REIT law.
3. Transferable shares or transferable certificates of beneficial owner-ship (which are equivalent to shares in a corporation) must be issued to at least 100 persons. The 100-person membership must be main-tained throughout the life of the trust (at least 335 days per year).
4. Five or fewer persons may not own more than 50 percent of the trust; that is, a trust cannot qualify as a REIT if it is a personal holding company.
5. The REIT may not be a dealer in real estate; it may not hold prop-erty primarily for sale to customers in the ordinary course of business. The REIT is intended to be a medium for public investment in real estate and it must not be an active participant in a real estate business or venture. It must be a "passive" entity.
6. At least 75 percent of the total value of the assets or investments of the REIT must be in real estate, cash, or government securities. A further limitation restricts the security of any one issuer to an amount not greater in value than 5 percent of the total assets of the trust and may not represent more than 10 percent of the voting securities of the issuer.
7. There are three limitations placed on the gross income of the REIT which tend to assure the passive nature of its income. These limita-tions are as follows:

    a. At least 90 percent or more of the annual gross income must come from dividends, interest, rents from real property, and gains from the sale of stock, securities, and real property.
    b. On top of the 90 percent rule is the rule that at least 75 percent of the annual gross income must come from real property, interest on mortgages, gains from the sale of real property, and other real estate sources. This means that the largest share of the income must come from real estate. Only 15 percent may come from stocks, dividends, or gain from the sale of stock or other securities, and 10 percent may come from any source.
    c. Not more than 30 percent of the annual gross income may come from the sale of securities held for less than 6 months or from the sale of real estate held for less than 4 years, except for involuntary conversions.

8. The REIT must distribute as dividends, not including capital gains dividends, at least 90 percent of its taxable income.
9. The REIT must be organized legally as either an unincorporated association or trust.

Tax Benefits

The special income tax benefits of the REIT arise from its treatment, if it meets the necessary qualifications, as a "conduit" or pass-through with regard to its income distributed (at least 90 percent) to its members or beneficiaries. The latter pay tax on their individual distributions. The REIT pays no income tax on income which it distributes; it thus avoids the double-taxation feature of the ordinary business corporation.

Advantages

The tax conduit treatment is, of course, the main benefit of the REIT to the investor. There are other economic benefits—some derived from the conduit treatment—of this form of ownership of real estate.

1. The REIT is most suitable and appealing to, and, indeed, primarily intended for, the small investor who wants the economic and tax advantages of real estate that might not ordinarily be available to him. Such an investor is usually primarily interested in current annual income, the good return from real estate as an investment, and lastly the benefits of any capital appreciation in the value of his holdings. The REIT is a kind of mutual fund in real estate which, along with the above benefits, has such features as diversification, centralized professional management, transferability of shares, and an ability to acquire large properties beyond the reach of the individual investor acting on his own.

2. The REIT has generally been accepted by the investing public and has through its broader base of shareholders established a reasonably good market for its shares. The market is undoubtedly stronger than the rather limited market for limited partnership syndicate shares or other forms of ownership. Adding to this general acceptance is the fact that most REIT's have generally been well managed, and all are, of course, subject to strict regulations.

3. A general benefit to the economy resulting from the creation of the REIT is the additional source of funds made available for real estate development and investment.

4. Capital gains in a REIT may be passed through directly to the shareholder when a property is sold at a profit. No tax is paid by the trust. Also, all distributions of capital gains are long-term in nature to the shareholder and may be reported as such on his tax return regardless of his individual holding period. This is in contrast to the corporate organization form where the corporation pays the capital gains tax and the shareholder is

taxed at ordinary income rates on his pro rata share of any distribution of the gain to him.

5. While the REIT is primarily directed at the small investor, the large investor may nevertheless find it advantageous. Certain features of the REIT are not available in other organizational forms. The REIT may be created to acquire and market a property with limited market appeal as a single parcel but which can be marketed more easily through the sale of shares. Or, a single parcel of income-producing property may be held in the REIT form. The unique tax and economic advantages of the REIT may be attractive to any investor who can adapt these advantages to his investment objectives and capabilities.

Disadvantages

Like other forms of real estate investment ownership, the REIT has its comparative limitations. Its usefulness as a syndication form must be considered in light of the factors set forth below.

1. The REIT must observe strict and complex federal and state rules and regulations regarding its organization and operation if it is to maintain its favored tax status. While such control may be beneficial to the shareholders in giving them a degree of protection, the REIT promoters may find that another form of organization, such as the corporation, gives a greater freedom and ease of operation. Further, the organization and operation of the REIT entails considerable expense in the way of accounting and legal services.

2. The qualification of at least 100 owners eliminates the REIT from consideration in any real estate venture where enlistment of this many owners is not feasible. It may be desired that control of the venture be concentrated in only a few owners; or a sufficient number of participants may not be available to meet the qualification. Also, if there is a possibility that the 100-member qualification cannot be maintained, it may be best to select another ownership form initially. If the REIT loses its status as a trust because of failure to meet this qualification at any time, regaining REIT classification (from that of a taxable corporation) may be difficult.

3. The tax benefits of certain deductions cannot be passed through the REIT to its beneficiaries. Operating losses, taxes, and interest deductions are consumed in the REIT and are of no direct benefit to the shareholder. While the REIT may make tax-free distributions to its shareholders if such arise, depreciation deductions cannot be passed through to the shareholders so as to permit the latter a shelter or offset against other income, such as would be possible in a noncorporate partnership or individual ownership form.

This inability of the REIT to pass through losses and other deductions to its beneficiaries means that it is not a practical entity for holding property for eventual development and appreciation, or for projects in which losses are expected in the early stages of development. Tax-loss property is of little, if, any, benefit to the REIT.

4. The REIT is not suited for active real estate operations—development, construction, management. This is because of the qualification that it must be a passive entity and not an active, operating real estate operation.

5. The REIT cannot, like a corporation, accumulate income. Whether this limitation might retard the growth potential of the REIT is a factor to consider.

6. While the REIT may acquire a single parcel of property, it is probably not the best organization form for such an acquisition. The syndicate in the form of a limited partnership may be more suitable. This is because of the manner in which single parcels are acquired by promoters (contract or option) and then transferred to the syndicate group in exchange for partnership—ownership units. The promoters are usually brokers who also act in such a capacity for the syndicate's real estate as well as serve as management agents for the group. Such an arrangement is not possible with the REIT, or at least very hazardous in light of the strict regulations surrounding the REIT and its operations.

7. As pointed out previously in this discussion, the REIT is primarily a current-income entity for the small investor and this should be the major objective of any investor considering participating in the REIT. However, the REIT is similar to the public real estate corporation, which also offers certain advantages to the investor. While the latter organization form has "double-taxation," this must be weighed against other benefits of the corporation as well as against the tax disadvantage of the REIT in that losses may not be passed through to the beneficiary. The latter factor may heavily outweigh the advantage of the conduit treatment of the REIT. From the promoter's point of view, the REIT is probably unsuited except for a large undertaking or situation.

Further Readings and References

Conlee, Cecil D. "A Developer Discusses Joint Ventures," *The Mortgage Banker*, May, 1969, 59–61.

Doggett, Aubrey C., Jr. "Considerations in Forming A Trust," *The Mortgage Banker*, September, 1970, 43–46, 52–58. The entire September issue is a "Special Real Estate and Mortgage Investment Trust Issue."

Hussander, Martin. *Real Estate Syndicator's Manual and Guide.* Englewood Cliffs, N. J.: Prentice-Hall, Inc., 1969.

Ives, J. Atwood, and William S. Green. " 'REIT's'—Enigma or Opportunity," *The Commercial and Financial Chronicle*, July 9, 1970, 1, 14–16.

Kratovil, Robert. *Real Estate Law*. Fifth Edition. Englewood Cliffs, N. J.: Prentice-Hall, Inc., 1969.

Rabinowitz, Martin J. "Realty Syndication: An Income Tax Primer for Investor and Promoter," *The Journal of Taxation*, August, 1968, 92–98.

Tidwell, Victor H. "Subchapter S v. Partnership: A Guide to Their Contrasting Tax Treatments," *The Journal of Taxation*, September, 1968, 174–178.

6

Commercial
Leasehold
Financing

Commercial real estate development utilizing the long-term ground lease and leasehold financing is not new, but the use of the lessee's interest (the leasehold) as a financing device has received particular attention and increasingly widespread use in recent years. Almost every kind of commercial building can be developed and financed under the leasehold arrangement—office buildings, shopping centers, warehouses, restaurants, hotels, motels, department stores, and apartment buildings.

The arrangement typically is concerned with the financing of commercial property on unimproved land, or land where obsolete buildings are to be removed. The developer leases the land from its owner and then seeks to obtain funds from an institutional lender, usually a life insurance company, for the erection of improvements. The lease between the land owner and the developer is known as a "ground lease," with the owner's or lessor's

This chapter originally appeared as an article by the author, "Commercial Leasehold Appraising," *Valuation*, Official Journal of the American Society of Appraisers, January 15, 1967.

interest referred to as the "underlying fee" or simply "fee," and the developer's or lessee's or "tenant's" interest referred to as the "leasehold." Ground leases are usually for long terms—many for 75 years or more—and are "net" to the lessor; that is, the lessee is responsible for paying all expenses of the property. When the developer leases space in his buildings, the lease between the developer and tenant is referred to as the "sublease" or "space lease" and the occupant is known as the "subtenant" or "space tenant."

URBAN COMMERCIAL DEVELOPMENT

Ground leases are particularly attractive to both land owners and developers in fast-growing and highly built-up urban areas so characteristic of our economy now and due to be even more so in the years ahead. Quite frequently, much of the choice commercial land in heavily populated urban areas is held by individuals or institutions who for any number of reasons do not want to or are not able to sell it outright, or who are not themselves in a position to properly improve the property, such as property held in trusts and estates. Or, the value of the land may have become so high that it is not feasible for a developer both to buy the land and also to improve it with a building. The ground lease offers a practical solution in both situations.

Owners of choice commercial land which has substantially increased in value since they acquired it are faced with a large capital gains tax if the land is sold outright. If the land, however, is leased on a long-term basis, the income to the owner is stretched over many years and the tax burden is minimized. Moreover, the owner still has his land on which he is now receiving a presumably attractive net rate of return, and his position as lessor is further enhanced by the capital improvements which the lessee makes on the land and which revert to the owner at the expiration of the lease term.

The arrangement is attractive to the lessee–developer. Instead of purchasing a high-priced parcel of land which would require a large capital outlay for an asset on which there is no depreciation allowance for income tax purposes, the ground lease keeps the developer's investment in land to a minimum and the ground rental becomes a tax-deductible business expense. His funds are released to apply to the improvements on the land or to other uses. He is assured of the long-term use of the land and after erection of the improvements anticipates an excellent rate of return on his equity through the cash flow from the improvements. As a practical matter, the owner has in effect made a "loan" of the land to the lessee–developer; instead of interest payments on a loan from an outside lender, periodic rent is paid on the lease. If the developer had to obtain a loan from conventional outside sources, the loan-to-value percentage he could borrow would be something less than the full value of the property; there would be a cushion of safety in the loan. Through a subordinated ground lease, the developer has in effect acquired a full loan on the land value and the security is his lease covenant to improve the land in a stated manner. The developer has also acquired an asset—his leasehold—which can increase in value and perhaps be sold at a profit or can itself be used as security for a loan.

FINANCABLE AND MARKETABLE FEATURES

The commercial developer leases land for the purpose of erecting improvements thereon which will generate a cash flow returning to him an attractive income on his investment. In addition, he will probably wish to sell or refinance his investment when the cash flow has reached a given point. To accomplish these objectives the developer will want to obtain the maximum loan possible from an institutional lender with provisions to meet his needs. The lender, of course, needs provisions to protect the security of the loan. Both parties, however, have a mutual interest in negotiating a financable and marketable investment, and it is with this objective in mind that attention is now focused on certain characteristic features of this increasingly important form of financing.

Subordination

The developer's interest in the land under the ground lease (his leasehold) may serve as the security for his loan from an institutional lender. Since the lender's security is the leasehold, the lender could lose the security in the event of default by the developer and termination of the leasehold in any manner. Such a leasehold mortgage is referred to as being "unsubordinated" (or "nonsubordinated," or "without subordination"), meaning that the owner of the land has not subordinated his underlying fee interest to the lender's mortgage and his rights are thereby superior to those of the lender. Under this arrangement, a leasehold mortgage is actually a second mortgage.

Such loans are not particularly attractive to most lenders, but there are certain provisions which can give the lender a sufficient degree of protection to make them acceptable. The lender must have protection in the event of default by the developer on his ground lease with the land owner. Various arrangements are used for this protection, but basically the lender secures the right to receive prompt notice from the owner of any default by the developer and is granted ample time to step into the lessee's position and cure the default and pursue its remedies under the mortgage. Probably the most important protection for the lender after the notice-and-right-to-cure feature is whether the leasehold can be assigned. Any limitations on assignability can affect marketability (particularly important to the lender in the event of foreclosure) and hence value. The lender will certainly want the right to sell the leasehold interest in the event of foreclosure. Leasehold rights should be freely transferable and any unreasonable restrictive control on this feature by the owner of the land lessens their quality as loan security. Assignability without continuing liability is particularly important to institutional lenders.

Under a "subordinated" ground lease (or "subordinated fee"), the owner of the underlying fee has agreed to subordinate or to make his interest inferior to that of the lender's mortgage. The effect is to bring the lease up to a fee status. The fee owner is required to sign the loan deed but not the promissory note; his liability is limited to the loss of his land. The ground lease permits the lessee–developer to require the owner to subordinate the owner's underlying fee interest as security for a loan. Both the land and its improvements will now serve as security for the loan. In the event of foreclosure, the owner forfeits his interest in the property to the lender. It might be said—and with a large element of truth—that the leasehold is financable right at this point; the lender has a fee ownership security and all other security features of the transaction are simply side dressing.

The subordination feature, like the ground lease concept itself, is not new, but land owners in the past generally have been reluctant—indeed, often have absolutely refused—to consider subordination of their fee. Widespread recognition and increasing acceptance by owners of subordination as being advantageous to both owner and developer is of relatively recent origin. Subordination may permit an owner to capitalize fully on the value of his land. The developer may be able through subordination to obtain a loan which might not otherwise be available because of the lender's established policy or practice of not lending against unsubordinated leaseholds or because of regulatory statutes prohibiting this class of loans for certain types of lending institutions. Erection of proper improvements should, of course, enhance the owner's investment position. Further, the amount of the loan available from the lender is larger with the subordination feature. The owner might, in exchange for the subordination feature, be able to negotiate attractive features elsewhere in the lease, such as higher rentals (normally 20 percent more than without subordination) or participation in the profits generated by the improvement.

Condemnation

One of the most important and most difficult-to-negotiate provisions of a ground lease to be used as a security for a loan is the one dealing with condemnation. Condemnation action could damage the loan security by reducing its income-producing ability and thereby its value. Shopping center lending, for instance, depends heavily upon selling volume and overage rents. Condemnation for adjacent street widening could absorb a sufficient number of a center's parking spaces to adversely affect store volumes, especially at peak seasons such as Christmas when all the spaces the center can get are needed. Or, substantial footage may be taken off the front of an office building to provide a sidewalk, thereby reducing the rentable square footage of the building and hence its value.

The lender is clearly interested in seeing that the condemnation provision spells out the effect of a taking on the lease (such as the right of the lessee to cancel), who is to receive the award, and the basis for the division of a lump sum award. The lender would like, if legally permissable, to be in a position to receive the tenant's portion of an award in the event of total condemnation. In the event of partial condemnation, the lease should continue in force with a rental reduction. Provision in a ground lease for arbitration of any differences is usually acceptable to the lender; this keeps him out of court.

The lender is better protected with—and indeed, should at the time of original negotiations insist upon—a mortgage provision. This gives the lender the right to receive the borrower's share of any award and to apply it to the balance of the mortgage debt or have it reinvested in the leasehold improvements in order to maintain the leasehold value through the repair or replacement of the buildings, unless the balance of the loan is adequately secured by the remaining property. Or, it may be that a condemnation action is anticipated prior to construction of any improvements, and allowance for such can be made in the lease. One developer, for example, knew that the expressway authority was planning to add another lane to the feeder road immediately in front of his office building site. Consequently, additional land was allowed in his planning for parking space around the building so that there would be no impairment of the rentability of the building when the partial taking of land occured. The mortgage spells out that the award in this instance will go to the developer since he put in the extra land. The situation, however, would be different if the taking had affected the rentability of the building in any way. The lender would in effect not be holding the same quality of security as prior to the taking and would elect to apply the borrower's award money to reducing the balance of the mortgage debt. Usually, if condemnation materially affects the value of the property, the lender will claim the borrower's award to be used to reduce the mortgage debt.

The right of the space tenant to cancel his lease upon condemnation should be clearly defined; otherwise, he might have a right to cancel his sublease regardless of the size or effect of the taking. In fact, the space tenant may have been looking for a way out of his lease if business has not been going well for him. The sublease clause would usually state that if over a certain percentage of the property is taken, or if a substantial percentage is taken so that it is not practical for the space tenant to operate his business within the remaining space, then he has the right to cancel his sublease.

Rental Achievement

The granting of a mortgage loan, and particularly a leasehold mortgage loan, is usually contingent upon the developer–borrower's accomplishing the leasing of a stated amount of space in the building on a stated basis. A loan commitment might read:

> The annual rental of office space shall not be less than $550,000 from not more than 140,000 square feet of the rentable office space at an average rental of at least $3.50 per square foot, and from not more than 300 garage spaces at an average rental of $12.00 per space per month, and the space rented shall be rented on a basis so that if the building were 100 percent rented, the annual rental would be at least $632,000 from office space and $65,000 from garage space.

The developer would provide a certified rent roll indicating the tenants, the space, and the annual rentals, and the loan-servicing agent would certify that he had checked the occupancy of the building to establish the accuracy of the rent roll statement.

If after the completion of the building the developer has not achieved the rent roll requirement, a floor loan for a reduced amount will be disbursed. Additional sums are then later disbursed as the rental schedule submitted with the loan application is met; however, this must be done within a specified time, usually 1 to 2 years after the closing of the floor loan.

An appraisal for a proposed building might state that it will rent for a given amount per square foot. Should it not be possible to achieve the estimated rental because of changes in economic conditions or the market and it becomes necessary to lower the rental—say, $3.50 to $3.25 per square foot—then it would also be necessary to reduce the carrying charges of the building. The total rent or carrying charges needed to carry the building is determined by adding together the total expenses for the building and the debt service. A lower loan amount is given by the lender when it is determined that a given rental level cannot be achieved. The lender usually wants a 20 percent safeguard in the floor loan, which is typically 75 to 80 percent of the full payout.

Prepaid Ground Rent

Prepaid ground rent is a security feature for the lender which is found particularly in unsubordinated leasehold mortgages and which is used by a developer to try to obtain a maximum loan. The normal leasehold loan, one that is unsubordinated, does not allow the developer the maximum loan percentage permissible because the main security is the leasehold, which is junior to the rights of the land owner. A normal loan might be 75 percent of market value, whereas a loan of only 60 to 65 percent of leasehold value may be allowed on an unsubordinated leasehold mortgage. The lender seeks to build in a margin of protection.

Prepaid ground rent is a way of setting up the loan so that the lender has adequate protection to make the full loan amount to the developer. Prepaid ground rent for the term of the loan would eliminate the possibility of money defaults, except payment of ad valorem taxes. The result is about the same as fee security.

Assume that the developer has at the end of a 10-year period a stated price at which he can purchase the land. It is known, therefore, that there is a 10-year period in which ground rent must be paid rather than the land being purchased. The amount of ground rent it would take to cover the 10-year period is computed. Also taken into consideration is the fact that during the 10-year period there would be a certain amount of amortization of the loan; in fact, the amortization would basically be more than enough—if the loan was refinanced—to purchase the ground under a specified purchase option, thus limiting the lender's exposure. For example, assume that the total loan made on an office building was $3 million at 6 percent to be fully amortized in 20 years. At the end of 10 years the payback has equalled in excess of one-third the amount of the original loan, or approximately $1,065,000.00. If the purchase option at the end of the 10-year period is for $500,000.00, then the amortization to date would more than cover the depreciation and purchase price of the fee.

The agreement usually provides for the deposit of U.S. Government bearer bonds of a stipulated amount with an escrow agent before disbursement of any loan amount by the lender. Any time the market value of the bonds on deposit falls below a given amount, the developer must deposit additional bonds to restore the account to the proper amount. When the ground rent is paid each year by the developer, the escrow agent refunds the amount to him from an account. In the event of a foreclosure of the mortgage, the bonds remaining on deposit with the escrow agent are turned over to the lender and the proceeds are applied in reduction of the mortgage debt or toward payment of ground rent or purchase of the fee.

This arrangement is between the borrower and the lender and technically is not prepaid ground rent but is more in the nature of an escrow fund (similar to the escrow funds for taxes and insurance) or security to guarantee payment. The arrangement does not affect the liability of anyone, and as between the owner (as landlord) and the developer or the lender (as tenant), it does not protect the tenant against default under the lease except to make money available to cure the default. In other words, the terms of the ground lease are still the sole rights that the developer or the lender have insofar as the owner is concerned.

The lender gives the developer credit on the appraisal for the prepaid ground rent. This amount is added to the building and improvement value, which results in the developer receiving a higher-percentage loan on the improved property.

Option To Purchase

A purchase option can be used to the advantage of the land owner, the developer, and the lender. With the lessor or owner it can provide that the land must be improved with a building or improvement of a certain value by a specified date or the owner can at his option require the developer to purchase the property at a stated price, or the lease may be terminated.

As for the developer or lessee, the purchase option can be given to him at a stated price to be exercised on or after a specified date. When the developer puts improvements on the land, he will create a substantial increase in the value of the property. The purchase option permits him to purchase the property at a value set prior to the time he created additional value through his improvements. Furthermore, this allows the leasehold owner to accumulate funds from the income of the property sufficient for the purchase. A corporation, for instance, cannot, under the federal income tax laws, accumulate earned surplus in excess of $100,000 without paying reasonable dividends, unless it can prove that these funds are needed for a specific feasible purpose. Otherwise, the corporation may be subject to the penalty of an accumulated earnings tax. The majority of buildings are still owned in corporate form, although individual joint ventures and partnerships are becoming increasingly popular so as to obtain maximum tax advantage from depreciation.

The lender or mortgagee finds the purchase option advantageous because he then knows what he would have to pay for the land at a specific date. His liability for rent payments in the future can thus be terminated and the loss in the event of foreclosure tends to be minimized.

A lease agreement might provide, for example, that the lessee shall spend $675,000 in improving the subject property before September 1, 1976, or at option of lessor, lessee shall be required to purchase the land for $500,000. It might further provide that the lessee shall have a purchase option between September 1, 1981, and August 31, 1991, for $525,-000; between September 1, 1991, and ending date of the lease at $575,000.

The time spreads in the option and the determination of the prices to be paid at the different intervals are matters of negotiation between the parties, and there are numerous methods or formulas that might be used. The important point here is that the option to buy be obtained if at all possible—it can benefit all parties—and in all probability the land will always be worth more than the buy figure in the lease even if the latter does appear high at the moment.

Escrow

There are two types of escrows in making loans, one of which is included in the loan deed. The latter is the escrow of monthly deposits for taxes and insurance. This has become more important to the large institutional lenders and in over 90 percent of the loans it is included in the loan deed. However, in many instances the lender may waive this requirement by separate letter for a specific borrower stating that the escrow will be waived so long as the property is owned and controlled by this borrower and so long as no terms in the mortgage are in default and if payments for taxes and insurance are paid by the due date.

The other type of escrow is the one set up between lender and borrower for completion of unfinished space. For example, in a $1 million loan which has a floor of $800,000.00 based upon a rent requirement of 75 percent occupancy at $3.50 per square foot, the borrower may have met the conditions for the full payout. However, the unrented space is rarely ever completed until it is leased; therefore, the lender will require that the funds needed for completion be put in an escrow account until completion of the unfinished space.

Escalation—Rental Adjustment

Escalation is concerned with the adjusting of the rental over the term of a lease because of increases in taxes, operational expenses, or both. The lender's commitment normally requires that the space leases provide for escalation on the part of space tenants. Such a provision in the commitment might state that each lease (for space) for a term of not more than 5 years, including renewal terms, shall contain provisions requiring the tenant (space tenant) to pay additional rent for his proportionate part of any increases in taxes and operating expenses of the real property after the first lease year or any year set as the base year; and that the tenants' proportionate part shall be a fraction, the numerator of which is the number of square feet of floor area in its demised premises and the denominator of which is the total number of rental square feet of floor area in the building.

Or, another quite similar provision used in the leasing of the improvements (or space), after setting forth the annual base rental and its per-square-foot breakdown on a floor level basis, states that the rental is not to be adjusted for the first 5 years, but in each of the following years shall be adjusted on a square-foot basis to cover increases in ad valorem taxes which exceed those during the fifth lease year. Adjustments are to be the annual base rental plus (a) rent adjustment increase, allocated on a square-foot basis, or (b) up to a stated amount.

Escalation or rental adjustment provisions may also be found in the ground lease. These adjustments are usually accomplished by one of three methods: graduated (step-up), reappraisal, or index. Under the graduated or step-up method the parties agree in advance on the amount by which the rent is to be increased each period and at what intervals the adjustment will take place. For example, a 75-year ground lease provides that the rental for the first 10 years shall be $1,250.00 per month, or $15,000.00 per year. Thereafter, the monthly rent is increased or stepped up at 10-year intervals in an amount equal to 1 percent per year of the original $1,250.00 per month—that is, $1,500.00 per year—until expiration. The yearly rent for the second 10-year period, for instance, will be $16,500.00; for the final 10-year period, $24,000.00.

The reappraisal method provides that at stated intervals during the term of the ground lease the property will be reappraised. An adjusted rental would then be negotiated based upon the new valuation.

The index method ties the rental adjustment to a specified index, such as the Consumer Price Index, more popularly known as the "cost-of-living" index. The lease may place limits on the index—such as maximums or minimums, or both. It is simpler to use percentage increments as a basis for adjustments.

It is questionable whether the index method is a satisfactory method of rent adjustment, particularly in fairly relating the rent to the value of the property. The value of the property, as is well known, can increase and decrease considerably—and indeed in a very short span of time. The value of a property could be down, yet the rent increased as a result of an increase in the cost-of-living index. Or, the value of the property could have increased much more than the increase in the index. The government could decide to abandon the index, in which case it would be necessary to provide a new index, which could cause great conflict among the parties to the ground lease, as was the case when the index was based on the gold content of the dollar.

The same limitations could apply to the reappraisal method. Values may rise or drop sharply between appraisal intervals and the rental on the property may become inequitable in relation to its value. Moreover, there could be disagreement among the parties at each interval as to a final value. Provision should be made in the ground lease for submission of differences to arbitration.

The graduated or step-up method does have the advantage of setting forth the rent amounts once and for all in the lease, although it suffers from the same limitation as the other two methods—namely, vulnerability to sharp changes in the value of the property between adjustment intervals. Lenders usually prefer the rent amount to be established, or at least be fairly predictable, during the mortgage term.

Annual Reports

A rather common practice now is for the lender to require in its loan commitment that the developer annually furnish the lender with audited statements, prepared by a Certified Public Accountant, showing the annual rent roll, other income, and the detailed operating expenses of the property securing the loan. These reports go through the servicing agent and provide an actual operating history of the property, which is normally very difficult to obtain. These reports are useful to the servicing agent in that they provide a background to prove to out-of-town institutional investors what the per-square-foot operating costs are for a given type of building in the agent's area. These costs vary widely among different areas of the country.

Furthermore, these statements are useful when the building is refinanced. Most commercial buildings are usually refinanced at the end of, say, a 5- to 7-year period, and if audited statements have been obtained annually, a complete operating record of the property is available to show its income history.

Tri-party Agreement

The developer, upon accepting a commitment from an institutional lender for the permanent financing, will then be ready to seek his construction funds. The permanent-loan lender will put a provision in its commitment specifying that a tri-party agreement will be worked out with reasonable promptness between it (the permanent lender), the interim lender (usually a commercial bank or other source of construction funds), and the borrower, providing essentially for the following: joint use of the loan documents by the interim lender and the permanent-loan lender; agreement by the interim lender that it will not accept payment from the developer or assign the loan documents to other than the permanent lender; and transfer by assignment of the loan from the interim lender to the permanent lender within a stated period of time and after compliance with the terms and conditions of the commitment.

The effect of this agreement, in addition to its obvious benefits of facilitating the closing of the loan and minimizing the costs thereof, is to protect the permanent lender against some lenders' practice of "raiding" commitments before the permanent loan is closed. Interest rates do fluctuate between the time the commitment is issued and the time of the actual payout by the permanent lender. The raiding lender approaches the developer and offers him more attractive terms than those under the existing commitment. The tri-party agreement seeks to prevent the interim lender from selling the loan to anyone else or permitting it to be purchased by anyone except the permanent lender named in the agreement.

A recent commitment to the developer of a speculative office building, for a loan of $550,000.00, required a rental achievement of $3.25 per square foot. The developer actually accomplished a rental of $4.00 per square foot, which obviously would make the building qualify for a more attractive loan than when it started out speculatively; a building actually rented and at an excellent rate is, indeed, prime loan security. The permanent lender feels that if it takes the speculative risk in the beginning, it should be protected from the developer going out and securing a more favorable loan. However, in many instances the lender will agree to increase the loan amount if there has been a substantial increase in the actual rent structure compared to the estimated rent projection.

Prepayment Option

Lenders on the security of commercial leasehold property are reluctant, as are other lenders, to permit prepayment in the early stages of the loan. In periods of tight money, investors try especially hard to stretch out or delay the prepayment as long as possible. Prepayment options vary among lenders, but the following is typical of how such an option might read in the lender's commitment:

> The borrower shall be permitted to prepay up to 10 percent of the original principal sum in any year, not cumulative, and after 7 years from the start of amortization the borrower may prepay the loan at 103 percent of par value, and after 10 years the borrower may prepay at 101 percent of par value, and after 15 years prepayment at par.

Or, a variation may read:

> Borrower is to have the privilege of prepaying, in multiples of $1,000, up to 10 percent of the original principal amount of the loan in any one year from the anniversary date of the mortgage. Such privilege shall be noncumulative. The borrower is to have the additional privilege of paying the loan in full after the first 5 years. Such prepayment, however, shall be accompanied by a prepayment fee computed as a percentage of the sum of the unpaid principal balance of the loan plus any optional prepayments made during the preceding 12 months. If the loan is prepaid during the sixth year of the life of the loan, said prepayment fee shall be at the rate of 5 percent of such sum, which rate shall decline thereafter at the rate of one-half of 1 percent each year, reducing to 1 percent during the fourteenth year and thereafter.

Interest Equalization Tax

The Interest Equalization Tax Act (U.S. Public Law 88–563) enacted in 1964, and still not widely known, imposes a severe tax of up to 15 percent of the loan amount when the borrower is a nonresident alien individual or a foreign (alien) corporation or partnership. The purpose of the Act is to restrain the flow of money out of the country. Commitments may contain a provision stating that the lender will not be obligated to purchase the loan unless satisfactory evidence is furnished that the transaction is not subject to the interest equalization tax.

Bankruptcy

There is nothing that a lender can do to have a bankruptcy of the developer dismissed, and it would be a "noncurable" event of default if the lease specifies bankruptcy of the lessee as a basis for default. In such event, the lease would be terminated and all rights accruing to the developer or lender would cease. It is best to omit (or eliminate) bankruptcy from a ground lease as an event of default; the absence of a bankruptcy clause is important to the lender. Events of default should be limited to items which can be "cured" by the payment of money, such as for rent, taxes, and assessments. Also, the lease agreement must provide for notice to the lender, with adequate time, to cure the default in the case of unsubordinated leases.

Personal Liability

The developer would like to put his ground lease in a shell corporation which would eliminate his being personally liable over the long life of the lease for its obligations. The owner–lessor hesitates at permitting this release from personal liability until the improvements are finished. Thereafter the lessor could look to the improved real estate for security and be willing to release the lessee from personal liability.

Cash Flow and Constants

Commercial income-producing property is typically bought, developed, and sold on a cash flow basis. A developer, for instance, might estimate the cash flow from a proposed office building as follows:

Income:
Office:

Terrace level	10,000 sq ft at $5.00 =	$	50,000
1st floor	10,000 sq ft at 6.00 =		60,000
Floors 2–15	140,000 sq ft at 4.00 =		560,000
Floors 16–25	100,000 sq ft at 4.50 =		450,000
	260,000 sq ft		$1,120,000
	95% *occupancy:*		1,064,000

Parking:
>> Under building—
>> >> 200 cars at $25.00 per month $ 50,000

>> >> >> >> Total income: $1,114,000

Disbursements:

>> Mortgage—$6,500,000 at 8.5% constant $552,500
>> Land rent   50,000
>> Operating—
>> >> $1.50 sq ft occupied
>> >> $0.50 sq ft vacant   377,000

>> >> >> Total disbursements: 979,500
>> >> >> >> >> *Cash flow:* $ 134,500

This cash flow is then related to the developer's equity in the investment and the return on his equity is computed (cash flow divided by the equity amount). Since the developer's equity is reduced to a minimum when he has leased the land, leasehold financing will show a higher return on equity than if the fee were mortgaged in the conventional manner. Moreover, subordination of the underlying fee results in the developer obtaining a maximum loan (lender considers both land and building as security), which reduces the developer's equity even more and thus further increases his rate of return on equity.

The preceding illustration used an example of an 8.5 percent mortgage "constant." Constants refer to the total of principal and interest paid in any one year. A low constant increases cash flow and value, and a higher constant has the reverse effect. Ideally, the debt-service constant should be no more than the rate of return on a free and clear basis.

In commercial lending, the constant is really more important to the developer than is the interest rate: it is the constant that affects the cash flow. If the interest rate increases but the constant remains the same, the net cash flow is greater; the larger portion of the amortization payment is income-tax-deductible interest. To keep the same constant with an increased interest rate, it is necessary to extend the term or length of the loan.

The developer, in negotiating a loan, may not wish to go over a 6 percent interest rate, while the lender may be insisting upon a 6¼ percent interest rate. The developer could agree to the increase if the lender would agree not to increase his constant above 8 percent. If the loan was kept on a 20-year, 6 percent interest-rate basis, which is an 8.6 percent constant, and the interest rate is raised to 6¼ percent but the loan term was left at 20 years, the effect would be to increase the constant, or the amount of the annual mortgage payment, considerably.

Constants are being increasingly used in the mortgage business, especially in times of market changes. Interest rates which formerly were 6 percent are now 7 percent and above. However, it should really make little difference to the developer, since income-producing property sells on a cash flow basis and the developer is interested in his cash flow. The lender can charge a 7 percent interest rate but extend the term of the mortgage sufficiently to reduce the constant back to the level it would have been under a 6 percent interest rate. There is really, therefore, no loss to the developer.

It might be pointed out that there is a technical difference between the terms "cash flow" and "cash throwout," although in practice they are used interchangeably. Cash flow is an accounting term which refers to the amount of money in pocket on April 15 after paying corporate or individual taxes and taking advantage of depreciation. Cash throwout is a real estate term which means the number of dollars in pocket as of December 31 after paying operating expenses and debt service but before taxes and depreciation.

INCREASE IN USE

As is evident throughout this presentation, a properly negotiated leasehold financing arrangement offers a sound and flexible form of financing commercial improvements. A wide variety of commercial structures can be financed under the arrangement. The rapid growth of metropolitan areas and the resulting demand for commercial development of all types point to a continued increase in this type of financing in the years ahead.

Further Readings and References

Bohon, Davis T. *Complete Guide to Profitable Real Estate Leasing.* Englewood Cliffs, N. J.: Prentice-Hall, Inc., 1969.

"The Economy: Its Effect on Leasing in Today's Market," *NIREB's Division Reports,* No. 9, February, 1970. Sponsor: Realtor Robert E. Walker. Chicago: Commercial and Investment Division, National Institute of Real Estate Brokers of the National Association of Real Estate Boards, 1970.

Flanagan, Charles P. "Financing of Leasehold Estates," *The Appraisal Journal,* July, 1968, 383–92.

Gunning, Francis P. "A Primer for Mortgageable Ground Leases," *The Mortgage Banker*, March, 1967, 35–41.

Myers, John H. *Reporting of Leases in Financial Statements*. Accounting Research Study No. 4. New York: American Institute of Certified Public Accountants, 1962.

McMichael, Stanley L., and Paul T. O'Keefe. *Leases—Percentage, Short and Long Term*. Fifth Edition: Englewood Cliffs, N. J.: Prentice-Hall, Inc., 1959.

National Institute of Real Estate Brokers of the National Association of Real Estate Boards. *Ground Leases*. Sponsor: Byron W. Ererice, Jr. December, 1965. Chicago: National Institute of Real Estate Brokers, 1965.

O'Keefe, Raymond T. "The Why and How of Making Mortgages on Leaseholds," *The Mortgage Banker*, June, 1962, 31–33.

7

Creative

Financing

Creative financing is the solving of unusual and special financing and investment needs, both of borrowers and of lenders, for which traditional techniques are in themselves inadequate. It is the creation of new approaches to provide satisfactory loans in situations which would be difficult or impossible to finance under normal loan patterns. One authority on the subject, Milton Podolsky, writing on "Creative Financing of Industrial Properties" in the October, 1968, issue of the Society of Industrial Realtors' *Newsletter*, describes creative financing as follows:

> It is a matter of taking the new materials of a problem in financing, combining them in a new way, separating them in a new way, or adding new ingredients; thereby coming up with an acceptable and palatable product which can be purchased by lending institutions.

REASONS FOR USE

Creative financing is prompted by a number of interrelated factors. Both borrowers and lenders may face in periods of inflation and tight money

---

This chapter originally appeared as an article by the author, "Creative Financing of Real Estate," *Economic Leaflets*, Bureau of Economic Research, University of Florida, March, 1970.

the problem of needing higher yields from their projects and investments. Lenders are squeezed between a declining purchasing power of their investment portfolios and increasing operating expenses. Traditional financing using the long-term mortgage with a fixed interest rate may not be attractive to all institutional lenders in such times, and attention is turned to techniques which generate higher yields.

Another factor contributing to the need for creative financing is the increase in the dollar amount of the individual loans, brought about by the increasing size and complexity of projects. Developers have required large amounts of capital; at the same time they have wished to provide the incentive for both developers and lenders to take on the additional risk exposure of large loans.

The liberalization of statutory lending restrictions has also encouraged creative financing. Institutional lenders may now engage in financing situations which were not permissible several years ago.

KICKERS

Creative financing nearly always involves the use of "kickers" or "sweeteners." This means that the financing is arranged to provide the lender an income beyond a fixed return—a yield in addition to the straight interest rate. The kicker is an extra privilege attached to the obligation so as to make it more attractive to lenders; it is often the incentive that makes an unusual situation acceptable to the lender.

A variety of kickers is possible. Generally, they fall into four categories, and there are many combinations of the categories:

1. The lender may participate in the income of property.
2. The lender may participate in the profits of the venture.
3. The lender may share in the equity ownership of the project.
4. The lender may charge nonrefundable fees and discounts.

BENEFITS TO BORROWERS

By means of these creative techniques of financing, the borrower, who may often in effect take on the lender as a partner, is able to obtain in exchange up to 100 percent financing for a project, thereby increasing his financial leverage. Developers are interested in obtaining the highest possible loan, and creative financing has enabled lenders to accommodate this need. Frequently, the technique used will provide the developer with an income that is almost totally tax-sheltered.

Borrowers further benefit by obtaining larger capital sums, which enable them to engage in the development of larger projects than their resources might otherwise permit. Participation in these larger projects can, of course, also benefit lenders by giving them investment outlets as well as higher yields.

CRITICISM

Creative financing is not readily accepted by all lenders and developers. Some institutional lenders feel that the techniques are merely gimmicks which will disappear when money becomes more available. It is also felt by some that, if inflation is brought under some degree of control, the need for creative financing will be reduced and normal mortgage financing will be acceptable to the lender. Some developers have expressed a feeling that lenders in some instances make yield demands which are not in accord with the degree of risk assumed.

The Mortgage and Real Estate Executives Report, Vol. 2, No. 3, May, 1969, quotes comments by Richard A. Plehn, of the New York real estate financing concern bearing his name, as follows:

> . . . this type of financing almost always diminishes the resale value of the property. Prospective purchasers are often interested in (1) benefiting from future rental increases; (2) benefiting from refinancing; and (3) the ultimate pleasure of owning the fee simple free and clear of any encumbrances. Property subject to [sophisticated] types of financing denies these benefits in lesser or greater degree.

USURY

The question of usury—charging more than the legal rate of interest—may be raised in certain creative financing techniques. For instance, does application of the usury law apply to situations where the lender participates in the income stream or equity of a project? Does such participation constitute additional "interest" from the viewpoint of the usury law? The question remains unanswered in some areas and there does not seem to be unanimous agreement among the courts.

One knowledgeable legal counsel, Mendes Hershman, Associate General Counsel of the New York Life Insurance Company, as reported in *The Mortgage and Real Estate Executives Report*, Vol. 2, No. 7, September, 1969, suggests that

> until the law is further clarified . . . equity participations be limited to situations where (1) the lender uses a subsidiary to acquire the equity interest; (2) the applicable usury law imposes a ceiling that permits the participation, even where it is deemed interest; (3) the transaction comes under an exemption to the usury statute (as where the borrower is a corporation).

TECHNIQUES

The possible patterns of creative financing techniques have been increased mightly by the imagination, versatility, and ingenuity of parties to the transactions. The spectrum ranges from minor "sweeteners" or "kickers" to joint venture participations. There probably have not been two transactions which utilized exactly the same pattern. It is possible, however, to identify the general features of certain techniques and arrangements.

Wraparound Mortgage

The wraparound mortgage, sometimes called a blanket mortgage or an extended first mortgage (although it is a second mortgage), is one in which a lender, such as a life insurance company, advances funds to a borrower in excess of an existing first mortgage on a property without requiring that the existing mortgage be paid off. The new "wraparound" second mortgage leaves any existing encumbrances on the property undisturbed and includes the total of all encumbrances. The wraparound lender assumes the existing loan and takes over its periodic payments, advances additional cash to the developer, and originates a mortgage of longer term and higher interest rate for the entire amount outstanding. The second mortgagee puts out in his own cash only the amount of additional funds granted over and above the remaining balance of the mortgage. The borrower makes periodic payments covering all of the mortgages to the wraparound lender and has no further direct dealings with the lender of the original first mortgage. The wraparound or second mortgagee makes the debt-service payments on the first mortgage to its holder. The second mortgagee retains the balance of each payment, which is composed of interest at the higher rate, amortization of the cash actually put out (amount above the balance of the first mortgage), plus an amount equal to the difference in interest rates on the two mortgages on the amount not advanced.

The wraparound mortgage may be useful to the developer to acquire additional cash where the income from the project will justify the addition. The original lender may not make further advances under the existing mortgage; the borrower is locked in to the existing mortgage by a long-term prepayment clause (institutional lenders generally are demanding longer lock-ins) or one which imposes a heavy penalty for prepayment.

Variable-rate Mortgage

The interest rate on a variable-rate mortgage can shift up or down over the term of the mortgage, depending upon the fluctuations of the indicator or index to which its rate is tied. The index may be either external, as the interest rate on long-term government bonds, or internal, as a lending institution's rate paid on its saving accounts or certificates. In the latter case, the originating lender has a degree of control over the index.

Several patterns of variable interest rates are possible. The rate may be tied to the lender's weighted average cost of savings money and the rate varies with changes in that index. *Savings and Loan News*, in an article entitled "Variable Rate Mortgages: A Way to Ease the Squeeze?" August, 1969, describes one savings-and-loan association that ties its interest rate for mortgage loans

> to the association's weighted average cost of savings money as of March 31 and September 30 each year. When the savings cost moves .25 percent either way from the figures in effect when the borrower signs his mortgage note, the loan rate moves too.

Further, this association's rate

> can vary by no more than 1 percent above or below the original interest rate over the life of the loan. A borrower with an 8 percent contract rate will therefore never pay more than 9 percent nor less than 7 percent, even if the association's cost of savings money increases, for example, by 2 percent.

The same article describes another savings-and-loan association which uses two approaches to the variable rate: one for commercial and multi-family loans and one for single-family loans. The former rate is tied to the bank prime rate (specifically, that of a major New York City bank); the association's loan rate changes with movements in this prime rate. On single-family mortgages, the association reserves the right to move the interest rate either up or down by a maximum of 1 percent; the rate is not tied to an index of any kind. The association gives the borrower 4 months' written notice, during which time he can prepay the loan without penalty.

Divided Amortization Schedule

The schedule of amortization may be divided so that there is a faster maturity on one part of the loan and a longer maturity on another part of it. Or, there may be only interest charged for several years and a complete amortization schedule developed from that point on. This type of divided schedule provides a quicker return of capital to the lending institution.

Bondable Net Lease

The bondable net lease technique may also be referred to as a mortgage bond or a financing net lease. The arrangement is essentially a direct 100 percent loan in which the lender must look primarily to the credit of the tenant rather than to the real estate itself for security. The long-term lease is treated in effect as a bond. The tenant usually leases a major portion of the property and the lease is sufficient, net with the rental income from the tenant, to amortize the loan completely within the lease period. This technique may be used by a major corporation which sets up a separate real estate subsidiary holding title and leasing to the parent corporation. The guarantee of the parent corporation will make the lease eligible for 100 percent financing even if the subsidiary has no credit standing itself.

Basket-clause Loans

A basket-clause loan is not, technically, a type of loan; rather, it is a provision in some state regulations for insurance companies which permits life insurance companies to make a small percentage of their loans in a

category that cannot be assigned to any of the traditional real estate classifications. The wraparound mortgage and a mortgage secured by a lease
rather than by a mortgage document are two examples of basket money
or leeway provision money. Other types of creative financing techniques
and kickers could carry the "basket" designation.

The incentive for this type of loan is usually a higher-than-normal yield.

Piggyback Loans

The piggyback loan is used primarily in residential financing, although
this form of lending need not be restricted to only one field. The technique
involves two or more lenders sharing or participating in a single loan, with
the result that a higher-than-normal loan may be made.

An institutional lender, such as a savings-and-loan association, originates
the loan, say for 90 percent of the appraised value of the property. The
originating lender supplies 75 percent of the money (a normal or typical
loan-to-value ratio) and a private or noninstitutional lender supplies the
top 15 percent. The private lender will obtain private mortgage insurance
on its portion of the loan and the insurance will continue in force until
the loan is reduced to a normal ratio. The originating institutional lender
(prime investor or primary investor, as this lender is sometimes called)
keeps the documents for both lenders and holds the senior position or
claim under the loan, except for the mortgage insurance, which the private
lender took out to cover his top 15 percent position in the loan. The piggyback is in essence a form of junior—or second—mortgage financing with
the prime investor owning 75 percent of a 90 percent mortgage and another
investor owning a subordinated 15 percent interest.

There are other variations of the piggyback concept, all of them having
the objective of enabling institutional lenders to grant higher-than-normal
loan-to-value ratios. For instances, the collateral or additional security for
the "excess" part of the loan may be put up by the borrower or by a third
party, and the lender may put up the entire amount of the loan from its
own funds. The "top" or "excess" of the loan is secured by collateral
other than the real estate. Two forms of collateral which might be used
are the time deposit and the guarantee by an outside institution. The time
deposit is also known as a "share collateral pledge agreement" or a "pass-
book loan agreement." The borrower deposits with the lender an amount
to secure the excess amount of the loan. The account draws interest, which
the borrower can withdraw, but the principal sum cannot be withdrawn
until the loan is reduced to the normal amount that would have been
granted under a standard first mortgage, such as 80 percent. The excess
portion of the loan might be guaranteed by an outside institution, for in-

stance, an educational institution. A loan may also be backed with collateral by assignment of stock, certificate of deposit, or a letter of credit. Such collateral makes the lender's position more secure, even though he has greater exposure on a large loan or an unusual property.

Lenders' Joint Pool Financing

Several lenders may participate in a large project and work out a joint loan agreement for the pooling of funds to provide interim construction financing for big projects. A notable example is reported in *Savings and Loan News*, November, 1968, "Joint Ventures: A Way to Compete for the Big Ones," which describes a high-price, high-rise condominium in a major city financed by a $7,350,000 construction loan from three savings-and-loan associations in the same local market areas. The article states:

> Construction funds come from a "money pool," to which each association contributes equally. The money pool the three associations have created is actually a joint loan origination, with each association committing an equal share of the interim loan at the project's inception. There is one mortgage and three notes. . . . There is no joint financing agreement for the permanent loans, however. Rather, each association has given a mortgage commitment on each apartment in a pre-assigned group of living units in the condominium.

Stock Ownership and Options

A lender's participation in a project may be in the form of stock ownership or stock options. When a lender takes a minority stock ownership in the developer's corporation, there is a possibility that dividends will not be declared by the majority stockholders for many years, and the lender will not participate in income during that early time. Furthermore, dividends are subject to the usual double taxation, first to the corporation, and then to the lender upon receipt. In circumstances where the receipt of preferred or common stock or of stock warrants make participation attractive, the borrower generally should be a corporation of substantial size with an established market for its stock.

The use of stock, stock warrants, options, and convertibility features create a variety of situations in which a lender may participate in the income from the property. For example, a development corporation may enter into an agreement with the institutional lender whereby the latter will have the right to convert the unpaid balance of its mortgage to common shares of the corporation at a given conversion price over a specified period of time. Under these circumstances, the lender grants the development corporation a more favorable interest rate in exchange for this conversion and participation feature in the project.

Joint Venture

The joint venture may be described in terms of either a creative financing technique or a form of ownership for investment in real estate. In the joint venture, the developer supplies the land and the construction, leasing, and management expertise, while the lender supplies the money for the project. The joint venture entity, which may be either a general partnership, a limited partnership, or a corporation, is formed as a subsidiary of the lender and developer to limit liability; the capital of each is nominal. After the building—say, an apartment structure—is completed, the lender receives a portion of the net income as a yield on development costs (interest plus amortization or recapture), the developer receives a percentage yield based on the market value of his land, and any remainder of the net income is split between the developer and the lender, usually on a 50–50 basis.

House & Home, December, 1968, gives an example of a hypothetical joint venture. Assume a land valuation of $200,000 and development costs of $800,000—a total "physical" valuation of $1,000,000. The completed project is expected to generate a net income of $90,000, which when capitalized at, say, 9 percent, indicates an "economic" valuation of $1,000,-000 for the project. Assume also that the lender receives a constant rate of development costs of 8.87 percent and that the developer receives an 8 percent rate on the market value of his land. The net income of $90,000 will then be distributed as follows: to the lender—8.87 percent on $8,000,-000, or $70,960; to the developer—8 percent on $200,000, or $16,000; a total distribution of $86,960. The remaining net income of $3,040 is split between the lender and the developer 50–50.[1]

Separation of Fee and Improvements

There is a wide variety of techniques utilizing the separation of fee and improvements whereby each of these interests in a property may be financed separately. A commonly used technique is for the land under a building to be sold to the lender and then immediately leased back to the developer. A mortgage loan is then placed on the leasehold. This gives the developer the use of 100 percent of the land value as capital and a 75

---

[1] Reprinted by special permission from the December, 1968, issue of *House & Home* copyrighted © 1968 by the McGraw-Hill Publishing Co., Inc.

percent leasehold loan on the building cost. The technique can be of advantage to both borrower and lender. While the lender puts up a larger share of the capital for the project, he obtains a higher yield. He is also able to participate in increases in income from the property as well as having a potential gain on the sale of the property. The developer is able to obtain more capital for his project, namely, 100 percent of the land value plus a 75 percent loan on the improvements. In addition, there can be some tax-shelter benefits as well as improved cash flow return on the equity.

Sale–Buyback

A sale and repurchase, or "buyback," under an installment sales contract is a variation of the sale–leaseback technique. The advantage of the former over the latter is that the owner–developer may retain depreciation while still obtaining the major benefits of a sale–leaseback.

Under the sale–buyback scheme, the developer sells a property to a lender, such as a life insurance company, and the latter simultaneously sells it back to the developer for the same price under an installment sales contract for a specified period of years. The lender retains title to the property, but the developer also retains an equitable interest in the title, and this feature enables him to retain the important tax advantage of depreciation deduction. The developer is obtaining maximum leverage through the borrowing of 100 percent of his cost and also has the benefit of a tax-sheltered income stream.

Balloon Loan

A balloon loan, sometimes called a "hangout," occurs when a long-term loan exceeds the term of the lease. For example, if a lease with a company has been negotiated for 30 years, and a loan has been committed for 35 years, the 5-year difference is referred to as a "hangout." When the balance of the loan is to be paid at the expiration of the lease, the loan is referred to as a balloon loan.

The Annual Constant

The annual constant is the amount of interest and principal needed to pay off a loan. It is the debt service stated as a percentage of the original debt, and includes the interest rate and the principal reduction rate.

The required annual amount is applied first to interest and the balance to principal. The total amount of the loan is divided into the number of years to determine the equal payments, which are constant during the term of the loan. In the early years of the loan, a greater portion of the payment will be allocated to interest and a smaller proportion to principal; in the later years of the loan, a greater portion of the payment will be allocated to principal and a smaller proportion to interest.

The constant may be utilized as a creative financial technique in that it may be arranged so as to solve a problem of financial yield both for the borrower and the lender. The principal and interest portions of the constant may be planned to give the lender a particular rate of return, and at the same time to give the developer the debt-service factor which he desires.

Milton Podolsky in his article, "Creative Financing of Industrial Properties" in the Society of Industrial Realtors' *Newsletter*, October, 1968, gives the following example of the use of the constant:

> . . . a twenty-year loan at 7 percent would have a constant factor of 9.31. The same loan at 7.5 percent would need twenty-two years and two months to have the exact same factor. If a borrower needed a loan of $1,000,000 and could acquire a 7 percent loan for twenty years, the payments would be $93,100 per year. If the company warranted nothing less than 7.5 percent then creative financing comes into being. The borrower would determine that he could pay this interest rate and still pay $93,100 per year, but for two years and two months longer. He then has two choices: have the tenant take a longer lease, or accent a future risk so that he can make a deal today.

OUTLOOK

Creative financing techniques will probably continue to be utilized in financing real estate, although the extent of their utilization will vary with economic conditions, particularly conditions which contribute to tight money. There will always be financing problems to solve—unusual properties or extremely large projects—which will not be attractive to lenders through traditional financing with its fixed-rate mortgage. Yields must be attractive to both borrower–developer and lender, and the market must be willing and able to pay the price to support the yields. The market is the ultimate judge, the acid test, of the future of "kickers," component financing, variable interest, and similar techniques.

Further Readings and References

Eglit, Howard C. (ed.). *Creative Real Estate Financing*. Volume II, Creative
    Business Library. Ann Arbor, Michigan: Institute of Continuing Legal
    Education, Hutchins Hall, 1968.
Gunning, Francis P. "New Techniques in Financing," *Shopping Center Report
    No. 17*. New York: International Council of Shopping Centers, 1966.
"How to Syndicate Real Estate." *NIREB's Division Reports*, No. 7, June, 1969.
    Sponsor: Realtor David R. Marrion. Chicago: Commercial and Invest-
    ment Division, National Institute of Real Estate Brokers of the National
    Association of Real Estate Boards, 1969.
McCord, Jim (ed.). *Real Estate Financing: Business and Legal Considerations*.
    Herman M. Glassner and Kurt W. Lore, Chairmen. Real Estate Law and
    Practice, Transcript Series No. 1. New York: Practising Law Institute,
    1968.
Opperman, John C. "Lender–Developer Participation," *The Mortgage Banker*,
    September, 1968, 30–38.
Podolsky, Milton. "Creative Financing of Industrial Properties," *Newsletter
    of the Society of Industrial Realtors*, October, 1968, 1, 3–6. Chicago: So-
    ciety of Industrial Realtors of the National Association of Real Estate
    Boards, 1968.
Real Estate Syndicates and How They Work, June, 1957. Sponsor: Richard L.
    Jones. Chicago: National Institute of Real Estate Brokers of the National
    Association of Real Estate Boards, 1957.
Rose, Cornelius C., Jr. "Equity Participations," *The Mortgage Banker*, June,
    1968, 44–47.
Sonnenblick, Jack E. "The Art of Intricate Financing," *Real Estate Today*,
    July, 1969, 26–35. Chicago: National Institute of Real Estate Brokers of
    the National Association of Real Estate Boards, 1969.

8

Financial
Analysis
and Projection

The yield from a real estate investment may be computed in a variety of ways, and there does not appear to be any one technique or concept utilized by all investors. One of the more common methods of analysis used by many brokers and investors is referred to as the traditional or conventional method and involves several computations or standards of measurement. Before discussing the traditional method, a brief description of the concept of leverage is given, since this concept is closely tied to the rate of return on the equity in the investment.

LEVERAGE

Leverage or trading on the equity is a basic financial concept which is widely employed in real estate. It refers to a situation whereby a person acquires a property with as little of his own cash as possible and borrows as much of the purchase price as possible; that is, only a small percentage of the purchase price is paid in cash and the balance is financed, traditionally with a mortgage. Certain creative financing techniques also generate leverage. The objective is to increase the rate of return on the cash invested.

Leverage and financing are key factors in most real estate investments. Through the use of other people's money, a large investment may be controlled with only a small amount of equity capital; and a small cash outlay can return a substantial profit. Most if not all of the large fortunes in real estate have been created through the interplay of leverage and financing within the framework of federal income tax laws and a growing economy.

Seldom is investment real estate acquired for all cash or "free and clear"; almost always, funds are borrowed to complete a transaction. One reason, of course, is that the purchaser simply does not have sufficient funds of his own to acquire the property on a 100 percent cash or equity basis.

Secondly, and perhaps more important, the purchaser will usually not want to buy for all cash even if he has it. If money can be borrowed on the property at a lesser rate than the rate earned on it (and the yield from most real estate investments is usually greater than the expense of borrowing funds), the investor can increase the overall net return on his equity by the use of borrowed money. The greater or larger the amount of borrowed funds in relation or proportion to the total investment, the greater is the leverage.

Institutional lenders on first mortgages, such as savings-and-loan associations, life insurance companies, commercial banks, mutual savings banks, and mortgage companies, are willing to accept a smaller rate of return (interest) than accrues to the provider of the cash or equity capital because the institution's creditor position as first-mortgage holder gives it a first claim on the income from the property. There is less risk, and therefore less return, in the first-mortgage position as contrasted with that of the equity holder. The latter has a secondary or residual claim on income and principal and seeks a greater rate of return for his more speculative and greater-risk-taking position in the investment.

Extraordinary Impact in Real Estate

Real estate is a highly desirable form of investment for leverage. There are several reasons accounting for this popularity:

1. Generally, more money can be borrowed on real estate than on most other kinds of investments. Loans are usually available on most real estate for at least 50 percent of its market value with much financing running to 60, 70, or 80 percent of value on a long-term first-mort-

gage basis. Additional funds frequently may be obtained through secondary financing or by the seller agreeing to take back a purchase-money mortgage from the buyer for part of the purchase price. The availability of such liberal financing sources means that an investor could acquire property with very little, or even none, of his own funds.

2. The attractive financing generally available on real estate when combined with tax depreciation and value appreciation creates a combination of factors which can produce a very high return on investment. Depreciation is computed on the full value of the property when acquired, which includes mortgages as well as cash. Appreciation is almost a certainty in real estate. The depreciation deductions tax-shelter the operating income and give a substantial cash flow. The equity of the investor is increased to the extent that the cash flow is used to amortize the mortgage. The cash gain on the disposition of the property will be increased. All of these factors are available for only a small cash investment relative to the total value of the property.

Limitations and Strengths

Leverage is not without its limitations. While the opportunities for substantial gains are enhanced, so also are the opportunities for substantial losses. A mortgage can increase the leverage of the investor's money, but it is essential that the property earn a return sufficient to pay the charges on the mortgage. The success of leverage depends upon the accuracy of the net-income estimate and the portion of the income which is pledged to the lender on the mortgage.

A large mortgage increases the percentage return on equity when the income from a property increases or the property appreciates in value. Conversely, a decline in income or value can quickly erode the return on equity, and the owner may have to put up additional cash from his own resources if he wishes to keep the property. It may be possible to obtain a cash flow without any equity investment—leveraging to infinity with 100 per cent debt financing or "mortgaging out." The property is said to be built for the mortgage in such a situation. The owner of a mortgaged-out property could be quickly wiped out by a slight decrease in net income from it or by a small change in the economy that caused a decline in the value of the property.

Leverage should take into consideration factors of safety, economic soundness, and good judgment. Leverage is a very useful, effective, and extraordinary financial tool which, used with discrimination, can create wealth for both the user and the economy. It is essential, however, that it be used constructively in economically sound projects which fulfill a community need. A differentiation must be made between irresponsible promotion and responsible promotion and growth; the acid test will come when there is a recession or decline in the economy.

Leverage attracts genuine entrepreneurs interested in sound and feasible projects as well as loose promoters who start unsound and infeasible projects. Leverage is only as sound as the materials or ingredients that go into the deal; a poor situation is accentuated by leverage, likewise a good one. One of the most difficult aspects of real estate loan analysis is distinguishing between sound and unsound projects which are highly leveraged. Leverage is academic if an investment is basically unsound in an economic sense.

TRADITIONAL METHOD

Attention is now focused on the traditional or conventional method of financial analysis of a real estate investment. This method is sometimes referred to as the broker's method of analysis. The following computations are involved:

    I.   Net operating income
    II. Taxable income (or loss)
   III. Spendable income (cash flow)
        A. Percentage of cash return on initial investment
   IV. Equity growth

An analysis of a 4-story apartment house under construction is given below to illustrate the above computations. The computations are illustrated first without figures.

I. *Net Operating Income*

Gross Income from All Sources	xx
Less: Allowance for Vacancy and Collection Losses	xx
	—
Effective Gross Income	xx
Less: Operating Expenses	xx
	—
Net Operating Income	xx

II. *Taxable Income (or Loss)*

Net Operating Income		xx
Less: Mortgage Interest	xx	
Depreciation	xx	xx
Taxable Income (or Loss)		xx

III. *Spendable Income (Cash Flow)*

Net Operating Income	xx
Less: Mortgage Payments	xx
Gross Spendable Income	xx
Less: Income Tax	xx
Net Spendable Income	xx
% of Cash Return on Initial Investment	xx

IV. *Equity Growth*

Annual Mortgage Amortization	xx
Plus: Original Investment	xx
Total Equity	xx

EXAMPLE

4-STORY APARTMENT BUILDING
UNDER CONSTRUCTION

Gross Rental Income (from rent schedule)		$82,560.00
Miscellaneous Income—Laundry Vending Machines		600.00
Total Income		$83,160.00
Vacancy and Rental Loss (5%)		4,158.00
Effective Gross Income		$79,002.00
Estimated Operational Expenses		
Electricity	$ 880.00	
Gas	1,000.00	
Water	880.00	
Pool-maintenance Contract	780.00	

Elevator-maintenance Contract	360.00
Exterminator Contract	240.00
Landscaping	480.00
Resident Manager:	
Salary & Payroll Tax	1,250.00
Apartment	1,620.00
Utilities (Phone & Electricity)	450.00
Professional Management	3,600.00
Maintenance and Replacement Reserve	6,500.00
Taxes:	
Real Estate, City & County	8,800.00
Taxes:	
Pers. Prop., City & County	880.00
Insurance	1,200.00

		28,920.00
(I) *Net Operating Income* (First Year)		$50,082.00
Net Operating Income		$50,082.00
Less: Mortgage Interest *	$24,916.00	
Depreciation †	43,032.00	67,948.00
(II) Taxable Income (Loss) (First Year)		($17,866.00)
Net Operating Income		$50,082.00
Less: Mortgage Payments *		34,096.00
Gross Spendable Income		$15,986.00
Less: Income Tax (Loss)		–0–
(III) Net Spendable Income (First Year)		$15,986.00
(III-A) % of Cash Return on Initial Investment		19.98%
Annual Mortgage Amortization (First Year)		$ 9,180.00
Plus: Original Investment		80,000.00
(IV) *Equity Growth* (First Year)		$89,180.00

---

* There is a first mortgage on this property in the amount of $270,000.00, payable $2,008.00 per month, or $24,096.00 per year, including principal and interest at a variable rate dependent upon market conditions, but not to exceed 7% per annum. Owners have offered the property for sale at a total price of $440,000.00 and will accept as low as $80,000.00 cash down. The balance of the purchase price to be a purchase-money second mortgage, payable $2,500.00 per quarter, or $10,000.00 per year, including interest at 7% per annum, until paid.

† Double declining balance, including building improvements, and equipment. Breakdown not shown here.

INVESTOR'S TAX POSITION—FIRST 10 YEARS OF OPERATION

	1st Year	2nd Year	3rd Year	4th Year	5th Year	6th Year	7th Year	8th Year	9th Year	10th Year
(I) Net Operating Income	$50,082	$50,082	$50,082	$50,082	$50,082	$50,082	$50,082	$50,082	$50,082	$50,082
Less:										
Interest, 1st Mtg.	18,696	18,156	17,886	17,616	16,806	16,536	15,996	15,186	14,916	13,836
Interest, 2nd Mtg.	6,220	6,040	5,680	5,400	5,050	4,690	4,330	3,970	3,430	3,070
Depreciation	43,032	33,469	27,046	22,591	19,363	15,722	14,372	13,238	11,441	10,721
Total Deductibles	$67,948	$57,665	$50,612	$45,607	$41,219	$36,948	$34,693	$32,394	$29,787	$27,627
(II) Taxable Income (Loss)	(17,866)	(7,583)	(530)	4,475	8,863	13,134	15,384	17,688	20,295	22,455
Less Income Tax (30% Bracket)	—	—	—	1,342	2,659	3,940	4,615	5,306	6,088	6,736
Net Income After Tax (Loss)	$(17,866)	$(7,583)	$ (530)	$ 3,133	$ 6,204	$ 9,194	$10,769	$12,382	$14,207	$15,719
Plus: Depreciation	43,032	33,469	27,046	22,591	19,363	15,722	14,372	13,238	11,441	10,721
Cash Before Amortization	$25,166	$25,886	$26,516	$25,724	$25,567	$24,916	$25,141	$25,620	$25,648	$26,440
Less:										
1st-Mtg. Amortization	5,400	5,940	6,210	6,480	7,290	7,560	8,100	8,910	9,180	10,260
2nd-Mtg. Amortization	3,780	3,960	4,320	4,590	4,950	5,310	5,670	6,030	6,570	6,930
(III) Cash "Spendable" Income	$15,986	$15,986	$15,986	$14,654	$13,327	$12,046	$11,371	$10,680	$ 9,898	$ 9,250
(III-A) % of Cash Return on Initial Investment	19.98%	19.98%	19.98%	18.31%	16.66%	15.06%	14.21%	13.35%	12.37%	11.56%
(IV) Growth of Equity										
Annual Mtg. Amortization										
1st Mtg.	5,400	5,940	6,210	6,480	7,290	7,560	8,100	8,910	9,180	10,260
2nd Mtg.	3,780	3,960	4,320	4,590	4,950	5,310	5,670	6,030	6,570	6,930
Cumulative Mtg. Amortization	9,180	19,080	29,610	40,680	52,920	65,790	79,560	94,560	110,250	127,440
Plus: Original Investment	80,000	80,000	80,000	80,000	80,000	80,000	80,000	80,000	80,000	80,000
Total Equity	$89,180	$99,080	$109,610	$120,680	$132,920	$145,790	$159,560	$174,500	$190,250	$207,440

131

Limitations

Traditional analysis is certainly not sophisticated and lacks much possible refinement. Its simplicity, however, appeals to many investors who do not feel the need for or would not understand more mathematically oriented techniques. Traditional analysis produces several investment indices: return on market value, gross and net return on equity, return including equity growth, and so on. Such a variety of investment indices can be confusing, especially in comparing alternative investment outlets. Also, inadequate consideration is given to the time value of future cash flows, uneven cash flows, and the value of the equity reversion when the property is sold. Several other methods of analysis—some more sophisticated—seek to provide a more realistic reflection of market yields. The suggested readings at the end of this chapter were selected for their excellence in describing and explaining these other methods—namely: band of investment, discounted cash flow, mortgage equity and Inwood and Ellwood, and the role of computers in investment property analysis.

Further Readings and References

Akerson, Charles B. "Ellwood Without Algebra," *The Appraisal Journal*, July, 1970, 325–335.

Bockl, George. *How to Use Leverage to Make Money in Local Real Estate.* Englewood Cliffs, N. J.: Prentice-Hall, Inc., 1965.

Graham, Donald H., Jr. "Owner's Analysis of Yields on Major Real Estate Investments," *The Appraisal Journal*, October, 1965, 541–548.

Hodges, M. B., Jr. "Ellwood Plus (Or, Equity Yield After Taxes)," *The Real Estate Appraiser*, September–October, 1969, 11–22.

McMichael, James M. *Real Estate Investment . . . Analysis and Programing.* Fourth Edition. Los Angeles: California Real Estate Association, Exchange Division, 1965.

National Institute of Real Estate Brokers of the National Association of Real Estate Boards, Commercial and Investment Division. *How to Use Taxation and Exchange Techniques in Marketing Investment Real Estate.* Chicago: National Institute of Real Estate Brokers, 1969.

Nelson, Roland D., "Overall Rate—Band of Investment Style," *The Appraisal Journal*, January, 1969, 25–30.

Ratcliff, Richard U. (ed.). *Colloquium on Computer Applications in Real Estate Investment Analysis.* Monograph Series, Number 2, 1968. Vancouver, B. C.: Faculty of Commerce and Business Administration, University of British Columbia, 1968.

Ratcliff, Richard U., and Bernhard Schwab. "Contemporary Decision Theory and Real Estate Investment," *The Appraisal Journal*, April, 1970, 165–187.

Seldin, Maury, and Richard H. Swesnik. *Real Estate Investment Strategy.* New York: John Wiley & Sons, Inc., Wiley Interscience, 1970.

9

Land

Over the long term, land will always be in demand, and this demand—changing over time in strength, location, and form—will press against a fixed supply. Long-term growth factors cause land values to rise rather continuously, and historically, total land values have increased steadily for many years.

DEMAND FACTORS

Many factors contribute to the demand for land, and hence its value increases. A considerable amount of land is being absorbed by highways, airports, reservoirs, recreational facilities, industrial and office parks, growing metropolitan areas, housing subdivisions, and large-scale projects involving a variety of land uses within a given area. In addition, more land is being used per project in many instances: single-family homes are placed on larger lots; urban renewal areas and downtown redevelopment projects frequently require more land for parking, squares, and landscaping; commercial and industrial firms desire more land for their buildings and for parking, future expansion, and landscaping; professional buildings have moved to the suburbs and require single-story, spread-out structures with parking space and landscaping; and many other types of operations now require more land area—educational institutions, churches, apartments, and nursing homes and hospitals.

Further pressure is placed on land values by situations which tend to create a shortage of land. Restrictive zoning reduces the amount of land available for certain uses. Problems in local government finances may delay or prohibit the expansion of utilities and tend to limit the land area which can be used for building. Finally, in urban areas especially, there is much land held off the market in anticipation of higher prices.

Heavy investment in land by giant business corporations also generates additional demand and an increase in values. While many of these corporations are buying land simply to hold for an investment, others are entering into long-range development projects. Such activity will undoubtedly tend to increase the attractiveness of surrounding land.

There are at least three alternatives for investment in land: (1) raw acreage to hold "as is" for eventual resale at a profit; (2) raw acreage for subdividing into residential lots for single-family dwellings; and (3) individual scattered lots—residential, commercial, and industrial—which have already been subdivided and are for sale at retail prices. This chapter is concerned with raw acreage.

RAW ACREAGE

Raw acreage, like other real estate forms, offers a versatile investment medium. Acreage values range from a few dollars per acre to substantial sums; parcels may be a few acres to several thousand acres. Even in periods of tight money, it is possible to acquire acreage with a relatively low downpayment as contrasted with, say, securities.

Buying and holding raw acreage—land which has no established income —does involve considerable risks. Such a purchase anticipates a future market, and many factors, often unforeseeable, can affect its value. One cannot invest intelligently by simply buying raw acreage anywhere. Proper research is necessary, and all factors should be thought out carefully. Many of the risks can be tempered or eliminated with prudent investigation and judgment. Acquiring raw acreage to hold for future resale is a speculative activity, but it can and should be an intelligent speculation. There will always be opportunity for profit in a soundly conceived raw acreage investment. The potential lies in well-located, properly priced raw acreage of proper quality acquired and sold at the right time. Note the four important qualifications: location, price, quality, and timing. Many cities contain much land which has never been utilized and which will remain static. There is a limited demand for land which can be utilized for highly profitable uses, such as industrial and commercial; such land uses account for only a small fraction of the land area of the country. The investor must be selective in raw land acquisition; he must determine which specific locations represent the valuable sites of the future, and the selection of such areas is not a simple task.

LOCATION

The factor of location is the foremost consideration in the acquisition of real estate, and raw acreage is no exception. While acreage values continue to increase due to factors discussed earlier, there will be wide differences by area or location, and there will be vast areas in which no value increases will occur in the foreseeable future.

PRICE

A major error in purchasing raw acreage is to buy at too high a price (this pitfall is usually compounded by also buying too soon). The price at which acreage can be acquired is a key factor in its potential profitability, and high prices can only be justified by economic use. The price must be measured against future demand and need, with due consideration to community planning goals. Much acreage can be overpriced through successive speculative transfers, with the price representing values 5 or 10 years in the future. Certainly any potential immediate changes in the use of acreage, such as an imminent transition from a residential to a commercial zoning classification, will be reflected in its price. Further, excessive estimates of outlying acreage values may be caused by overoptimism about the quickness of its development.

QUALITY

Quality refers to the physical as well as the legal, economic, and environmental features of acreage. Since value is created by the potential use to which acreage may be put and the benefits it can offer a purchaser, the investor in acreage to hold for resale should seek to acquire tracts that offer the greatest potential for alternative uses with the fewest impediments. Acreage should be accessible, have good topography, and not require excessive development costs such as will be the case when rocky or swampy areas are present. Sewer and water mains do not have to be present, and in fact are usually not on outlying acreage. However, the investor should anticipate (and before others do) that lines will eventually be extended in the direction of the acreage. Most outlying acreage is zoned agricultural or some variation of a rural–fringe-area classification; uses permitted in the classification should be checked as well as the probable ease of obtaining a zoning change to a higher use in the future. Zoning trends, patterns, and attitudes should be investigated lest the investor acquire acreage with limited potential uses. Title should be checked and any legal defects cleared; also, an owner's title insurance policy is desirable.

It is preferable to acquire acreage in large tracts rather than in numerous small and scattered parcels for maximum profit potential. Larger tracts may usually be acquired at lower cost per acre and then broken up into smaller tracts. The latter tracts may be sold at a higher price per acre. Further, in the case of a developer–buyer, a large tract is easier to plan and work with and is frequently less expensive to develop; more can be done with it to make it attractive and create a wider market.

TIMING

Raw acreage acquisition as well as its ultimate disposal must be accurately timed or the holding period can prove too costly to maximize profits and may even result in a loss. Ideally, the purchase should be well ahead of the market and prior to the wave of speculative buying, but yet not too many years before expected growth takes place. There is considerable difference of opinion among investors and developers as to the holding period, and there is no standard time table. The waiting period may be 5 to 10 years, or even with the best of judgment it may be necessary to extend it to 10 to 20 years. Land values are difficult to forecast; increases may take place at short intervals, with the jump greater than the total value increases for the past five years. Or, there may be a gradual increase over a period of several years as land use patterns slowly change. Value increases can be predicted with careful analysis of the rate and direction of growth of nearby urban areas. Proper timing should include the avoidance of buying at the peak of large-scale speculative activity, where full future value is often added to the price in advance. It is best to look into inactive areas with good prospects of improvement.

EXAMPLE

OFFERING OF LAND INVESTMENT FOR APPRECIATION

A tract of 34.56 acres of land is offered for sale. Zoning of the tract is as follows: 5.35 acres—commercial; 29.21 acres—residential apartments. The tract is well located with respect to access roads, schools, churches, and shopping. It is within short driving time of a major metropolitan city. Public utilities—electricty, water, and sewer—are available adjacent to the site.

The terms of the offering are: price—$432,000 ($12,500 per acre, 28.7¢ per square foot); owner will consider a 20% down payment, 8% interest only on balance for 2 years, then 5 years amortization. Release clauses are negotiable. Cash required: $86,400.

The population of the metropolitan area in which the subject property is located shows a steady growth rate of slightly over 5% per year. Real estate values generally increase about 4 times the population growth rate in more populous areas, plus or minus the effect of adjacent land developments, new highway and street construction, and similar factors.

The growth rate of 20% for that portion of the subject property zoned "Commercial" is considered conservative, as is 17% for that portion zoned "Apartment." Also considered is the current sales price of property immediately to the north of the subject as well as the effect of ingress and egress ramps to a proposed circumferential expressway. Probable 1976 prices of $1.00 per square foot for commercial zoning and $0.85 per square foot for apartment zoning are used here for projections of net return and net gain.

PROJECTED NET RETURN IN 7 YEARS

5.35 *Acres* Zoned Commercial—233,046 sf

Projected Price in 7 Years @ $1.00 sf	$233,046
Less: Acquisition Cost @ $16,413/acre	87,810
Less: Development Cost	0
Net Return	$145,236

29.21 *Acres* Zoned Apartments—1,272,388 psf

Projected Price in 7 years @ $0.85/psf	$1,081,530
	$1,081,530
Less: Acquisition Cost @ $16,413/acre	479,430
Less: Development Cost @ $3,300/acre (paving, water mains, sanitary & storm sewers)	96,393
Net Return	$ 505,707
Less: Assessment for Paving of Blvd., Est.	27,000
Total Net Return	$ 623,943

EFFECT OF 7-YEAR OWNERSHIP & DISPOSITION

Sales Price— 5.35 Acres Zoned Commercial		$ 233,046
29.21 Acres Zoned Apartments		1,081,530
Total		$1,314,576

Less: Cost of Sale—(4.5%)

Real Estate Commission	$ 54,440	
Title Policy	3,460	
Survey & Legal	1,250	
		59,150

Less: Adjusted Cost Basis (Book Value)

Original Cost	$432,000	
Development Cost (Capitalized)	96,393	
		528,393

Recognized Gain		$727,033
Less: 25% Capital Gains Tax		181,758
Net Gain		$545,275

SUMMARY OF BENEFITS

Net Gain on Disposition		$545,275
Value of Deductible Expenses (to 60% bracket taxpayer)		
Interest Expense	$82,944	
Ad Valorem Tax Expense	?	
Paving Assessment, Blvd.	16,200	
		99,144
		$644,419

Benefits on Actual Investment
100 × $644,419 ÷ $528,393 =   118.89%
(Benefits ÷ Book Value)
or Actual Investment Returned + 118.89%

INVESTMENT ANALYSIS

Year	Principal	Interest	Principal & Interest	Balance	Cumulative Investment		
					$	$/acre	¢ psf
1968	$	$	$	$345,000	86,400	2,500	5.7
1969	0	27,648	27,648	345,000	114,048	3,300	7.6
1970	0	27,648	27,648	345,000	141,696	4,100	9.4
1971	69,120	27,648	96,768	276,480	238,464	6,900	15.8
1972	69,120	22,118	91,238	207,360	329,702	9,540	21.9
1973	69,120	16,589	85,709	138,240	412,411	11,933	27.4
1974	69,120	11,059	80,179	69,120	492,590	14,253	32.7
1975	69,120	5,530	74,650	0	567,240	16,413	37.7
	$345,600	$138,240	$483,840				

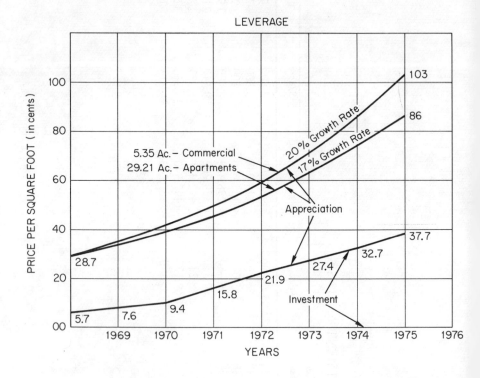

LEVERAGE

Further Readings and References

Casey, William J. *How to Buy and Sell Land*. New York: Institute for Business Planning, Inc., 1962.

Drachman, Roy P. "The High Cost of Holding Land," *Urban Land*, October, 1968. Washington, D. C.: Urban Land Institute, 1968.

Hoyt, Homer. "The Changing Principles of Land Economics," U. L. I. Technical Bulletin No. 60. Washington, D. C.: Urban Land Institute, 1968.

Hoyt, Homer. "Dynamic Factors in Land Values," U. L. I. Technical Bulletin No. 37. Washington, D. C.: Urban Land Institute, March, 1960.

"Land: Farms and Ranches as Investments With Special Emphasis on Tax Implications." St. Louis: Doane Agricultural Service, Inc., n.d.

Miller, Frank. "Land—Its Potential," *The Appraisal Journal*, April, 1970, 240–252.

Nelson, Richard Lawrence. "Land Values in the United States," *Urban Land*, Vol. 28, No. 2, February, 1969. Washington, D. C.: Urban Land Institute, 1969.

Pearson, David. "The Challenge of Rising Land Costs," *Urban Land*, Vol. 27, No. 6, June, 1968. Washington, D. C.: Urban Land Institute, 1968.

Rapkin, Chester. "Economic Patterns of Urban Land Use," *The Appraisal Journal*, April, 1970, 227–239.

"Raw Land: How to Find, Finance and Develop It." Special 12-page report. Englewood Cliffs, N. J.: Prentice-Hall, Inc., n.d.

10

Industrial
Property

Industrial property may take several forms. The single-tenant, owner–user industrial plant provides an entrepreneurial profit opportunity for the developer–builder of the plant. The building itself may provide an investment opportunity if and when it is disposed of by its owner–user, although industrial real estate is characterized by a slow turnover.

Another kind of industrial property is the single- or multiple-tenant building erected by a developer on a contract or speculative basis for sale or lease or sale–leaseback to the tenant or tenants. Profit opportunity here includes the developer's profit as well as almost the entire spectrum of yields in a real estate investment package: cash flow, mortgage amortization, tax shelter, and value appreciation potential. Industrial parks, loft buildings, and warehouses are discussed in this chapter, with emphasis on the industrial park.

THE INDUSTRIAL REAL ESTATE MARKET

A properly located, well-planned, and well-constructed industrial building can be an excellent investment, but industrial property is a highly risky venture for the uninformed investor. Several general features of the industrial real estate market should be considered by the prospective investor:

1. Industrial buildings are often constructed as a custom-made specialized facility for a particular user, combining both building and equipment into an integrated unit, sometimes for a particular manufacturing process. Such special use can—although not necessarily—limit the market for the property and increase the risk of investment. An industrial property is usually not easily converted to other uses, and when it is vacant another industrial tenant must be found.

2. Another feature of the market is the rapid rate of functional obsolescence of buildings, machinery, and manufacturing processes. Industrial technology can change fast, with resulting obsolescence in plant and equipment design. Further, major highway patterns can change. Also, amenities desired by industry tend to change over time. Advance planning and constant attention to trends is essential to reduce investment risk as much as possible.

3. Industrial real estate provides a good market for the use of borrowed money and employment of the entire spectrum of traditional and creative financing techniques. Industry does not generally like to tie up capital in real estate for its own use; the funds can usually earn a higher return as working capital in the business. Therefore, heavy reliance is placed on the financing and leasing of facilities, and industrial real estate provides excellent opportunities for the lender and nonuser–investor who seeks a good yield and other benefits of investment in real estate. Creative financing techniques can usually solve most financing situations, particularly during periods of tight money, but it should be remembered that the project must initially be economically sound and meet a market demand.

4. Industrial development is generally taking place in the outlying areas of cities, following arterial and interstate highways. In these locations land is available at reasonable prices and property taxes are lower, and skilled labor likes the suburban locations with the attractive environment and ease of access by automobile.

5. Industrial parks should be a major factor in the industrial property market for the foreseeable future, especially for warehousing and distribution activities and for small- and medium-sized light-manufacturing firms. A properly planned and economically justifiable park can be an excellent investment.

6. The demand for industrial space depends upon general economic

conditions, the position of the economy in the business cycle, and the supply of existing and proposed competitive space. Demand can fluctuate sharply. Rapid industrial expansion in the economy generates construction of industrial space at a rate which usually exceeds demand. When industrial production slows, the oversupply of space results in a lowering of rentals and other concessions to keep space occupied, and a search is started for alternative uses for many buildings, which may not be easy to create.

7. The industrial tenant is usually considered a good one by the investor. He is a businessman and understands a business transaction. While investors may prefer short-term leases in an inflationary economy, a triple-A industrial tenant on a long-term lease is a desirable investment. Industrial tenants, once satisfactorily located, hesitate to make expensive moves to other buildings. Further, the industrial property is not as quickly or as adversely affected by neighborhood changes as other types of property might be.

8. Industrial property usually offers attractive income tax benefits to the investor, particularly depreciation deductions. The value of the buildings are usually high in relation to the land, assuming that the land has been acquired at a reasonable price.

THE INDUSTRIAL PARK

A number of interrelated factors have contributed to the growth of industrial parks. Among the more prominent are the following: (1) the general rapid growth of manufacturing and distribution activities in the economy and the need for space to accommodate them; (2) the trend toward one-story industrial buildings occupying larger sites than the earlier multistory structures; (3) downtown traffic and parking congestion; (4) shortage of large tracts of land downtown and the increasingly high costs of acquiring such land; (5) expansion and improvement of highways; (6) industry following the flight of the population to the suburbs; (7) appeal of aesthetic values and controlled compatibility of industries in a park-like environment; and (8) availability of prepared sites and, usually, immediately available speculative buildings that can be easily finished to particular requirements.

DEFINITION

Industrial parks are diverse in character, and no standard description will cover all of them. The industrial park is generally recognized as a large area subdivided into sites to accommodate industry. It is an industrial sub-division or community of independent industries developed according to a comprehensive plan which provides for protective control of the district. The character of the park is one of low-density occupancy with park-like attractiveness; architectural, landscaping, and other aesthetic considerations are given emphasis so as to promote a harmonious environment. Along with aesthetic considerations, functional utility and efficiency of the park is also stressed so that maximum use will be permitted. Streets, utilities, rail facilities, and other improvements are installed before individual sites are marketed to prospective tenants. In brief, the park is a large tract of land zoned for industry and engineered with a planned layout designed for maximum efficiency, economy, and aesthetic appearance.

TYPES OF TENANTS

The average size of an industrial park is between 400 and 500 acres. Individual sites vary in size, but 2- to 5-acre parcels are commonly in demand. Various types of tenants may be found in industrial parks, but this kind of development is probably best suited to warehouse and distribution firms, including firms which perform the assembly–storage function. Sites are expensive, lease rentals are substantial, the locations are usually excellent; warehouse and distribution firms are usually the ones who can benefit most from the locational aspects of the park and from the park-like amenities. Heavy industry, particularly with large site requirements, is probably the least suited for the industrial park, although a park could be developed exclusively for such use. Research groups and office structures may also fit into the industrial park, but these uses are typically found in their own parks.

SITE SALES

Sites in an industrial park may be marketed in several ways. The park developer may erect a speculative building either for sale or lease to a prospective tenant. Or, the site may be sold or leased to a tenant who constructs its own building. Or, the developer may improve a site, and then construct a building on a lock-and-key basis for a specific occupant.

GENERAL FACTORS OF VALUATION

In evaluating a proposed industrial park, the investor should consider the present supply of land zoned for industry, the quantity and the quality of new industrial use land coming on the market, and the demand or rate of absorption for such land. The income and development expenses, including the developer's profit, must be estimated as if the park were completed. Several basic factors should be remembered about an industrial park:

1. Direct and indirect or interim costs of development are substantial, and are incurred over an extended period of time; park development must be carefully planned and scheduled.
2. It is difficult to project specific space needs for industrial firms. The park, therefore, must have a large degree of flexibility in its layout and size of individual sites.
3. Profit returns from an industrial park do not come in the early stages of development. The planning and development period is long and costly, proper timing is essential in all phases of development, and the rate of absorption of sites may be slow. Land must initially be purchased at the right place. Interest cost must be charged to improvements during the development period. Certain expenses, such as interest costs on borrowed money and property taxes, continue from the start.
4. Financing of an industrial park is based largely upon the credit and financial strength and reputation of the developer and the tenants of the park; 100 percent financing is possible through joint venture arrangements between developer and institutional lender such as a life insurance company. Nevertheless, for such a large-scale project it is desirable that the developer have a substantial reserve of cash himself; financial ability is a must.
5. A feasibility study made by an independent professional firm should be ordered in advance of definite land acquisition. The study would, among other things: analyze the demand-and-supply relationship for industrial land in the area; study the economic base of the community; determine the type of industry best suited for the proposed park; check such items as local property tax trends, governmental and community attitudes toward an industrial park, zoning trends, and labor supply; and analyze the financial aspects of the proposed park.

    Proper advance planning of a park is as essential as proper financing. Such factors as site size, location of park, kind of park, and providing amenities wanted by industry must be correctly projected. The park must be related to the community in which it is located.

6. An industrial park is designed primarily to serve a growing population market where there is a definite need for warehouse and distribution activity and light-manufacturing and assembly operations. The park is oriented to a market and its justification for existence is its ability to efficiently and economically service that market.

SPECIFIC FACTORS OF VALUATION

Specific factors of analysis for an industrial park, both proposed and existing, cover a wide range. Among the basic considerations are the following:

1. *Accessibility and Location.* Good arterial roads, both to the park and within it, are essential. Visibility of the park from a major road is a plus factor. Most new parks are located in or near suburban areas and on a major road, such as an expressway where easy access is possible at nearby interchanges.
2. *Utilities.* A park is seldom developed without access to public utility services—electricity, water, natural gas, telephone, sanitary sewer lines, and storm sewers. Private utilities for the park may be considered in some instances, such as a sewage-treatment plant, but generally public connections are more desirable, and cheaper in the long run. Remember to adapt the utilities to the potential users of the park—capacity, load requirements, special connections, and expansion needs.
3. *Transportation.* Raw materials and other goods must be delivered to the park occupants and products must be distributed from the park. Proximity to major expressways, interstate highways, and local arterial roads is essential, particularly where firms in the park rely heavily upon trucking services. Availability of rail service at the park is desirable and a must in most locations. Also attractive is proximity or easy access to a commercial airport served by scheduled airlines.
4. *Soil, Subsoil, and Topography.* The land for an industrial park, which will encompass several hundred acres, should be as level as possible and entail a minimum of features requiring costly correction, such as extensive filling in, sinking of piling, or extensive grading. Sometimes it is possible in the case of very valuable land to purchase the rough land at a good price, perform the expensive preparation re-

quirements (clearing rock, filling, grading) and still make a profit. Topography should be considered in relation to preparation costs, including natural drainage.

5. *Property Taxes.* Present and potential property tax trends in the community should be studied. An industrial park can be a heavy taxpayer, and reasonable and fair assessments are essential to a successful park.

6. *Labor Supply.* An industrial park will need a variety of different kinds of labor, ranging from blue-collar to managerial. The availability of the labor supply in the community should be checked, along with wage and salary levels, labor unions, skills, and the ability of the community to attract and accommodate labor.

7. *Restrictions and Amenities.* Amenities of an industrial park include well-maintained landscaping of grounds and foundation plantings, clean streets, architecturally attractive buildings, a pleasing and easily negotiated street pattern, and a park-like atmosphere. Easily seen street-name and directional signs are an attraction. Good street lighting is a plus factor.

DEED RESTRICTIONS

Deed restrictions are a basic ingredient of an industrial park. They are designed to insure control over the functional aspects of the park as well as over aesthetic values. Through effective and properly enforced controls, the park environment is maintained, property values are maintained, and tenant compatibility is protected. Restrictions may vary with geographic regions, and they must be adapted to the type of industry to be located in the park, but they commonly cover the following factors:

1. Buildings-and-grounds maintenance
2. Parking
3. Signs
4. Building construction and design
5. Waste disposal
6. Loading and unloading facilities
7. Storage
8. Compliance with building and zoning codes of community
9. Use of sites
10. Expansion and improvements
11. Land-to-building ratio
12. Maintenance of landscaping

PROPOSAL FOR JOINT VENTURE DEVELOPMENT
OF AN INDUSTRIAL PARK

Assume that the site is well located from an accessibility and visibility standpoint and meets all criteria for an industrial park. The developer plans to (1) sell sites for development; (2) develop buildings for lease to both single and multiple tenants; and (3) build and sell buildings on a lock-and-key basis to occupant–owners. Further, the developer intends to retain architectural control on all buildings erected in the park and will refuse to sell to a speculative builder, who would be in competition with his own buildings in the park.

For the purpose of establishing a joint venture relationship, the commercial bank advises that it will consider the development of the park on the following basis:

1. The joint venture will own 50% of the land devoted to leased buildings.
2. 25% of the land is to be sold for development to owner–occupants.
3. 25% of the land to be devoted to buildings to be sold on a lock-and-key basis to owner–occupants.

The basic ingredient of the joint venture is the purchase of approximately 55.33 useable acres comprising Industrial Park for $18,000 per acre or $950,000. It is contemplated that a 5-year acquisition-and-development loan would be arranged with the National Bank in the approximate amount of $500,000, with the remainder of the purchase price being provided by XYZ Life Insurance Company. The injection of the $450,000 could be all or partly in the form of a loan from XYZ Life Insurance Company. All loans will accrue interest at a rate of at least 7%.

The joint venture would have initial paid-in capital of $100,000 provided by both parties on a 50–50 basis at the beginning of the venture. A pro forma balance sheet in Exhibit "A" (p. 149) shows the beginning status of the venture.

The $100,000 cash paid into the venture will serve as a buffer for the first year's operating expenses and interest on loans. These expenses are estimated as follows:

1. Interest on $500,000 first mortgage
    @ 7% + 1% fee   = $40,000
2. Interest on $450,000 loan from

	National Bank @ 7%	= 31,500
3.	Management fee to John Doe @ 2%	= 18,000
4.	Real estate taxes	= 6,100

Total Expenses, First Year $95,600

XYZ Life Insurance Company and John Doe will be equal partners. Each will own one-half interest in the property.

Net sale proceeds will first be applied to the payment of interest and principal of the joint venture indebtedness to the National Bank up to a total of $10,000 per acre released. When this debt, on a pro rata basis, is satisfied, net sale proceeds will be applied as follows: $8,000 per acre released to be applied against the joint venture to XYZ Life Insurance Company, the remainder divided equally between John Doe and XYZ Life Insurance Company. When all debts are retired, all cash flow will be divided equally between the partners.

It might be noted on the income and cash flow projections that, when the total debt is repaid in 1974, 27.67 acres of developed land remain in the venture with a projected value at that time of $3,861,000, including improvements. The deduction of permanent loans of $2,700,000 leaves a net value of $1,161,000, with an annual cash flow of $62,291.00 after debt service and expenses for ensuing years.

EXHIBIT A

JOHN DOE–XYZ LIFE INSURANCE COMPANY
JOINT VENTURE
INDUSTRIAL PARK
CITY AND STATE

Assets

Cash	$ 100,000.00
Real Estate (at Market value)	965,000.00
Total Assets	$1,065,000.00

Liabilities

1st Mortgage, National Bank	$ 500,000.00
2nd Mortgage, XYZ Life Insurance Company	450,000.00
Total Liabilities	950,000.00
Paid-in Capital	100,000.00
Appraisal Surplus	15,000.00
Total Liabilities and Net Worth	$1,065,000.00

EXHIBIT B

INCOME AND CASH FLOW PROJECTION

	1970		1971	
Land Sales				
(Exhibit "C")	$ 55,320.00		$ 58,086.00	
Less: Lot Release Payments	49,788.00		49,788.00	
Gross Profit on Land		$ 5,532.00		$ 8,298.00
Lock-&-key Bldg. Sales				
(Exhibit "D")	$386,100.00		$386,100.00	
Less: Cost (& Bldr's Profit)	277,158.00		277,158.00	
Gross Profit on Land & Bldg. Sales		$108,942.00		$108,942.00
Bldgs. Built for Lease at Cost				
(Exhibit "E")	$554,352.00		$554,352.00	
Less: Permanent Loans				
@ 70% Loan to Value	$542,000.00		$542,000.00	
Total Gross Profit		($ 12,352.00)		($ 12,352.00)
Less:				
Operating Expense	$ 18,000.00		$ 15,000.00	
Interest	71,500.00		56,450.00	
Taxes	6,100.00		5,500.00	
Total Expenses		($ 95,600.00)		($ 76,950.00)
Net Income, Sales & Bldg.		6,522.00		20,670.00
Net Income from Leased				
Buildings		–0–	$ 96,525.00	
Debt Service on Leased Bldgs.			77,837.00	
Cash Flow to Leased Bldgs.		–0–		$ 18,688.00
Net Income to Venture		$ 6,522.00		$ 39,358.00
Total Loans Outstanding	$950,000.00		$750,812.00	
Cash Applied to Loans	199,188.00		199,188.00	
Net Loans Remaining		$750,812.00		$551,624.00
Return to XYZ Life Ins. Co. Investment		7%		10.9%

	1972		1973		1974	1975
$ 77,448.00		$ 82,980.00		$ 88,512.00		
49,788.00		49,788.00		38,303.00		
	$ 27,659.00		$ 33,191.00		$ 50,209	
$386,100.00		$386,100.00		$386,100.00		
277,158.00		277,158.00		265,673.00		
	$108,942.00		$108,942.00		$120,427	
$554,352.00		$554,352.00		$531,382.00		
$542,000.00		$542,000.00		$542,000.00		
	($ 12,352.00)		($ 12,352.00)		$ 10,618	
$ 11,000.00		$ 7,000.00		$ 3,000.00		
41,400.00		26,350.00		11,300.00		
4,800.00		3,200.00		2,000.00		
	($ 57,200.00)		($ 36,550.00)		($ 16,300)	
	67,049.00		93,231.00		164,954	
$171,600.00		$246,675.00		$321,750.00		
138,378.00		198,891.00		259,459.00		
	$ 33,222.00		$ 47,784.00		$ 62,291	$62,291
	$100,271.00		$141,015.00		$227,245	
$551,624.00		$352,436.00		$153,428.00		
199,188.00		199,188.00		153,428.00		
	$352,436.00		$153,248.00		–0–	
	21.4%		35.6%		82.7%	63%

EXHIBIT C

LAND USE SCHEDULE

Total Land   55.33 acres
    Land Sales   13.83 acres
    Lock-&-key Sales   13.83
    Buildings Owned & Leased   27.67

    Total   55.33 acres

2.766 acres sold per year for 5 years
2.766 acres per year devoted to Lock-&-key Sales for 5 years
5.534 acres per year devoted to Leased Buildings

EXHIBIT D

LAND SALES

1970	2.766 @ $20,000 per acre	=	$ 55,320.00	
1971	2.766 @ $21,000 per acre	=	58,086.00	
1972	2.766 @ $28,000 per acre	=	77,448.00	Commercial Frontage
1973	2.766 @ $30,000 per acre	=	82,980.00	Commercial Frontage
1974	2.766 @ $32,000 per acre	=	88,512.00	Commercial Frontage

Total Proceeds from Lot Sales = $362,346.00

EXHIBIT E

LOCK-&-KEY SALES *

1970   2.766 acres + 42,900 sq ft Warehouse—Total Cost $277,158
    Sales Price @ $386,100.00
1971   2.766 acres + 42,900 sq ft Warehouse—Total Cost $277,158
    Sales Price @ $386,100.00
1972   2.766 acres + 42,900 sq ft Warehouse—Total Cost $277,158
    Sales Price @ $386,100.00
1973   2.766 acres + 42,900 sq ft Warehouse—Total Cost $277,158
    Sales Price @ $386,100.00
1974   2.766 acres + 42,900 sq ft Warehouse—Total Cost $277,158
    Sales Price @ $386,100.00

* Assumptions:
1. 15,500 sq ft of Warehouse space per acre of Land Used
2. Cost of Construction = $5.30 per sq ft
   (using an estimated 10% office space requirement—this price includes construction loan interest and fees and a 7½% builder's profit)
3. Sales price of property based on a multiple of 9.5 × an economic gross income of $.95 per sq ft of a package price of $9.00 per sq ft of building area

DEBT RETIREMENT SCHEDULE

		Total Debt	*Paid Off*	*Debt Remaining*
1970	National Bank	$500,000.00	$110,660.00	$389,340.00
	XYZ Life	450,000.00	88,528.00	361,472.00
				$750,812.00
1971	National Bank	$389,340.00	$110,660.00	$278,680.00
	XYZ Life	361,472.00	88,528.00	272,944.00
				$551,624.00
1972	National Bank	$278,680.00	$110,660.00	$168,020.00
	XYZ Life	272,944.00	88,528.00	184,416.00
				$352,436.00
1973	National Bank	$168,020.00	$110,660.00	$ 57,360.00
	XYZ Life	184,416.00	88,528.00	95,888.00
				$153,248.00
1974	National Bank	$ 57,360.00	$ 57,360.00	–0–
	XYZ Life	95,888.00	95,888.00	–0–
				–0–

INCOME & EXPENSE SCHEDULE—LEASED BUILDINGS

1971	128,700 sq ft @ $.95	$122,265.00
	Expense & Vacancy @ $.20 per sq ft	25,740.00
		$ 96,525.00
	Less: Debt Service @ 9.60 Constant on $6.30 per sq ft	77,837.00
	Cash Flow	$ 18,688.00
1972	228,800 sq ft @ $.95	217,360.00
	Expense & Vacancy @ $.20 per sq ft	45,760.00
		$171,600.00
	Less: Debt Service (same as above)	138,378.00
	Cash Flow	$ 33,222.00

1973	328,900 sq ft @ $.95	312,455.00
	Expense & Vacancy @ $.20 per sq ft	65,780.00
		$246,675.00
	Less: Debt Service (same as above)	198,891.00
	Cash Flow	$ 47,784.00
1974	429,000 sq ft @ $.95	407,550.00
	Expense & Vacancy @ $.20 per sq ft	85,800.00
		$321,750.00
	Less: Debt Service (same as above)	259,459.00
	Cash Flow	$ 62,291.00

COMMITMENT FOR PROPOSED SALE-AND-LEASEBACK OFFICE-AND-WAREHOUSE PARK

Development Corporation will sell said property to Insurance Company and Insurance Company will leaseback said property to Development Corporation upon the following terms and conditions:

1. Upon completion of a mutually acceptable development plan designed by a qualified land engineer showing streets and utility layouts, grades, engineering tests and plotted survey, Development Corporation will convey said property to Insurance Company for a purchase price of $21,000 per acre; and, Insurance Company will pay the cost of development upon completion in accordance with said development plan; provided, however, that the total sum paid as the purchase price and development cost by Insurance Company shall not exceed the sum of $26,000 per acre.

2. At the time said property is conveyed by Development Corporation to Insurance Company, Insurance Company, as lessor, and Development Corporation, as lessee, will enter into an Indenture of Lease, whereby said property is demised, upon the following terms and conditions:

(a) The lease term shall be for 30 years commencing on the date of execution of the lease and Development Corporation shall have an option to renew this lease for additional term of 20 years provided Development Corporation gives Insurance Company 12 months prior written notice and provided the lease is not in default when notice is given nor in default at the end of the initial term.

(b) The rental shall be payable as follows: (i) The sum of 10% of the total purchase price plus development costs as set out in Condition 1 hereof shall be payable as annual rental during the entire term of this lease in equal monthly installments beginning on the commencement of the term of the lease and continuing on the first day of each month thereafter; provided, however, that until the development costs are determined, the rental shall be calculated on the basis of $26,000 per acre with appropriate adjustment by reimbursement to lessee of any excess rental paid in the event the development costs are less than $5,000 per acre; (ii) in addition to the base rent payable under the lease, Development Corporation will pay Insurance Company as additional rent, 25% of the cash flow generated from the development of the property. (Settlement of the cash flow due Insurance Company for the first 3 years will be deferred until the end of 3 years, after which settlement will be on a quarter annual basis.) "Cash flow" to be defined as the gross receipts received from the development project less all charges including ad valorem taxes, hazard and liability insurance, repairs, leasing commissions, debt services, ground rent, and other charges incurred in the operation of an office–distribution park but exclusive of depreciation, all as determined in accordance with generally accepted principles of accounting applicable to the business conducted in the development. Said additional rental shall be payable at the end of each quarter of Development Corporation's fiscal year with appropriate adjustment to the additional rental payable each year within 60 days of the end of each of Development Corporation's fiscal year during the term hereof.

(c) Insurance Company will agree to subordinate its reversionary interest in individual parcels of land constituting a portion of the entire premises demised by joining in the execution of a mortgage for each individual tract for the purpose of securing one construction loan and one permanent loan on each tract; provided, (i) that neither the construction loan nor the permanent loan shall exceed 75% of the appraised value of the tract and building for mortgage loan purposes as determined by XYZ Mortgage Company; (ii) that Insurance Company shall be given the right of first refusal on all permanent loans before any permanent loan commitment is accepted; (iii) that Insurance Company will have the right to approve all permanent financing on each improvement; (iv) that each mortgage shall provide that Insurance Company shall be given notice of any default declared by the lender under the mortgage, with the inherent right to cure such default within 30 days after receipt of notice of default before any lender shall have the right to proceed to exercise any remedies under each mortgage; (v) that the indebtedness evidenced by each mortgage shall not provide for a maturity beyond the initial lease term without the prior written approval of lessor; and (vi) that Insurance Company shall not be liable for the indebtedness secured by said mortgage but will join in the mortgage for the sole purpose of fulfilling its obligations under the lease to subordinate its reversionary fee simple title and neither such subordination nor foreclosure of such mortgage shall in any way affect the obligations of the lessee under the lease.

(d) Insurance, including casualty and liability coverage, in such amounts and companies as approved by lessor, shall be maintained at all times on the premises by the lessee.

(e) All ad valorem taxes and assessments of any nature whatsoever and all license fees are to be paid by lessee.

(f) Lessee shall complete construction of all improvements consisting of office and distribution buildings totaling at least 350,000 square feet of gross area as follows: (i) during the first year of the term of the lease, 100,000 square feet; (ii) during the second year, 125,000 square feet; and (iii) during the third year, 125,000 square feet.

(g) The lease is to be a net lease.

(h) The obligations of the lessee under the lease are to be personally guaranteed, jointly and severally, by (name).

3. At the time the property is conveyed to Insurance Company, Insurance Company will issue to Development Corporation its permanent loan commitment on two buildings containing a total of 50,000 square feet. Said buildings will be of the office- and distribution-type with the design, plans, and specifications to be approved by Insurance Company. Said loan to be in the sum of $325,000 with interest at the rate of 8% for 23 years in monthly installments of $2,580.50 each. In the event Development Corporation does not achieve average rental of $1.25 per square foot on leases satisfactory to Insurance Company covering 75% of the net rentable area, then the loan shall be for $250,000 and there shall be appropriate adjustment in monthly payments of principal and interest thereunder.

Our commitment will be in the form of a bankable commitment and at our option, we have the choice of either taking the loan or asking XYZ Mortgage Company to place the permanent loan with another permanent lender.

4. Insurance Company and Development Corporation shall enter into a development agreement which shall provide:

(a) That Development Corporation shall have the right to sell vacant land in the development up to, but not to exceed, 25% of the net usable land area of the property after deducting that portion of the property which is used for streets and utilities; provided, however, such sales are for cash (or if the sale is upon terms, then Development Corporation must secure the prior written approval of Insurance Company as to the terms), and further provided that Insurance Company is paid its total cost per acre at the time Insurance Company is called upon to execute any deed of conveyance, and further provided Insurance Company is paid 50% of the sum over and above its total cost per acre. The "total cost per acre" as used in the preceding sentence shall be determined by dividing the total purchase price and development cost of Insurance Company by the net usable acres after deducting that portion of said property that is used for streets and utilities.

(b) In the event Insurance Company agrees to approve any refinancing, then Insurance Company shall receive 50% of all net new money created by such refinancing.

(c) In the event there is a sale of the vacant land area, then such sale is to reduce the base rental payable under the lease by 10% of the corresponding reduction of the purchase price and development cost theretofore paid by Insurance Company and Insurance Company, as lessor, and Development Corporation, as lessee, shall enter into an amendatory agreement establishing the new base rental under the terms of the lease.

5. Notwithstanding anything in Condition 1 hereof to the contrary, the total sum paid by Insurance Company as the purchase price and development cost shall not exceed the sum of $676,000.00.

6. Title to the premises, all legal documents, agreements, or other instruments used in conjunction with this transaction, including the loan commitment, deed of conveyance, and ground lease, shall have the prior approval of Insurance Company.

7. XYZ Mortgage Company is our representative in the area and all negotiations regarding this property, including all negotiations during the term of the lease, are to be channeled through them.

8. We have appointed the law firm of A, B, C, and D as our legal representatives to handle, on our behalf, all matters regarding title examination, preparation of the lease, loan papers in conjunction with loan commitments issued by us in conjunction with the development of the project, and any other documents required in the development of the project. Actual legal work will be handled by Mr. John Doe and Mr. Doe John of that firm.

9. All expenses involved in the development of the project, including without limitation all legal fees, title insurance premiums, real estate commissions, conveyance taxes, and intangible taxes, shall be paid by Development Corporation.

10. Insurance Company will require that a $10,000 good-faith deposit be put up upon the acceptance of this agreement. Acceptance must be received by Insurance Company no later than 10 days from the date of this agreement.

JOINT VENTURE PROPOSAL
OFFICE-AND-WAREHOUSE PARK

PROPOSAL:

To develop approximately 26 acres at the SEC of Belt Road and Route 66 with 350,000 square feet of office and warehouse space over a 3-year period as follows:

First Year	100,000 sq ft
Second Year	125,000 sq ft
Third Year	125,000 sq ft
Total	350,000 sq ft

GENERAL PLAN:

The owner, Development Corporation, will sell to investor the 26 acres of land graded with streets in based on $21,000 per acre plus development cost. Total cost is not to exceed $26,000 per acre. The investor will leaseback the 26 acres to Development Corporation at 10% annual return net of all charges for a term of 25 years with one option to renew for an additional 25 years. The investor will be entitled to receive 25% of the cash flow generated from the development.

GENERAL CONDITIONS:

1. Investor will purchase 26 acres from developer for a price not to exceed $26,000 per acre and will leaseback at a 10% annual return net of all charges.

2. The developer will build 350,000 square feet of office and warehouse space over a time period of approximately 3 years.

3. Investor is to agree to issue a permanent financing commit-

ment for the first two buildings, which will contain a total area of approximately 50,000 square feet. Investor may elect to issue a take-out commitment and finance the property through another institutional lender.

4. Investor is to be granted a second lien on all improvements erected on the property.
5. Investor will agree to subordinate its interest in the land to the construction lender and initial long-term lender.
6. Investor will have right to approve the permanent financing on each deal.
7. Investor receives 25% of all cash flow from the project.
8. Investor receives 50% of net new money created by refinancing.
9. In the event of land sales, profits above $26,000 per acre are to be divided on a 50–50 basis, sales limited to 25% of land area.
10. XYZ Mortgage Company will have the right of first negotiation in connection with permanent loans on a basis competitive as to terms and conditions. XYZ Mortgage Company will also have a nonexclusive right to negotiate leases for a full 5% commission and will have equal sign rights.

PRO FORMA DEVELOPMENT STATEMENT

COST:
Land cost (graded with all utilities and streets in) not to exceed $26,000 per acre $ 676,000

IMPROVEMENTS:
350,000 sq ft of office- and distribution-type buildings
at estimated cost $6.00   2,100,000
Interest and ad valorem tax during construction   50,000

Total Cost $2,826,000

INCOME AND EXPENSE:
350,000 sq ft of one-story office- and distribution-type
buildings at avg. rental value $1.25/sq ft $437,500
Less: 5% vacancy allowance   21,875

Gross Dependable Income $415,625

Expenses:
Taxes $42,000
Insurance   5,250
Agents commissions   20,780

Structural repairs	3,500	
Expenses		71,530

NET INCOME BEFORE DEBT SERVICE AND GROUND RENT: $344,095

GROUND RENT: 67,600
DEBT SERVICE: $2,275,000 ($6.50/sq ft), 7¾%, 20 years
  9.86 constant   224,315

CASH FLOW (EST.): $0.15/sq ft $ 52,180

CASH FLOW DEFINED

Cash flow is net income after all charges, including ad valorem taxes, hazard and liability insurance, repairs, leasing commissions, debt service, ground rent, and other charges normal to the operation of an office-and-distribution park, but exclusive of depreciation.

OFFERING TO FOREIGN INVESTORS
OF XYZ COMPANY
WAREHOUSE-AND-OFFICE BUILDING

LOCATION:

Commercial and industrial center of a large metropolitan area. The tract is adjacent to the Southern and Northern Railroad.

LAND:

8.01 acres valued at $15,000 per acre = $120,000. Parking areas are paved with asphalt.

IMPROVEMENTS:

Newly completed 115,600-sq-ft building with interior rail spur, truck cauls, warehouse, offices, and freezer–cooler (7,000 sq ft). The building is dock high and is suitable for any general warehousing or manufacturing use. Walls are of insulated metal panels on structural steel frame 20-year built-up roof. Warehouse area is 20 feet clear height with fluorescent lighting and year-round heating.

LESSEE:

The XYZ Company is a large wholesale grocery firm operating in
Florida and several other southern states. It was established in 1920,
celebrating its fiftieth anniversary this year. Sales have steadily increased.
Present volume over $80,000,000 annually. The Company's net worth
exceeds $3,000,000.

LEASE:

25 years at a net rental of $75,000 annually, payable monthly. Tenant
pays all utilities, taxes, insurance, maintenance and repairs, so rental is
absolutely net. Tenant has two 10-year options to renew at the same
rental. Lease gives tenant the right to purchase the property for
$1,050,000 during the first 5 years, and to purchase the property for
$917,000 during the remaining term of the lease. The higher figure
for the first 5 years was inserted to insure that the option would not be
exercised until after 5 years.

MORTGAGE:

$600,000 at 7% interest. Constant payments of $50,940 per year will
retire this mortgage in full over the 25-year term of the lease.

PURCHASE PRICE:

The Sellers have agreed to sell the property for $886,000—$236,000
cash and a second mortgage of $50,000, 7% interest only for 10 years.

At the end of 10 years, the first mortgage will be reduced to $476,479.
We would plan to refinance at that time for $525,000, paying off the
$50,000 second mortgage from the proceeds of this loan.

INVESTMENT BY PURCHASER:

Purchase Price—Net Cash to Seller	$236,000
Cost of Forming Foreign Corporation, Legal & Other Expenses & Working Capital	4,000
Cash Required	$240,000

ACCOUNTING EXPENSES:

If this property is acquired by investors who do not live in the United
States, it is suggested that they employ an affiliate of Realty Company—
Realty Management, Inc.—to keep the books and records of the owning
corporation and to attend to corporate details. The annual cost of this,

including fees paid to the foreign corporation director, will be $900 per year—which will reduce the net income to $74,100.

PROJECTION OF CORPORATE INCOME & EXPENSES:

We recommend that title to this property be taken in a foreign (name of country) corporation. Our nonresident client's investment will be represented by

400 Shares Capital Stock	$40,000
Paid-in Capital	40,000
8% Notes	160,000
	$240,000

Our accountants have prepared a 15-year projection showing the direct cash return and the indirect (mortgage-reduction) return which we believe can reasonably be expected from this investment. These returns are summarized below.

SCHEDULE OF BENEFITS

	1st 5 Years	2nd 5 Years	3rd 5 Years	Totals
DIRECT BENEFITS:				
Note Interest	$64,000	$64,000	$ 64,000	$192,000
Taxable Dividends	—	7,737	41,836	49,573
Nontaxable Dividends	34,300	25,890	19,810	80,000
Total	$98,300	$97,627	$125,646	$321,573
Average per Year	$19,660	$19,526	$ 25,129	$ 21,438
RETURN ON INVESTMENT OF $240,000	8.19%	8.14%	10.47%	8.93%
INDIRECT BENEFITS:				
Mortgage Reduction	$51,412	$72,109	$ 61,861	$185,382
Average per Year	$10,282	$14,422	$ 12,372	$ 12,359
RETURN ON INVESTMENT OF $240,000	4.28%	6.01%	5.16%	5.15%
COMBINED RETURN	12.47%	14.15%	15.63%	14.08%

CAPITAL GAINS PROFIT IF OPTION TO PURCHASE IS EXERCISED:

If Lessee exercises its option to purchase for $1,050,000 at the end of 5 years, the capital gains profit would be $215,412. However, we assume that the XYZ Company will not repurchase at this time, for by waiting until the sixth year the purchase price will be $917,000.

If the option to purchase is exercised between the sixth and tenth years, the capital gains profit will be:

	Mortgage Balance	Profit	Average Yearly Profit on $240,000	
6th year	$582,049	$ 94,951	$15,825	6.59%
7th year	$568,632	$108,368	$15,481	6.45%
8th year	$554,276	$122,724	$15,341	6.39%
9th year	$538,915	$138,085	$15,343	6.39%
10th year	$522,479	$154,521	$15,452	6.44%

RECOMMENDATIONS:

The Realty Company recommends the Warehouse and Office for the following reasons:

1. It is a very conservative investment that does not involve management. The lessee is a large wholesale grocery firm with a volume of over $80,000,000 annually and whose net worth exceeds $3,000,000.
2. This property contains 8 acres of land on which there is a new 115,600-sq-ft building. The railroad has a spur track leading directly into the building. This type of property has a very long useful life.
3. This property yields a cash return of 8.19% during the first 5 years, 8.14% second 5 years, and 10.47% third 5 years (after refinancing) on an investment of $240,000. In addition to this cash return, over a 15-year period there should be a mortgage reduction of $185,382, which represents an average additional return of 5.15% on the cash invested. The buyer can thus expect a combined return totaling 14.08% over the 15 years.
4. It is highly probable that the tenant will exercise its option to repurchase the property. In this event, the minimum capital gains profit to the purchaser will average 6.39% per year in addition to the 8.93% cash return.

1st Mortgage $600,000—7% Interest—$50,940 Annual Constant
2nd Mortgage   50,000—7% Interest only
Refinanced Mortgage   525,000—7% Interest—$47,250 Annual Constant

	1st Year	2nd Year	3rd Year	4th Year	5th Year
Net Operating Income	$ 74,100	$ 74,100	$ 74,100	$ 74,100	$ 74,100
Deductions:					
Interest on 1st Mortgage	42,000	41,374	40,705	39,988	39,221
Interest on 2nd Mortgage	3,500	3,500	3,500	3,500	3,500
Interest on Refinanced Mortgage	—	—	—	—	—
Interest on Notes	12,800	12,800	12,800	12,800	12,800
Depreciation	19,650	19,650	19,650	19,650	19,650
Total Deductions	$ 77,950	$ 77,324	$ 76,655	$ 75,938	$ 75,171
Taxable Income	(3,850)	(3,224)	(2,555)	(1,838)	(1,071)
State Income Tax *	—	—	—	—	—
Federal Income Tax	—	—	—	—	—
Net Income	(3,850)	(3,224)	(2,555)	(1,838)	(1,071)
Add Back: Depreciation	$ 19,650	$ 19,650	$ 19,650	$ 19,650	$ 19,650
Proceeds from Refinancing	—	—	—	—	—
Cash Available for Mortgages	$ 15,800	$ 16,426	$ 17,095	$ 17,812	$ 18,579
1st-Mortgage Principal Payment	8,940	9,566	10,235	10,952	11,719
2nd-Mortgage Principal Payment	—	—	—	—	—
Refinanced-Mortgage Principal Payment	—	—	—	—	—
Surplus Cash	$ 6,860	$ 6,860	$ 6,860	$ 6,860	$ 6,860
Accumulated Surplus Cash	6,860	13,720	20,580	27,440	34,300
Mortgage Principal Balance—1st	591,060	581,494	571,259	560,307	548,588
Mortgage Principal Balance—2nd	—	—	—	—	—
Mortgage Principal Balance—Refinanced	—	—	—	—	—
Taxable Dividends	—	—	—	—	—
Nontaxable Dividends	$ 6,860	$ 6,860	$ 6,860	$ 6,860	$ 6,860
Total Dividends	$ 6,860	$ 6,860	$ 6,860	$ 6,860	$ 6,860
Direct Benefits (Interest & Dividends)	19,660	19,660	19,660	19,660	19,660
Indirect Benefits (Mortgage Reduction)	8,940	9,566	10,235	10,952	11,719
Combined Benefits	$ 28,600	$ 29,226	$ 29,895	$ 30,612	$ 31,379

* Corporate income tax law pending

LOFT BUILDINGS

The loft building is a multistory (typically 2 to 10 stories) building with unfinished interior space, located adjacent to the downtown core, and originally built for light-industrial use. Over the years, location requirements of light manufacturers have changed from the downtown area and the loft building is now generally obsolete.

The loft building may, however, still provide a good investment oppor-

			Paid-in Capital	40,000
			Stock	$ 40,000
	XYZ COMPANY		Notes (8%)	160,000
	WAREHOUSE-AND-OFFICE BUILDING			$240,000

6th Year	7th Year	8th Year	9th Year	10th Year	Refinancing	11th Year	12th Year
$ 74,100	$ 74,100	$ 74,100	$ 74,100	$ 74,100	—	$ 74,100	$ 74,100
38,401	37,523	36,584	35,579	34,504	—	—	—
3,500	3,500	3,500	3,500	3,500	—	—	—
—	—	—	—	—	—	36,750	36,015
12,800	12,800	12,800	12,800	12,800	—	12,800	12,800
19,650	19,650	19,650	19,650	19,650	—	19,650	19,650
$ 74,351	$ 73,473	$ 72,534	$ 71,529	$ 70,454	—	$ 69,200	$ 68,465
(251)	$ 627	$ 1,566	$ 2,571	$ 3,646	—	$ 4,900	$ 5,635
—	—	—	—	673	—	1,078	1,240
(251)	$ 627	$ 1,566	$ 2,571	$ 2,973	—	$ 3,822	$ 4,395
$ 19,650	$ 19,650	$ 19,650	$ 19,650	$ 19,650	—	$ 19,650	$ 19,650
—	—	—	—	—	$525,000	—	—
$ 19,399	$ 20,277	$ 21,216	$ 22,221	$ 22,623	—	$ 23,472	$ 24,045
12,539	13,417	14,356	15,361	16,436	476,479	—	—
—	—	—	—	—	50,000	—	—
—	—	—	—	—	—	10,500	11,235
$ 6,860	$ 6,860	$ 6,860	$ 6,860	$ 6,187	(1,479)	$ 12,972	$ 12,810
41,160	48,020	54,880	61,740	67,927	66,448	79,420	92,230
536,049	522,632	508,276	492,915	476,479	—	—	—
—	—	—	—	—	50,000	—	—
—	—	—	—	—	—	514,500	503,265
—	$ 627	$ 1,566	$ 2,571	$ 2,973	—	$ 3,822	$ 4,395
$ 5,700	7,393	5,294	4,289	3,214	(1,479)	9,150	8,415
$ 5,700	$ 8,020	$ 6,860	$ 6,860	$ 6,187	(1,479)	$ 12,972	$ 12,810
18,500	20,820	19,660	19,660	18,987	(1,479)	25,722	25,610
12,539	13,417	14,356	15,361	16,436	1,479	10,500	11,235
$ 32,199	$ 33,077	$ 34,016	$ 35,021	$ 35,423	—	$ 36,272	$ 36,845

tunity. These buildings have excellent locations in relation to the downtown core, and in many metropolitan areas land close to the core is scarce. Some loft buildings may be undervalued simply because they are situated in a fringe area, and these properties may be desirable acquisitions to hold for future appreciation.

The loft building can also be a good investment for income. Rentals can be lower than in buildings with finished interior space, and there are many firms which can use loft-type space. In fact, while loft space is still predominantly occupied by light manufacturers, the volume devoted to this

XYZ COMPANY WAREHOUSE-AND- OFFICE BUILDING (Continued)	Land	$100,000
	Building	786,000 40-year life—S/L
		$886,000

	13th Year	14th Year	15th Year	Total— 15 Years
Net Operating Income	$ 74,100	$ 74,100	$ 74,100	$1,111,500
Deductions:				
Interest on 1st Mortgage	—	—	—	385,879
Interest on 2nd Mortgage	—	—	—	35,000
Interest on Refinanced Mortgage	35,229	34,387	33,487	175,868
Interest on Notes	12,800	12,800	12,800	192,000
Depreciation	19,650	19,650	19,650	294,750
Total Deductions	$ 67,679	$ 66,837	$ 65,937	$1,083,497
Taxable Income	$ 6,421	$ 7,263	$ 8,163	$ 28,003
State Income Tax *	—	—	—	—
Federal Income Tax	1,413	1,598	1,796	7,798
Net Income	$ 5,008	$ 5,665	$ 6,367	$ 20,205
Add Back: Depreciation	19,650	19,650	19,650	294,750
Proceeds from Refinancing	—	—	—	525,000
Cash Available for Mortgages	$ 24,658	$ 25,315	$ 26,017	$ 839,955
1st-Mortgage Principal Payment	—	—	—	600,000
2nd-Mortgage Principal Payment	—	—	—	50,000
Refinanced-Mortgage Principal Payment	12,021	12,863	13,763	60,382
Surplus Cash	$ 12,637	$ 12,452	$ 12,254	$ 129,573
Accumulated Surplus Cash	104,867	117,319	129,573	—
Mortgage Principal Balance—1st	—	—	—	—
Mortgage Principal Balance—2nd	—	—	—	—
Mortgage Principal Balance—Refinanced	491,244	478,381	464,618	—
Taxable Dividends	$ 8,913	$ 12,452	$ 12,254	$ 49,573
Nontaxable Dividends	3,724	—	—	80,000
Total Dividends	$ 12,637	$ 12,452	$ 12,254	$ 129,573
Direct Benefits (Interest & Dividends)	25,437	25,252	25,054	321,573
Indirect Benefits (Mortgage Reduction)	12,021	12,863	13,763	185,382
Combined Benefits	$ 37,458	$ 38,115	$ 38,817	$ 506,955

* Corporate income tax law pending

use is declining and the trend is toward greater commercial usage.

Operating costs of the multistory building can be lower than in some other types of buildings. Tenants demand fewer services, less maintenance is required, and fewer employees are needed in the operation of the building.

Tenants may be attracted by the lower rents of the loft building as construction costs and rent levels increase in new buildings. Floor areas in a typical loft building may be remodeled into usable space for firms with small space requirements.

The loft building should be at least in an overall fair condition and structurally sound. Efficiency of operation is essential; expenses must be controlled carefully. Availability and cost of hazard insurance should be checked. Professional management is desirable. Also to be checked are such items as sprinkler system; zoning and building restrictions; elevator capacity; floor area, capacity, load capacity, and flexibility of space arrangement.

WAREHOUSES

There is generally a good demand for warehouse properties, although, like any industrial property, the demand can fluctuate depending upon the amount of existing space available in the market and economic conditions. In many locations, the construction of modern warehouses has not been sufficient to meet the demand.

There are several kinds of warehouses: (1) the large regional warehouse; (2) the city or statewide distribution warehouse; and (3) the small city or neighborhood warehouse. The amount of square feet, special equipment, and proportion of finished office space will differ with each type of warehouse. Location and physical features and requirements will also differ.

A modern warehouse must provide convenience, efficiency, and maximum utility for the storage and distribution of goods. The centrally located, multistory warehouse found in many places is obsolete except for limited purposes, such as temporary-transfer storage. These old warehouses have obsolete elevators, low ceilings, small doors, inadequate office space, and are generally not suitable for the efficient movement of goods.

The investor should observe the warehouse market from the viewpoint of the general and local trends in transportation, materials-handling methods, storage, and distribution of goods. Changes in these factors can cause a warehouse to quickly become obsolete. In addition, more specific information about warehouses is also needed for an intelligent investment decision. Particular data to consider in analyzing a specific investment proposal would include the following items:

1. Current income (lease rentals) and expense data and trends on various kinds of warehouses.
2. Vacancy data and trends; warehouses will inevitably incur vacancies as market locational and physical requirements change over time.
3. Locational trends, particularly in relation to trends in materials handling and distribution in an area.

4. Actual sales of warehouses and sales of land zoned for warehouse use.
5. Costs of construction of different kinds of warehouses. These costs will cover a rather wide range due to different physical features of warehouses. Cost estimates should also include special equipment and its maintenance.
6. Zoning requirements and deed restrictions should be carefully reviewed. Sometimes these can have the effect of limiting the market and hence the value of a given warehouse.

The investor should remember that the use to which a warehouse may be put is affected and often determined by its physical features. Many items need to be checked, such as location and spacing of bays, ceiling height, office space, railroad siding, and truck docks.

Further Readings and References

Beaton, William R. "Appraisal Analysis of Land Allocation for Industrial Use," *Valuation*, December, 1967, 11–22.

Beer, A. Robert. "Syndication of Industrial Properties," *Newsletter* of the Society of Industrial Realtors, June, 1969, 3–4. Washington, D. C.: Society of Industrial Realtors of the National Association of Real Estate Boards, 1969.

Boley, Robert E. "Rx for Successful Industrial Park Development," *Urban Land*, Vol. 26, No. 6, June, 1967. Washington, D. C.: Urban Land Institute, 1967.

Gates, Niles. "Industrial Property Investments," *Developing, Selling and Syndicating Real Estate Investment Property*. Los Angeles: California Real Estate Association, 1964.

Goodbody & Company. *Industrial Aid Financing*. New York: Goodbody & Company, 1965.

Herrmann, Cyril C. "The Outlook for Industrial Land Use In America," *Urban Land*, Vol. 28, No. 8, September, 1969. Washington, D. C.: Urban Land Institute, 1969.

Kinnard, William N., Jr. *Industrial Real Estate*. Washington, D. C.: Society of Industrial Realtors of the National Association of Real Estate Boards, 1967.

Korb, Irving, and Harold G. Trimble, Jr. *Real Estate Sale–Leaseback—A Basic Analysis*. Washington, D. C.: Society of Industrial Realtors of the National Association of Real Estate Boards, 1966.

Murray, Thomas F. "Industrial Real Estate Financing," *Newsletter* of the Society of Industrial Realtors, August–September, 1967, 1, 3–4. Washington, D. C.: Society of Industrial Realtors of the National Association of Real Estate Boards, 1967.

Schraub, Edgar D. *How to Invest in Industrial Property*. Englewood Cliffs, N. J.: Prentice-Hall, Inc., 1968.

11

Shopping
Centers

In considering a proposed urban shopping center, an economic feasibility study is usually the first step. An example of such a study is given below. Following this study is a shopping center projection worksheet used by one Realtor–developer. An offering of a shopping center property is then shown to illustrate one way of analyzing this type of property.

ANALYSIS OF ECONOMIC FEASIBILITY
and
RETAIL SALES POTENTIAL
PROPOSED SHOPPING CENTER

Mr. John Doe, President
Doe Development, Inc.
Street Address
City and State

169

RE: Proposed Shopping Center Site
Apex Drive at East Expressway
Jackson County, _____

Dear Mr. Doe:

In accordance with your request, we have made a study of the economic background of the trade area environing the captioned location, for the purpose of analyzing the retail sales potential available to the proposed center, as the basis for an estimate of economic feasibility.

In summary, my opinion is that sufficient retail sales potential exists at the present time to warrant immediate plans for the construction of approximately 70,000 square feet of sales space. Adequate sales potential is available for the "core" group, which would consist of a major grocery supermarket, a junior department store, a drugstore, and a variety store. This group would consist of approximately 60,000 square feet of space. In addition, approximately 10,000 square feet of space for small service and specialty shops should be provided.

Our analysis of the area indicates that the surrounding trade area is an area of much-higher-than-average income level and that the area is closely contained in a small geographical radius. Population growth within the area is proceeding at a rate much higher than the average for the metropolitan area, and the quality of the income level is trending upward at the same time.

Our method of investigation involved actual house count within the general trade area, in addition to verification by means of statistical data available from public agencies. The estimated population within the trade area as of September 1, 1965 is 2,628 households, and approximately 8,856 persons. The projected rate of growth, based upon the trends found in our investigation, indicates a growth to approximately 12,800 persons by September 1, 1968 and approximately 15,500 by September 1, 1970.

The retail sales volume potential available to the proposed center's principal lines is estimated, as of September 1, 1965, in excess of $2,000,000 for the supermarket; approximately $885,000 for the junior department store; approximately $400,000 for the drug store; and approximately $250,000 for the variety store. The service and specialty shops should do a corresponding volume, as detailed in the enclosed report.

Sales volume projections as of September 1, 1968 indicate a volume of approximately $3,000,000 for the supermarket; $1,300,000 for the junior department store; $580,000 for the drugstore; and approximately $360,000 for the variety store.

Details of our investigation, together with the data and method of evaluation upon which the opinions summarized above are based, are detailed in the attached report of our survey and analysis.

In summary, it is my opinion that the economic background of the general trade area surrounding the proposed center is of sufficient potential to warrant plans for immediate construction of the proposed center, starting with a sales space of approximately 70,000 square feet.

Sincerely yours,

Henry J. Doe

Table of Contents

I

Purpose

II

Location, Street Pattern, and Access

III

Trade Area and Population Background
    Determination of Trade Area
    Existing Competitive Facilities
    Estimated Trade Area Population

IV

Economic Background of Trade Area—Estimated
    Income and Expenditures

V

Projected Sales Volume Estimated for the Proposed Center

VI

Conclusions

VII

Underlying Assumptions

Addenda

Exhibit A—Estimated Effective Household Incomes in
    Selected Subdivisions in the Trade Area
Exhibit B—Building Permits Issued in Trade Area

List of Tables

Table
I   Housing Units, Population Estimates, and
        Growth by Census Tracts

LIST OF MAPS

I   PURPOSE

The purpose of this study is to analyze the economic potential in terms of estimated retail sales volume available to a proposed shopping center to be located at the northwest intersection of Apex Drive and the East Expressway. The proposed site consists of approximately 13 acres, and preliminary planning indicates a center of approximately 98,500 square feet of area and approximately 1,078 parking spaces. The site is bounded on the east by Apex Drive; on the south by the westbound on-ramp to the East Expressway; on the west by vacant land zoned for apartment development; and on the north by Apex Woods Drive.

The analysis will be concerned specifically with estimates of retail sales volume that can reasonably be expected to be generated by the trade area surrounding the subject site.

The method of analysis involves the estimating of present population by means of the statistical data available through public agencies and trade publications, and the verification of current population by inspection of the trade area. Projections as to future population and income levels are based upon trending the historical statistical data into future projections based upon current levels and the trends found.

II   LOCATION, STREET PATTERN, AND ACCESS

The site of the proposed shopping center is in an unincorporated area of Jackson County, in the southeastern section of the metropolitan area.

The areas adjoining the subject to the west and north consist of single-family residential subdivisions developed during the past 5 years, and ranging in price levels from the $16,000–18,000 range in the earlier developments, increasing to $22,000–25,000 in the more recent developments. These contiguous areas west and north of the subject are approximately 95% developed at the present time. This portion of the subject area consists of an excellent residential neighborhood of higher-than-average income quality bordered on the west by Julington Creek; the north by Barnett Road; and the east by Apex Drive.

The areas northeast and east of the subject, east of Apex Drive, lying between Apex Drive and Julington Road consist of developing subdivision areas, the development of which started approximately 2 years ago and is continuing at an increased rate at the present time. Homes in these subdivisions are in the $20,000–27,000 price range, and the area at this time is approximately 65% developed.

The areas south of the subject consist of sparsely developed tracts of land, most of which have been purchased by subdivision developers, and at this time the area is in an early stage of subdivision development in a somewhat higher price range than the areas north of the expressway, generally speaking from $20,000 to as high as $32,000. This area is the expansion area within the subject trade area. At the present time, the area is only approximately 10% developed, but development is under way at an unusually rapid rate.

The subject site enjoys excellent accessibility from the densely populated residential areas north and northwest of the subject site via residential collector streets and Apex Drive. Access to the subject site from areas south of the expressway is excellent via Sunset Drive, with its residential collector streets and Apex Drive. Access to the proposed center from the northeast is principally via residential collector streets feeding westward into Apex Drive from the residential areas developed east of Apex Drive.

The two main thoroughfares in the area consist of Apex Drive, which is a principal north–south thoroughfare leading from the business district to the subject area, and the East Expressway. The principal east–west thoroughfare is the East Expressway to the central business district. The expressway intersection with Apex Drive is a "half-diamond," with a westbound on-ramp and an eastbound off-ramp. The interchange does not have a westbound off-ramp or an eastbound on-ramp. Consequently, access to the subject site from the east via the expressway is not good. However, this is offset by the fact that the boundaries of the trade area have taken this into account, and the principal means of access within the trade area would not involve use of the expressway at all.

In summary, the site appears to have the advantage of easy access from all parts of the trade area via existing principal thoroughfares and residential collector streets feeding into these thoroughfares. The trade area boundaries involve driving time of approximately 3 to 4 minutes from the subject site.

Information developed during our investigation indicates that at the present time, planning is underway for the extension of Apex Drive southward from its present end just south of Sunset Drive, to intersect with a new east–west street approximately one-quarter of a mile south of the Belt Line Highway. If constructed, this extension of Apex Drive would open up a considerable land area south of the subject that contains a high potential for rapid development during the next 3 to 5 years.

The location of the principal thoroughfares and residential collector streets are shown on the facing-page map. (Map omitted here.)

III   TRADE AREA AND POPULATION BACKGROUND
Determination of Trade Area

The boundaries of the effective trading area for the subject site were determined on the basis of housing development patterns, major street patterns and observed traffic flow patterns, and existing competition. At the present time, it appears that, due not only to the previously cited factors but also in consideration of the existing shopping habits that have developed because of heavy nearby competitive retail convenience facilities, the northern boundary of the trade area should be set at the south side of Barnett Road, in the area between Julington Creek and Apex Drive. The eastern boundary is set at Apex Drive between Barnett Road and Julington Road, running along Julington Road to the East Expressway; along Pine Valley Road to Rocky Shoals Road and along Rocky Shoals Road to its intersection with Cherry Road. This section of Rocky Shoals Road, from Pine Valley Road to Cherry Road, is also the southeastern boundary of the trade area. The western boundary of the trade area has been set at Julington Creek, which traverses this part of Jackson County in a general south and southeasterly direction. This has been a development barrier and probably will continue to be so for residential development, serving as a natural separator along the western edge of the trade area. This boundary was set, as a conservative method of delimiting, in spite of the fact that a bridge has been constructed on University Drive which could conceivably open up a considerably larger western area, but your consultant feels that this western area is too close to heavy existing competitive facilities at Oslo Road and Colonial Road and a heavy strip development along Oslo from Colonial to Barnett Road.

The boundaries of the trade area are shown on the facing-page map. (Map omitted here.)

After a careful study of the trade area which involved detailed inspection of each street and actual house count of every existing unit in the trade area, it is our opinion that the subject is the center of a high-quality trade area of better-than-average economic potential, contained within an unusually small geographic area.

As has been previously discussed, the subject is adjoined immediately on the north and west by a fully developed middle- to upper-middle-income residential area to the east and northeast which, being about 60%

developed, includes high expansion potential. The principal growth areas
are located east and south of the subject, with a large amount of currently
undeveloped area south of the expressway that will develop rapidly during
the next 3 to 5 years and provide a much-increased concentration of
available economic potential to the subject site.

The location of the existing new subdivision developments, most of
which are in early stages of development, having been started within the
past 6 months to 1 year, is shown on the facing-page map. (Map omitted
here.) In addition to the developments indicated on this map, our investigation indicates planning for a substantial number of additional subdivisions, which will involve groundbreaking during the next 12 to 24
months.

While many of the new subdivisions indicated on the map have only
recently started development, many of them have involved construction
of houses and sales patterns indicating a high rate of absorption of new
residential construction in this area. The newer construction involves
price ranges substantially above the previous pattern of development, and
indicates a much-higher-than-average median family income for all these
areas.

The extreme southern part of the trade area is principally undeveloped
at the present time, which, based upon historical trends of subdivision
development in this immediate vicinity, indicates excellent future potential for development purposes, as the supply of existing land in the
northern areas and eastern areas of the trade area is absorbed by currently
planned developments.

Existing Competitive Facilities

The trade area boundaries were set principally on the basis of existing
competition insofar as the western and northern boundaries of the trade
area are concerned. The principal shopping facility in this area of Jackson
County is the large development at Apex Drive and Bee Drive, consisting
of the Plaza Shopping Center, the Apex Mall, and the Town and
Country Shopping Center. These facilities combined have all the area
and features of a major regional shopping center, including three major
department stores and a full line of hard and soft goods, as well as service
facilities. This concentration is located approximately 3 miles north of the
subject site.

At this point in the analysis, it should be pointed out that the proposed shopping center must of necessity be a neighborhood convenience
goods center, having no potential involving major hard goods sales. The
facility should cater to necessities, conveniences, and services. A small to
medium neighborhood shopping center would constitute the highest and
best use of the subject site.

The principal competition for a neighborhood convenience goods
center at the subject site consists of convenience goods facilities located
at Oslo Road and Colonial Road, and strip-type convenience goods de-

velopment along Oslo Road from Colonial to Barnett Road. The Oslo–Colonial Shopping Center, a rather complete neighborhood convenience goods center, is the only well-planned facility in this area with adequate parking. The balance of the competitive facilities along Oslo Road suffer at the present time from a serious lack of adequate on-site parking as well as extremely heavy traffic congestion on Oslo Road. Oslo Road is only two lanes, and the poor planning that has resulted in the strip-type development causes a serious traffic congestion problem in this area. The existing facilities in the Oslo–Colonial through to Oslo–Barnett area are merchandising at maximum volume, even in the face of the poor traffic flow and parking situation.

It may well be that the subject site would draw from a much greater area to the west than the boundaries of this study indicate, considering the excellent traffic flow existing at the subject site due to the recent widening of Apex Drive to four lanes and possible access via the University Drive bridge over Julington Creek. Any change in the existing shopping habits, such as might be caused by interruption of merchandising along the Oslo Road strip due to possible widening or the obvious dissatisfaction with these facilities due to the traffic congestion, would probably result in permanent diversion of this market to the subject site. However, our study has not taken into account any trade potential from the area west of Rocky Shoals Creek.

In addition to the Oslo Road facilities, small facilities are located along Barnett Road in the area east of Apex Drive, with a Tops Supermarket located just north of Barnett Road on Apex Drive.

In our opinion, the boundary lines established for the subject trade area take the existing facilities into account fully, and, on this basis, a higher-than-average portion of the consumer dollar for convenience goods can reasonably be expected to flow to the subject facilities.

Estimated Trade Area Population

As a starting point from which to base the current trade area population and upon which to base future projections from trending, we have investigated the population estimates for the two census tracts in which the subject site is located. Estimates made by the U. S. Population Census in 1960 and as made by the Metropolitan Planning Commission for 1964 and 1965 are set forth in Table I, below.

While the subject site is located within these census tracts, these tracts contain a much larger area than the subject trade area, and the population figures in the census tracts have been investigated only as a check on a more detailed estimate by the building permit method, and to form a basis for trends in the overall area. The smallest growth occurred in tract B, which is almost completely built up and which adjoins the subject, being north of the expressway. The more rapid rate of growth occurred in tract A, which is the area south of the expressway and which involves much vacant land, the true growth of which has just started.

TABLE I

HOUSING UNITS, POPULATION ESTIMATES, AND GROWTH

Housing Units

Census Tract	1960	4/1/64	4/1/65	% Growth 1960–1965	Avg. Annual
A	1,896	2,970	3,464	82.7%	16.6%
B	3,158	4,026	4,405	39.5%	7.9%
Total	5,054	6,996	7,869*		

Population

A	6,667	10,217	11,642	74.6%	14.9%
B	11,355	13,963	14,595	28.5%	5.7%
Total	18,022	24,180	26,237*		

* Number persons per housing unit, 4/1/65, is 3.37.

Our investigation included a complete house count of the entire trade area, and the results of this investigation detailed by individual land lots is set forth in Table II, as follows:

TABLE II

CURRENT POPULATION IN TRADE AREA (9/1/65)

Land Lot	Housing Units	Population Estimate
1	46	155
2	340	1,145
3	477	1,607
4	100	337
5	8	27
6	40	134
7	236	795
8	60	202
9	129	434
10	91	306
11	10	34
12	26	87

13	28	40
14	59	10
15	0	0
16	13	43
17	80	269
18	10	33
19	4	13
20	18	60
21	40	134
22	61	205
23	32	107
24	36	121
25	27	91
26	10	34
27	57	192
28	421	1,419
29	169	570
Total	2,628	8,856

As a basis upon which to find the rate and trend of population growth in the trade area, building permits issued by Jackson County for the period January 1, 1962 through July 1, 1965 have been tabulated, and are set forth in Table III:

TABLE III

BUILDING PERMITS IN TRADE AREA

1962	175
1963	356
1964	229
to 7/1/65	207
3½-year total	967

Table IV sets forth the method of estimating growth rates in the trade area:

TABLE IV

GROWTH RATES IN TRADE AREA

Total housing units as of 9/1/65, including
82 under construction   2,628

Less: New construction since 1/1/62   967
                                            ————
Number housing units as of 1/1/62   1,661

Rate of growth (based on number of units since 1/1/62)

1962	10.5%
1963	21.4%
1964	13.8%
1965	24.9% (2nd 6 months projected)

Our investigation, as summarized in Table IV, indicates a historical growth rate for the period 1962 through July 1, 1965 at an average annual rate of 14.5%, based upon the estimated January 1, 1962 population. This is substantiated by the census tract data previously set forth in Table I. Considering the trends in force and the large amount of vacant land west and south of the trade area which is rapidly developing at the present time, as well as the fully developed contiguous area in which no growth will take place, a future growth rate averaging 15% per annum based upon current population appears to be a reasonable estimate for future projection of population growth.

Based upon this projected rate of growth, the projected population growth in the trade area for 3 years, 5 years, and 10 years in the future is set forth in Table V:

TABLE V

PROJECTED POPULATION GROWTH

Estimated trade area population as of 9/1/65	8,856
Estimated trade area population as of 9/1/68	12,840
Estimated trade area population as of 9/1/70	15,500
Estimated trade area population as of 9/1/75	22,100

IV   ECONOMIC BACKGROUND OF TRADE AREA—ESTIMATED
      INCOME AND EXPENDITURES

Based upon a careful investigation of research data contained in trade journals, census bureau estimates, and estimates by the Metropolitan Planning Commission, coupled with the available evidence of price ranges in existing housing and projected development housing, it is our opinion that a reasonable estimate of average annual income per household in the trade area is $8,500. Based upon this estimate of average income per household, the total gross income of the trade area for the current date and projected for 3 and 5 years in the future is set forth in Table VI:

TABLE VI

INCOME & BUYING POWER ESTIMATES

Date	Households	Gross Income
Current (9/1/65)	2,628	$22,300,000
9/1/68	3,810	32,400,000
9/1/70	4,599	39,000,000

In the light of the estimated gross income of the population group making up the trade area as set forth in Table VI, and based upon sales volumes in existing comparable convenience shopping centers, trade averages, and sales as reported in trade publications, the gross sales volume for the convenience good items considered as desirable for the subject site are estimated in Table VII. The allocations of the percentage of the total area sales to the subject are based upon the accessibility considerations, traffic patterns, and shopping habits pertinent to the competitive facilities previously discussed.

TABLE VII

SALES VOLUME ESTIMATES (9/1/65)

Item	Total Trade Area	% to Subject	Estimate for Subject
Food	$2,650,000	80	$2,120,000
Jr. Dept. Store	1,770,000	50	885,000
(General Mdse., Apparel, & HH Appliances)			
Drugs	442,000	90	398,000
Variety	310,000	80	248,000
Florist	17,700	75	13,000
Shoe Repair	26,500	75	19,900
Gift Shop	26,500	75	19,000
Beauty Shop	70,800	70	49,500
Barber Shop	44,200	50	22,100
Hardware	88,500	90	79,600
Laundry	44,200	75	33,000
Total	$5,496,400	Avg. 71%	$3,888,300*

* Equals $439 per capita, and $1,479 per household.

V   PROJECTED SALES VOLUME ESTIMATED FOR
THE PROPOSED CENTER

Based upon the economic data and competitive factors analyzed in
section IV, taking into account the projected population growth in the
trade area, the estimated sales volume potentials projected as of September 1, 1968 are as follows:

TABLE VIII

PROJECTED ESTIMATED SALES VOLUME FOR SUBJECT
AS OF 9/1/68

Food	$3,082,000
Jr. Dept. Store	1,284,000
Drugs	578,000
Variety	360,000
Florist	19,000
Shoe Repair	29,000
Gift Shop	29,000
Beauty Shop	72,000
Barber Shop	32,000
Hardware	115,000
Laundry	48,000
	$5,648,000

The projection 5 years from the date of the data contained in this
report is estimated as follows:

TABLE IX

PROJECTED ESTIMATED SALES VOLUME FOR SUBJECT
AS OF 9/1/70

Food	$3,720,000
Jr. Dept Store	1,550,000
Drugs	700,000
Variety	434,000
Florist	23,000
Shoe Repair	35,000
Gift Shop	35,000
Beauty Shop	87,000
Barber Shop	39,000
Hardware	139,000
Laundry	58,000
	$6,820,000

At this point, it should be pointed out that the foregoing projections of gross sales volume are *potentially* available, and the ability to capture the maximum from this potential depends upon aggressive merchandising and good management by the operators of the facilities. The estimates for the specialty service lines such as the beauty shop, barber shop, and gift shop are particularly dependent upon experience; and the operation must be carried on in accordance with good public relations and advertising policies.

VI   CONCLUSIONS

Our conclusions as to the economic feasibility of the proposed shopping center are based upon the analysis of the following factors, which have been presented in the foregoing portions of the report:

1.   Existing population in the trade area
2.   Population growth rates in the trade area
3.   Economic background of the trade area
4.   Existing street and traffic flow patterns
5.   Existing competitive facilities

The conclusions reached as to these specific factors are:

1.   The existing population is sufficient to support a new neighborhood shopping center facility of moderate size.
2.   Population growth rates indicate good future prospects for increasing sales volumes and increasing size of the projected center.
3.   The economic background of the trade area indicates an income level much higher than the Jackson County average.
4.   The existing street and traffic flow patterns indicate that the subject is strategically located in relation to the existing streets and the observed traffic flow patterns.
5.   The trade area has been limited, taking fully into account the existing competitive facilities. The resulting trade area which is the subject of this study is a closely knit area, all portions of which have quick accessibility to the proposed shopping center.

Based upon the projected sales volumes available as of September 1, 1965 and taking into account the growth which will occur between 1965 and 1968, it is our recommendation that plans be instigated for construction, as soon as possible, of approximately 70,000 square feet of sales space, to contain a grocery supermarket, a junior department store, a drugstore, and a small variety store. These facilities would require approximately 60,000 square feet, and in addition approximately 10,000 square feet of space for small service stores should be included.

Considering the population and economic growth as projected for the next 5 years, it is recommended that a long-range plan be considered for the expansion of the center to between 90,000 and 100,000 square feet by 1970. Adequate sales volumes for the lines typically needed in the neighborhood shopping center would be contained in the final space of approximately 90,000 to 100,000 square feet. This would consist of approximately 30,000 to 40,000 square feet of small service and specialty shops in addition to the "core" group of 60,000 square feet.

VII   UNDERLYING ASSUMPTIONS

The opinions expressed in this study and the projected sales volume potential available to the proposed shopping center are predicated upon the following assumptions which are basic to the opinions reached:

1. that the population growth in the trade area will continue in the direction and intensity averaged during the past 4 years;
2. that no long-term economic recession or depression will occur;
3. that present trends in wage and price levels will continue during the period of projection;
4. that the retail operators of the various lines of merchandise whose volume has been estimated will conduct an efficient and aggressive merchandising operation under good management and practice good public relations and advertising policies; and
5. that the developer of the proposed center will undertake an aggressive advertising and promotional campaign prior to opening, and that a program of promotion and advertising of the center with tenant participation will continue on a periodic basis throughout the period of projection.

EXHIBIT A

ESTIMATED EFFECTIVE HOUSEHOLD INCOMES IN
SELECTED SUBDIVISIONS IN THE TRADE AREA

Subdivision	Family Income Range
1. Apex Valley	$7,850 to $ 9,500
2. Riverside	7,850 to 8,500
3. Rolling Hills	7,850 to 8,500
4. Green Valley	7,200 to 7,850
5. Buckhead	7,200 to 7,850
6. University Valley	6,500 to 8,500
7. Avondale	6,500 to 8,500

8.	University Gardens	6,500 to	8,500
9.	Murray Hill	6,500 to	8,500
10.	Apex Woods	6,500 to	8,500
11.	Barnett Drive	6,200 to	7,850
12.	Red Oak	6,500 to	8,500
13.	South View	7,200 to	7,850
14.	Suburban Heights	7,850 to	8,850
15.	Beechwood	8,850 to	9,500
16.	Oak Lawn	8,050 to	8,900
17.	Carol Estates	8,850 to	9,850
18.	Black Acres	7,850 to	8,850
19.	Green Acres	9,500 to	10,500
20.	West Chapel	8,200 to	8,900
21.	Apex Meadows	8,550 to	9,500
22.	Willow Park	8,850 to	9,550

Note: Effective family incomes are after income taxes. Estimates based on price ranges of homes based on 20% of gross income for debt service, taxes, and insurance.

EXHIBIT B

BUILDING PERMITS ISSUED IN TRADE AREA FROM 1/1/62 TO 7/1/65

Land Lot	Total Bldg. Permits
62	6
67	44
68	18
69	1
70	4
90	0
91	28
92	28
93	35
94	46
103	1
102	20
101	24
100	5
121	3
122	2
123	13
124	53
125	24
136	5

135	96
134	62
133	55
132	22
153	7
154	116
155	119
156	132

SHOPPING CENTER PROJECTION—WORKSHEET

LOCATION: _____ ft on _____ × _____ ft on _____
_____ × _____ = _____ sq ft
of land

LAND SIZE: _____ sq ft of land (−) _____ square feet for
service station (or restaurant)
_____ sq ft of land remaining.
Building area = _____ sq ft
Walkways   = _____ "
Total   _____ "
Parking   = _____ cars Ratio = _____ to _____

ESTIMATED LAND COST:
Less: _____   (−) $ _____
_____
$ _____

ESTIMATED CONSTRUCTION COST:
_____ square feet @ _____ = _____
_____ square feet @ _____ = _____
(walkway) $ _____
Construction Cost   _____
TOTAL ESTIMATED COST: $ _____

PROPOSED FINANCING
TOTAL ESTIMATED COST
BEFORE FINANCE COSTS: $ _____
Net Site Cost $ _____
Estimated _____ sq ft
(Mortgage overall) $ _____

Estimated Mortgage Financing available: $ _____

ESTIMATED CASH REQUIRED $ _____

Mortgage Brokerage, Closing Costs, and $ _____
Interim Financing   _____

ESTIMATED CASH REQUIRED $ _____

NOTE: _____ Mortgage — _____ % — _____ years =
$ _____ per year
including principal & interest

PURCHASE PRICE (OR TOTAL PROJECT COST) $ _____
COMMITMENT POSSIBLE: $ _____
    $ _____ @ _____ % for _____ years   _____
CASH REQUIRED, or (_____ land value put in as equity) $ _____

===

GROSS INCOME $ _____
ANNUAL OPERATING EXPENSES:

Taxes $ _____
Insurance   _____
Maintenance   _____
Utilities   _____
Management   _____
Leasing fee—Nationals @ _____ %   _____
    "   " —Locals   @ _____ %   _____
TOTAL EXPENSES (Estimated high) $ _____

NET OPERATING PROFIT (Before Debt Service) $ _____
ESTIMATED DEBT SERVICE: INTEREST AND AMORTIZATION
    OF MORTGAGE ($ _____ months $ _____
            × _____ months)   _____
        NET CASH FLOW $ _____
The foregoing figures are correct, to the best of my knowledge.

===

RETURN ON ALL CASH—NET OPERATING PROFIT $ _____ _____%
                    TOTAL PRICE
RETURN ON CASH TO—NET PROFIT AFTER INT.
MORTGAGE   —   CASH TO MTG.
RETURN ON CASH AFTER—CASH FLOW $ _____ _____%
INTEREST AND AMORTIZATION—CASH TO MTG. $
TENANTS

1— _____ — _____ sq ft @ $ _____ = $ _____
2— _____ — _____ sq ft @ $ _____ = $ _____
3— _____ — _____ sq ft @ $ _____ = $ _____

4— _____ — _____ sq ft @ $ _____ = $ _____
5— _____ — _____ sq ft @ $ _____ = $ _____
6— _____ — _____ sq ft @ $ _____ = $ _____
, 7— _____ — _____ sq ft @ $ _____ = $ _____

GROSS FROM NATIONALS $ _____

Total Building = _____ square feet
Nationals = _____ " "
Balance for Locals _____
_____ square feet

THEREFORE

NET _____ %—After all expenses and amortization = $ _____
NET _____ %—After all expenses and amortization = $ _____
NET _____ %—After all expenses and amortization = $ _____

CONDENSED EXAMPLE OF AN
OFFERING OF A SHOPPING CENTER PROPERTY

The Center contains prime, nationally known chain-store tenants.

PRICE: $1,615,000
MORTGAGES: $1,150,000
CASH REQUIRED: $ 475,000

Annual Return on Investment:

Direct Return	$46,328	9.75%	(Average 10 Years)
Indirect Return	47,178	9.93	(Average 10 Years)
Total Benefits	$93,316	19.68%	(Average 10 Years)

LOCATION AND AREA DATA: Major metropolitan area.

BUILDINGS AND TENANTS:

The center was completed in March, 1961 and completely leased almost immediately. There are 20 stores with a total leasable area of 100,396 square feet. The major tenants are: a national chain variety store, a national chain drugstore, a regional chain supermarket, a national chain automotive supply store, a national chain cafeteria, and a national chain shoe store. A major national oil company service station at the southwest corner street intersection was purchased in June, 1968. The buildings are well constructed according to the Building Code Requirements established by the City. Schedules of tenants, lease data, and average rents paid are given below.

LAND AREA:

Plot size is approximately 615.4' × 638.66' for a total land area of 393,000 square feet. Parking space is available for 545 cars at one time.

ADDITIONAL RENTAL DATA

Total Overage Rent Paid

1965	$26,956
1966	$27,568
1967	$31,057

Overages Paid by Key Tenants, by Year	1965	1966	1967	1968
Cafeteria	$12,782	$13,140	$13,822	$14,207
Drugstore	5,804	5,207	7,092	7,632
Automotive Supply	–0–	–0–	1,096	4,076
Jeweler	6,812	7,844	8,890	*

* Lease modified in June 1968. Minimum rent was increased and overage percentage was reduced.

Rent Paid by Local Tenants	$ 53,325 =	24.8%
Rent Paid by AAA Tenants	161,508 =	75.2
Total Rent	$214,833	100.0%

Note: 75% of the rental income is from AAA rated tenants. Sales volumes of major reporting tenants have shown a steady increase as indicated by the steadily increasing overage rentals paid.

INCOME AND EXPENSE SCHEDULE

INCOME:

Minimum Rents	$182,433	
Percentage Overages	32,400	
Other Income	1,500	
Total Income		$216,333
Less: Vacancy Allowance 5% of Local Tenants		2,666
		$213,667

EXPENSES:

Taxes	$ 30,340

TENANT SCHEDULE

Tenants	Lease Term	Area in Sq. Ft.	Minimum Annual Rent	Overage Percentage Rent	Options to Renew
Shoe Store	3/1/61 to 2/28/71	4,200	$ 8,400	5% sales over $168,000	None
Supermarket	3/1/61 to 12/31/80	18,300	22,875	1% sales over $2,287,500	4-5 years same rent
Automotive Supply	3/1/61 to 3/31/70	9,800	15,750	3% sales over $455,000	2-5 years same rent
Variety Store	3/1/61 to 2/28/78	21,000	31,500	4% 1st $1 million, plus 3% excess (less $31,500)	5-5 years same rent
Poultry Store	1/1/61 month to month	2,000	2,500	5% sales less $2,500	
Drugstore	3/1/61 to 2/28/86 *	16,100	26,400	3% sales to $1.1 million, 2.5% next $650,000, 2% excess of $1,750,000	
Cafeteria	3/1/61 to 2/28/76	10,000	15,000	5% sales over $300,000	1-5 years same rent plus tax escalation
Dress Shop	3/1/61 to 2/28/71	2,625	5,906	4% sales less $5,906	
Barber Shop	3/1/61 to 2/28/71	900	2,400	6% sales less $2,400	1-5 years same rent
Beauty Salon	3/1/61 to 2/28/71	900	2,475	8% sales less $2,475	
Doctor	3/1/61 to 2/28/71	750	2,400		
Jeweler	3/1/61 to 7/31/73	1,500	6,000	5% sales less $6,000	
Laundromat	3/1/63 month to month	1,200	3,720	8% sales less $3,720	
Bakery	3/1/61 to 2/28/71	2,200	4,400	6% sales over $100,000	1-5 years same rent
TV & Appliance	Exp. 11/30/73	1,095	3,420		
Photography Studio	4/1/64 to 3/31/74	1,500	3,372	6% sales less $3,372	
Clothing Store	3/1/61 to 2/28/71	2,151	5,915	6% sales less $5,915	
Wig Shop	4/12/69 to 4/11/71	750	1,800	8% sales less $1,800	
Sewing Machine	3/1/61 to 1/31/71	1,600	3,200	3.5% sales less $3,200	
Gift Shop	3/1/61 to 2/28/71	2,625	5,400	5% sales less $5,400	1-5 years same rent
Service Station			9,600	2¢ per gallon less $9,600	
		100,396	182,433		

* National drug chain has right to terminate lease as of 3/31/71 with 12 months' notice and a $26,400 penalty. May also terminate at end of 15th year or 20th year with no penalty.

189

Maintenance, Repair	8,700	
Utilities	4,350	
Advertising, Promotion	3,480	
Insurance	3,208	
Management	9,000	
Janitorial	3,000	
Miscellaneous Supplies	533	
Corporate Management	1,500	64,111

Net Income Before Mortgage Payments		$149,556
Less Mortgage Payments:		
1st Mortgage	$ 98,914	
2nd Mortgage—$200,000—7% Interest		
Balance due in 10 Years	18,000	
Total Mortgage Payments		116,914
NET CASH FLOW INCOME		$ 32,642

INCREASED INCOME DUE TO INFLATIONARY TREND:

Over the past 10 years, the U. S. economy has continued its inflation at the average rate of 3% per year. Most of the leases have clauses providing that overage rents are to be paid based on a percentage of the gross sales volume for each tenant. Thus as the dollar volume of sales increases, the rent income should increase correspondingly. It is conservatively estimated that net income, after expenses, will increase at the rate of 1% per year, while mortgage payments remain constant. Thus the investor has a built-in hedge against inflation.

INCOME PROTECTION BY INCREASED BUILDING COSTS:

Costs of construction have risen 10% to 15% within the last year. Trade unions are just now negotiating new contracts for higher wages, which indicates more building-cost increases ahead. As costs of new buildings rise, the rental required must increase accordingly; thus new store buildings will require higher rents from merchants. This factor adds stability to the tenants on leases in the Center. Such higher rents on competing facilities will also be the basis for higher minimum rents when the present leases expire.

CASH INVESTMENT REQUIRED:

Price	$1,615,000
Less: 1st Mortgage (6% interest,	
$8242 month) Approximate	
balance—$950,000	
2nd Mortgage (7% interest—	
$18,000 year, due in 10 years)	

	$200,000	
	Total Mortgages	1,150,000

Equity Cash	$ 465,000
Closing expenses and working capital	10,000

TOTAL CASH INVESTMENT	$ 475,000

ESTIMATED PROFIT ON RESALE OF PROPERTY:

As present inflationary trends continue, the Center should be producing considerably more income 10 years from now, and the property should have a value considerably in excess of the price now being paid.

In estimating the capital gains profit which an investor client should receive, it is assumed that the price paid 10 years hence will be the same as presently paid. Here are the figures based on this extremely conservative assumption:

Resale Price	$1,615,000
Less: Balance Due on Mortgage in 10 Years	678,200
Proceeds	$ 936,800
Deduct: Original Cash Investment	475,000
Capital Gains Profit	$ 461,800
% CAPITAL GAINS PROFIT	97.2%

SCHEDULE OF BENEFITS

	1st 5 Years	2nd 5 Years	Total 10 Years
DIRECT BENEFITS—CASH RETURN			
Note Interest	$141,750	$141,750	$283,500
Taxable Dividends	12,180	86,429	98,609
Nontaxable Dividends	23,726	57,440	81,166
Total	$177,656	$285,619	$463,275
Average per Year	$ 35,531	$ 57,124	$ 46,328
CASH RETURN ON INVESTMENT OF $475,000	7.48%	12.03%	9.75%
INDIRECT BENEFITS			
Mortgage Reduction	$259,194	$212,589	$471,783
Average per Year	$ 51,899	$ 42,518	$ 47,178
RETURN ON INVESTMENT OF $475,000	10.91%	8.95%	9.93%
COMBINED RETURN	18.39%	20.98%	19.68%

SUPERVISORY AND CORPORATE MANAGEMENT:

If this property is acquired by an investor who is not a resident of the United States, it will be advisable to employ an affiliated company of Realty Company—Realty Management, Inc.—to keep the books and records of the owning corporation and attend to all corporate details. The charge for this service will be $1,500 per year.

We usually recommend also that nonresident investors employ Realty Continental Management Corporation to collect rents, pay all expenses, and generally manage the property. Realty Continental Management Corporation presently manages other centers in the subject property area, and thus the charge for this service would be only $9,000.

The fees for both companies are included in our expense estimate.

TAXES:

Real estate taxes were decreased approximately $2,000 in 1967; however, discussion with knowledgeable persons indicates that taxes will be increased approximately 15% within the next year or two. Therefore, real estate taxes have been estimated at 15% more than the 1968 figure.

MORTGAGE DATA:

The existing mortgage was placed with the Life Insurance Company on December 21, 1961 for $1,200,000, repayable $98,914 per year including 6% interest.

No prepayment privilege was allowed prior to January, 1969, with prepayment allowed thereafter with the following penalties:

After January 1, 1970 @ 3.0% unpaid balance
After January 1, 1971 @ 2.5% unpaid balance
After January 1, 1972 @ 2.0% unpaid balance
After January 1, 1973 @ 1.5% unpaid balance
After January 1, 1974 @ 1.0% unpaid balance
After January 1, 1975 @ 0.5% unpaid balance
After January 1, 1976 @ No Penalty

The principal balance due will be as follows on the dates indicated:

May 1, 1969	$952,841
June 1, 1969	$949,359
July 1, 1969	$945,863

A second mortgage is to be held by the seller in the amount of $200,000 payable at a 9% constant rate ($18,000) per year, including interest at 7% per annum. The entire balance will become due at the end of 10 years.

MORTGAGE BALANCES AND EQUITY FOR NEXT 10 YEARS:

End of Year	Mortgage Balances	Equity *
1	1,104,100	$506,900
2	1,055,406	555,594
3	1,003,747	607,253
4	948,943	662,057
5	890,802	720,198
6	829,120	781,880
7	763,681	847,319
8†	694,256	916,744
9	683,756	927,244
10	672,469	938,531

* Increased by reduction of mortgage balances due.
† Presume mortgages refinanced at end of 8th year with new mortgage for $700,000 at 7½% interest.

RECOMMENDATION:

Realty Company strongly recommends the purchase of the Center for the following reasons:

1. The Center is well located in one of the rapidly growing cities of one of the fastest growing states in the United States.
2. It enjoys a low interest mortgage (6%) in today's market of high interest mortgages, which range from 7¾ to 8½%.
3. The seller will carry a purchase-money mortgage at 7% interest for 10 years.
4. Over 75% of the tenants have AAA credit ratings.
5. Most of the leases have percentage overage clauses, which will produce additional rental income as prices and sales volume rise.
6. This investment has automatic protection from inflation since, as prices rise, the rental income will also rise.
7. After all corporate income taxes, our investor client should realize an average cash return from note interest and dividends of 9.75% average over a 10-year period.
8. In addition to the excellent cash return during the 10-year period, the mortgage debt will be reduced a total of $471,783— an average of $47,178 per year. This is an additional growth in equity of 9.93%, which will be realized when the property is resold or refinanced.
9. If the property is sold at the end of 10 years at the same price paid for it today, a client should receive a tax-free capital gains profit of $461,800. This recovery of 197% of the original investment is in addition to the yearly cash return.

10-YEAR ANALYSIS AND PROJECTION

	1st Year	2nd Year	3rd Year	4th Year
Net Operating Income—Projected	$149,556	$150,900	$152,400	$153,900
Less: Deductions For Taxable Income Computation				
Interest	99,350	96,556	93,591	90,446
Depreciation—Building	54,568	52,085	49,715	47,453
—Equipment	23,438	19,043	15,472	13,409
Total Deductions	$177,356	$167,684	$158,778	$151,308
Taxable Income	(27,800)	(16,784)	(6,378)	2,592
Less: Federal Income Tax	—	—	—	—
Net Income After Taxes	(27,800)	(16,784)	(6,378)	2,592
Add Back: Depreciation Deducted	78,006	71,128	65,187	60,862
Cash Available for Mortgages	$ 50,206	$ 54,344	$ 58,809	$ 63,454
Mortgage Principal Payments	45,900	48,694	51,659	54,804
Surplus Cash (Dividends)	4,306	5,650	7,150	8,650
Taxable Dividends	—	—	—	2,592
Plus: Nontaxable Dividends	4,306	5,650	7,150	6,058
Total Dividends	$ 4,306	$ 5,650	$ 7,150	$ 8,650
Add: Interest on Notes	28,350	28,350	28,350	28,350
Total Direct Benefits (Cash Flow)	32,656	34,000	35,500	37,004
Indirect Benefits (Mortgage Reduction) See 10-year Total →			—	—
Total Benefits	$ 78,556	$ 82,690	$ 87,159	$ 91,80

First Mortgage	$950,000	6%	$98,900	Annual	Constant
Second Mortgage	$200,000	7%	$18,000	"	"
Refinanced	$700,000	7½%	$63,000	"	"

h Year	6th Year	7th Year	8th Year	Re-financed	9th Year	10th Year	Total
55,400	$156,900	$158,400	$159,900	$	$161,400	$163,000	$1,561,756
87,109	83,568	79,811	75,825		80,850	80,063	867,169
45,294	43,233	41,266	39,389		37,597	35,886	446,486
13,409	13,409	13,409	13,411				125,000
45,812	$140,210	$134,486	$128,625		$118,447	$115,949	$1,438,655
9,588	16,690	23,914	31,275		42,953	47,051	123,101
—	—	441	9,363		15,529	17,692	43,025
9,588	16,690	23,473	21,912		27,424	29,359	80,076
58,073	56,642	54,675	52,800		37,597	35,886	571,486
68,291	$ 73,332	$ 78,148	$ 74,712		$ 65,021	$ 65,245	$1,351,562
58,141	61,682	65,439	69,425		—	—	
10,150	11,650	12,709	5,287	5,744	54,521	53,958	179,775
9,588	11,650	12,709	5,287	—	27,424	29,359	98,609
562	—	—	—	5,744	27,097	24,599	81,166
10,150	$ 11,650	$ 12,709	$ 5,287	$5,744	$ 54,521	$ 53,958	$ 179,775
28,350	28,350	28,350	28,350		28,350	28,350	283,500
38,500	40,000	41,059	33,637	5,744	82,871	82,308	463,275
—	—	—	—	—	—	—	471,783
96,641	$101,682	$106,498	$103,062	$ —	$ 93,371	$ 93,595	$ 935,058

Stock		$160,000	Land	$ 290,700	
Paid-in Surplus		315,000	Building	1,199,300	33-year life
Notes (9%)			Equipment	125,000	8-year life
		$475,000		$1,615,000	

Further Readings and References

"Feasibility Reports for Shopping Centers," *NIREB's Division Reports*, No. 5, February, 1969. Sponsor: Howard L. Green. Chicago: National Institute of Real Estate Brokers of the National Association of Real Estate Boards, Commercial and Investment Division, 1969.

Gunning, Francis P. "A Lender's Examination of Shopping Center Leases," ICSC Shopping Center Report No. 13. New York: International Council of Shopping Centers, 1969.

Gunning, Francis P. "The Wrap-Around Mortgage . . . Friend or U. F. O.?" ICSC Shopping Center Report No. 22. New York: International Council of Shopping Centers, 1969.

"How Mortgage Investment Trusts Are Set Up to Provide Construction and Development Loans," *ICSC Bulletin*. New York: International Council of Shopping Centers, 1969.

Hoyt, Homer. "Land Values in Shopping Centers," *Urban Land*, Vol. 28, No. 7, July–August, 1969. Washington, D. C.: Urban Land Institute, 1969.

Newman, Harry, Jr. "The Unsubordinated Groundlease," ICSC Shopping Center Report No. 12. New York: International Council of Shopping Centers, 1964.

"Seven Tested Steps in Leasing Small Stores," ICSC Shopping Center Report No. 21. New York: International Council of Shopping Centers, 1969.

"Shopping Center Guidelines," Part 1. *The Real Estate Analyst, Appraisal Bulletin*, March 24, 1967. St. Louis: Roy Wenzlick Research Corp., 1967. Part II of this Bulletin is in the following month's issue.

12

Office
Buildings

There are several kinds of office buildings. The most common are: (1) the multistory, high-rise buildings usually located in the downtown area; and (2) the smaller buildings situated on the periphery of downtown, on principal traffic arteries leading to the suburbs, and scattered in the suburban areas. While buildings in this second classification are usually free-standing, they may also be found in connection with shopping centers.

Office space is also found in converted loft buildings and old houses. Warehouses contain office space in varying amounts depending upon the type of warehouse. Suburban office parks may be found in many cities providing a wide range of space, from multistory buildings occupied by one tenant to numerous small structures.

Office space may be classified as to whether it is speculative or competitive space for sale in the open market; noncompetitive space built by private owners for their own use (owner–user), particularly institutions such as banks, insurance companies, and manufacturing corporations; space for occupancy by public and governmental agencies; and variations of the above, such as an institutional owner–user who puts a portion of its space on the open market. Office space may also be classified according to its quality, such as class-A space, and the quantity leased to individual users.

The above classifications indicate that analysis of the office space market must consider a variety of space types. Further, the sponsors and developers of office space have a variety of outlooks and objectives. Institutional owner–users generally take a long-term view, while speculative developers are more interested in the short term. Objectives vary, but typically are: entrepreneurial profit from the construction of the building; prestige or image in the case of some corporate owner–users; and financial and income tax objectives, such as leverage, depreciation, capital gain, and tax shelter, for investors.

Generalizations about the office space market are difficult to make and can be misleading. Office building construction has historically occurred in long-run cycles of underbuilding and overbuilding. The market in each city is unique, and comprehensive national data is lacking. The market is specialized and divided. Construction and ownership of buildings is widely dispersed among local investors and owner–users, local and national real estate syndicates, and real estate investment trusts. A long planning and construction period is usually involved for most office buildings, particularly the high-rise multistory structures. Standards of investment analysis vary. It is reasonable to say that most major office building promotion, construction, and ownership is conducted by large corporate investors and by sophisticated individual investors.

Vacancy rates must be considered for each project. Available statistics should be analyzed with care, since they may be misleading. Rates are usually based on the amount of space in existing buildings available for immediate occupancy. Not reflected in the rates is space being leased for future delivery, such as in new buildings yet to be completed, and space dependent on the moving out of existing tenants.

DEMAND-AND-SUPPLY CONSIDERATIONS

As pointed out above, generalizations about the office building market are difficult to make. Each market must be analyzed in terms of its own local environment with appropriate attention to national trends as they might apply to the local situation. Consideration is given below to factors which can generate demand for office space and factors which can influence the supply of this space. They all should be considered by any investor in any given market, although the extent of their application and influence will vary with the local market.

1. There has been a long-run trend toward an increase in the amount of office floor space occupied per employee. A part of this demand comes from the need to provide more space for office equipment and machines.
2. A trend in the economy toward a greater number of service-type businesses as contrasted with manufacturing firms generates an expansion of white-collar workers—administrative, technical, and professional—and a rise in the number of office employees. Also, as pointed out above, these employees tend to occupy increased amounts of floor space per worker.
3. Any general economic expansion of the economy tends to generate a demand for office space to accomodate the growth. Existing industries and firms expand; new businesses are born.
4. Demand is created by the desire of tenants to upgrade their space and to seek space of a better quality and location. Tenants of small business and professional offices usually want more and better space as they grow and prosper; the same is true of larger companies, which also frequently need more space for private offices as administrative staffs increase in size and rank.
5. Tenants displaced from buildings in urban renewal areas create demand for office space. Also, urban redevelopment programs may be promoted by civic groups or other downtown organizations and investors and business firms encouraged to locate in the new space as a matter of community promotion and interest.
6. New and modern facilities may be desired by companies as a matter of prestige and corporate image. The office building for many firms is more than simply a place to work; it is an attraction for employees, and emphasis is placed on total environment.
7. Consolidation of scattered offices can create a demand for space. Both private firms and public agencies may have space spread over several buildings, particularly in the downtown area. The bringing together of these offices into one location may necessitate the erection of a new building or the occupancy of a large block of space in an existing building if available.

DOWNTOWN VS. SUBURBS

Office buildings are found in both downtown and suburban locations. The suburban structure is usually a small, free-standing, 1- or 2-story, custom-built building designed for use by specific groups, such as medical and dental, or small business firms, such as insurance agencies and real estate brokers. Shopping center developers have found it profitable to provide office space in the center or in a nearby location connected with the center. Space may also be found in older houses converted to office use.

A major reason for a suburban location is the availability of land at a reasonable cost for parking space for employees as well as customers. Also, construction costs may sometimes be lower in the suburbs. Suburban locations frequently provide easy access to expressways and airports. The small investor with limited financial capabilities may find these outlying locations an attractive investment outlet, particularly if he joins up with several investors and the group acquires land and constructs the small office buildings for specified users. As with any office building investment, local trends must be studied; all cities do not necessarily experience a movement of office space to outlying areas.

Downtown in most metropolitan areas will probably always be the center for major office buildings; it is the financial and business core of the community. It has the attraction of shopping facilities, cultural and educational resources, civic centers, and restaurants. Further, downtown areas in many cities are quickly accessible by major expressways, and off-street parking is increasingly available, particularly with new office buildings. Also an attraction is the proximity to such facilities as the railroad station, bus terminals, government offices, and other business firms. The prestige of a downtown address is still an important consideration for many firms. The downtown core in many cities is going through a period of renewed growth and redevelopment, and investor interest in downtown is strong in these situations.

HOUSE CONVERSIONS AND SECOND-STORY SPACE

Office space may be created through the conversion of older houses where zoning permits such usage. Converted space is usually in a good location, such as on the periphery of downtown or on a main traffic street; location combined with lower rental rates enables it to compete successfully in the office space market. Many beginning business firms as well as small firms and professional men are attracted to this space. Many suburban areas have streets on which heavy traffic flow has caused them to go into transition from residential to commercial usage. Older residences on these streets make good investments, such as for doctors, dentists, attorneys, and trade associations who can use them for offices. Sometimes the upper stories of older houses may be rented to help offset the cost of acquisition and conversion as well as contribute something toward carrying costs. Later, the older buildings can be demolished and new modern office facilities constructed on the site. Land values usually increase as the areas develop into commercial usage, and investors benefit by acquiring locations in the early stages of the transition period. Each situation must be analyzed on its own merits. In some instances, a conversion may not be as profitable as combining and demolishing several older properties for immediate construction of a new, larger building. Existing buildings may no longer be the most profitable use of the land because of increasing land values.

Second-story office space over stores, or walk-up space, may be attractive to investors. Such space is useful to firms which do not require much public access as well as to firms attracted to the lower rents available on this type of space.

FINANCING

Soundly conceived office building projects—either new construction or existing buildings—are usually attractive collateral for institutional real estate mortgage lenders and to equity investors, such as syndicates, real estate investment trusts, and real estate corporations. All types of lenders will usually make loans on office buildings—mutual savings banks, life insurance companies, and pension funds for the larger projects; and savings-and-loan associations and commercial banks for the smaller and more numerous projects. Traditional mortgage lending patterns are used as well as creative financing techniques—leasehold mortgage, sale–leaseback, second mortgage, component financing, corporate stock and debentures, and private placements.

The payouts on most permanent mortgage loans on proposed privately owned office buildings are based on a specified rent attainment schedule. This means that a certain percentage of the space in the building must be leased before the lender will release additional funds. Such advance leasing —which can represent substantial dollar amounts—assures the building of future income, which is particularly important in the initial stages of its operation, when operating expenses are heavy.

Each lease must be weighed on its own merits. Lease terms and rental rates vary considerably in the office building field. Rental rates are usually quoted on a basis of dollars per square foot per year, or sometimes per month. Practices differ as to what services are included in the rate. Local markets have certain standard services included in the rate, and any other items granted are referred to as concessions. Services may or may not include air conditioning, utilities, janitorial services, partitioning, decorating, carpeting, drapes, and the like. Rates may vary according to the amount of space the tenant occupies; a full-floor occupancy by a single tenant may receive a lower rate than partial occupancy by several tenants.

As with all types of real estate, the availability of funds for financing office buildings is influenced by general monetary conditions. Tight money can have the effect of delaying plans for new construction, particularly for smaller office buildings. The impact on larger buildings may not be as severe, since financing of these buildings is usually based on long-term commitments whose terms remain the same regardless of changes in the money market. Further, funds may come from several sources—the firm's own funds in the case of large institutional buildings constructed for the owner's use—and from a wide variety of sources in the national money market rather than from primarily local sources. These factors tend somewhat to alleviate an immediate direct impact on office building investment when monetary conditions change.

REDUCTION OF RETAIL STORE SPACE

The growth of demand for downtown office space can have the effect of creating a shortage of retail store space in the area. As older buildings are demolished for large high-rise structures, the new buildings frequently have fewer store units than were available in the older buildings. Four store units may replace eight units prior to demolition, for instance, and developers may prefer national institutional tenants such as commercial banks or stock brokerage firms for the store space at street level. The latter-type tenants help give a prestige image to the building. Smaller merchants formerly situated on major traffic arteries and in the prime street level space are relocated on side streets.

COMPARATIVE ANALYSIS

The comparative attractiveness of an office building may be measured by several criteria. The factors given below are among the more important specific items to be analyzed about the building itself:

1. Class of tenants
2. Tenant services
3. Cost of building operation
4. Management
5. Prestige of building as an address
6. Length of leases and expiration dates
7. Elevators
8. Electric distribution system

9. Location of building with respect to other facilities, such as businesses, shopping, and financial
10. Surroundings of the building
11. Physical condition
12. Needed improvements and costs
13. Interior layout of floor space—building must provide maximum number of square feet of rentable area for efficient operation
14. Zoning and building regulations—any violation
15. Lighting
16. Windows and natural light
17. Air-conditioning and heating equipment
18. Corridors
19. Lobby
20. Parking for employees and customers
21. Public transportation
22. Any legislation affecting area in which building is located, such as urban renewal
23. Rental rates and services included in rate
24. Vacancy statistics for the subject building

SMALL OFFICE BUILDING
PROPOSED JOINT VENTURE

An experienced office building developer proposes to build a 100,000-square-foot, 3-story office building on a well-located site. There will be 10 spaces per 1,000 square feet of rentable area.

The developer proposes to borrow 75% of appraised value, or $3,-350,000, and offers to pay 8% interest with a 9% constant; or 8¼–8½% interest at a 9½% annual constant. The life insurance company would in addition to the interest receive 25% of the cash flow, which would yield an additional $26,750 per year. A proforma income and expense statement will illustrate the proposal:

ANNUAL INCOME:	95,000 sq ft @ $6.75 per sq ft		$641,250
	Less: Vacancy Allowance—5%		32,000
	Gross Dependable Income		$609,250
EXPENSES:	Taxes	$80,000	
	Insurance (Fire, extended coverage, OL&T)	4,000	
	Operating Expenses ($1.95 per square foot)	100,000	
			184,000

NET INCOME BEFORE DEBT SERVICE:	$425,250
DEBT SERVICE: $3,350,000, 8¼%, 9½% annual constant	318,250
CASH FLOW:	$107,000

The percentage of cash flow will increase the first-year return to the life insurance company by 0.8%. The return will increase each year thereafter as the debt is amortized.

An alternative proposal is for the developer to sell the land to the life insurance company at market value of $60,000 per acre or $792,000, and lease it back for 50 years at 10% net. The life insurance company would then make a leasehold loan of $2,800,000 at 10% constant on the improvements. The insurance company would be entitled to 50% of cash flows plus reversionary value of the land. Cash flow on this basis would run $66,000, and the one-half share of the insurance company would improve its overall return by 0.9% the first year.

DOCTORS' PROFESSIONAL BUILDING

1. The ownership of the building will be in the name of the owners as tenants-in-common.
2. The Doctors' Group will consist of six (6) doctors, each owning 5.55% of the building.
3. Each doctor will contribute $6,200 for his percentage ownership. The contribution will be made at the closing of the construction loan but not before (date).
4. Each doctor will obligate himself on a 20-year lease for space in the building. The lease will have a cancellation clause at the end of the 10th and 15th year with no penalty and at the end of the 5th year with a penalty of one year's rent. The lease will contain the normal increase provision to cover increases in taxes and operating expenses.
5. Each doctor is willing to pay a rent of $4.75 per square foot plus his pro rata share of the utility bill.
6. The lease for each doctor's space will be executed and the layout and location of each suite will be submitted by (date).
7. A joint venture agreement similar to the draft agreement already reviewed by each doctor will be executed by each doctor.
8. A financial statement supplied to each doctor will be submitted with his check for $500 made payable to Professional Building.

9. The State Trust Company or National Bank are both acceptable by all parties to the venture as lenders and depositories.
10. A mortgage loan of approximately $385,000 will be applied for. An anticipated rate of 8% and term of 25 years with a commitment period of 15 months will be requested.

PROPOSED PROFESSIONAL OFFICE BUILDING
(ONE-STORY)

Valuation

COST APPROACH:

Building	15,100 sq ft	@ $29.00 per sq ft	$437,900
Paving	21,400 sq ft	@ $ .30 per sq ft	6,400
Walks	5,400 sq ft	@ $ .50 per sq ft	2,700
Land	58,600 sq ft	@ $ 1.50 per sq ft	88,000

Total Value—Cost Approach $535,000

INCOME APPROACH:

14,330 net square feet @ $4.75 psf	$ 68,068
Less: Vacancy and Collection Loss (2.6%)	1,741

[Vacancy allowances calculated as follows:
7,000 net square feet (nsf) leased to Doctor–Owners at $4.75, no vacancy taken. 7,330 nsf (to be leased) at $4.75 psf = $34,818 × 5% = $1,741]

Effective Gross Income	$ 66,327

Expenses:

Taxes—45¢ psf	$6,880
Insurance—4¢ psf	604
Management—5%	3,316
Maintenance & Repair—10¢ psf	1,510
Janitorial & Cleaning—29¢ psf	4,156
Alterations & Redecorating—8¢ psf	1,208
Reserves for Replacements	800
Utilities—paid by tenants	–0–

Total expenses	$ 18,474
Net Income Before Recapture	$ 47,853

Capitalization by Building Residual

Net Income Before Recapture	$ 47,853

Less: Amount Charged to Land ($88,000 × 7¼%) $ 6,380

Income to Improvements $ 41,473
Capitalized @ 9¼%   448,357
Add: Land   88,000

Total Value—Income Approach $536,357
                                              say, $536,000

MARKET APPROACH:

Experience in the area of subject property indicates that buildings of this nature sell at approximately 7 times gross income. Subject's value is estimated after adding the utility charges (estimated at 50¢ per sq ft) to the gross income figure:

Gross Income	$ 68,068	
Plus: Utilities		
(paid by tenant)		
14,330 sq ft × 50¢	7,165	
	$ 75,233	
	× 7	multiple
Total Value—Market Approach	$526,631	
say,	$527,000	

CORRELATION:

Indications of value are:

Cost Approach	$535,000
Income Approach	$536,000
Market Approach	$527,000

In view of the income-producing nature of this property, the Income Approach to Value is considered to be most accurate. Therefore, it is the appraiser's opinion that the subject property has a market value, as of (date of appraisal), under assumptions given, of $536,000, allocated as follows:

Land	$ 88,000
Improvements	448,000
Total	$536,000

ONE-STORY OFFICE BUILDING
INCOME AND EXPENSE STATEMENT

Location: 4914 N. W. 18th Place, City and State.

Land: 24,000 sq ft (150′ × 120′; 50′ × 120′).

Improvements: A 11,000-sq-ft one-story office building (110′ × 100′) completed in October, 1970. Parking available for 25 cars.

Lease: October 1, 1970 to September 30, 1990 (20 years) at an annual rental of $25,300. Owner responsible for insurance, roof, exterior repairs of building, and real estate taxes up to $2,500 per annum.

                 XYZ Corporation (tenant) has D&B rating AAA1 with net worth in excess of $50,000,000.

Annual Income: $25,300

Expense: Taxes (Pegged) $2,500
                 Insurance   300
                 Structural Repairs   200
                                       ───────
                                                             3,000
                                                           ───────
Net Income Before Debt Service: $22,300

Loan: $200,000—24 years—7⅜% (Life Ins.
                 Co.) Annual Debt Service   17,808
                                                           ───────
Cash Flow: $ 4,492

Tax Statement:

	1st Year	2nd Year	3rd Year	4th Year	5th Year
Net Income	$22,300	$22,300	$22,300	$22,300	$22,300
Interest	14,640	14,400	14,160	13,920	13,680
Depreciation	9,960	9,407	8,936	8,494	8,074
Gain (Loss)	($ 2,300)	($ 1,507)	($ 796)	($ 114)	$ 546

Price: $65,000 for equity.

INVESTMENT SUMMARY OF OFFERING
OF EXISTING OFFICE SPACE
100 Main Street
Your City, State

This proposal is offering an income property with high leverage to create the possibility of high returns. The property contains about 800,000 square feet of office space. The investment provides a *current cash return* in the form of interest and considerable *growth potential* through equity participation.

PROJECTED RETURNS:

Case	Assumption	Yield (Before Tax)
Initial Cash Return		10.6%
Discounted Cash Flow (Conservative)	No sale or refinancing.	12.5
	Avg rent per sq ft in 1975 is $6.60	
Discounted Cash Flow (Optimistic)	1st Mortgage is refinanced in 1974; proceeds pay off 2nd Mortgage principal	20.5
	Avg rent per sq ft in 1975 is $7.41	

Schedules I, II, and III show detailed cash flows for conservative case.

DOLLAR REQUIREMENT:

There are two $965,000 units available.
Units consist of:

$900,000 (second mortgage which yields 9% cash) .
65,000 (5% equity interest which yields 32% cash)

Eight units have been sold to investors over the past 3 months.

Partner	Equity Interest
John Doe	25%
Henry Chac	25
Other investors (units)	40
Total	90%

Doe and Chac have invested a total of $350,000 for their 50% interest in the property.

STRUCTURE OF INVESTMENT:

Land and building are owned by Life Insurance Company, and leased back to 100 Main St. Company (Investment Partnership) until 2014 (46 years) at fixed rental.

Leasehold interest was purchased by 100 Main St. Company for $13,000,000 on 1/31/69 and will be financed by:

$ 3,000,000—1st mortgage (existing—Savings Bank)
    9,000,000—2nd mortgage
    1,000,000—equity

$13,000,000

Doe and Smith and ABC Realty Company receive 10% of 100 Main St. Company's net cash flow over $650,000. Attached schedules do not reflect this condition; however, effect on yield would be small, since significant amounts would not be earned under this clause until 1976–1977 based on projections in Schedule II.

RISKS:

Building is "headquarters" for many firms in the industry. Broad economic downturns in this industry could weaken the demand for space in this building.

"Downside" yield is probably in the 11–12% area, since it seems unlikely rents will fall below current levels.

Building is currently rented out at $5.00 psf. 86% of leases expire over next 6 years. This condition would seem to give favorable chances of significant rental increases to the $6.50–$8.00 area over next few years. This risk can be verified by checking comparables in the area.

TAX CONSIDERATIONS:

Depreciation of leasehold cost assures tax-free return of amortization on second mortgage, at least until first mortgage matures or is refinanced.

While some excess tax shelter is generated above amortization, the amount is small in relation to second mortgage interest income plus net profit.

Tax shelter is not the main attraction of this deal.

ATTRACTIVE FEATURES:

1. *12.5–20.5% return on investment.* This appears attractive in light of relatively low risks of deal: no development risks; prime

office space in this city should continue in strong demand, despite most ups and downs in economy.

2. *Good partners.* Doe & Chac are major factors in this city and the national real estate industry. Doe & Smith has good reputation in office building leasing in this city.

3. *Low capital turnover. Deal could put $965,000–$1,930,000 to work for up to 45 years.* No requirement to reinvest proceeds on 12–24 months basis, as in construction lending.

4. *Low demand on management time.* Since there is no development risk, since money could stay invested for long time at satisfactory return, and since money appears to be in "good hands" (Doe & Chac), this investment would appear to call for little or no management attention while money is invested.

5. *Reasonable liquidity.* Steady cash return plus growth potential means chances are excellent that investor could sell at cost within 90–120 days of decision to sell.

6. *Prime property.* Building is well located. Availability of sites for new office space in this area appears to be severely limited. This means demand for space in this building should continue strong. There are now many unsatisfied requests for space in subject building.

7. *Potential capital gains.* These could be realized through office rental increases, operating economies, and decreases in interest rates.

SCHEDULE I

DATE   100 MAIN STREET
                              (000's)

Investor's Net Cash Flow Based on Schedule of Lease Expirations

Year	Investment	2nd Mortgage	50% of Profits	Net Cash Flow
0	−$9,650	$	$	−$9,650
1		826	200	1,026
2		812	246	1,058
3		799	276	1,075
4		785	305	1,090
5		771	343	1,114
6		757	372	1,129
7		743	487	1,230
8		729	550	1,279

9	715	611	1,326
10	701	670	1,371
11–45	350*	1,021*	1,371
Column Number 1	2	3	4

Column:
1. Available in units of $965,000. Two units remain.
2. Column 4 from Schedule II.
3. 50% of column 9 from Schedule II.
4. Equals columns 1 + 2 + 3.

* Average annual amount for period.

SCHEDULE II

DATE

100 MAIN STREET
(000's)

Before-tax Cash Flows Based on Summary of Lease Expirations

Year		Gross Rent	Ground Rent	1st Mtg.	2nd Mtg.	Taxes	Expenses	Supervisory Fee	Total Expenses	Net C.F.
1	(1969)	$4,365	$1,125	$212	$826	$476	$1,281	$44	$3,904	$ 401
2	(1970)	4,507	1,125	212	812	476	1,345	45	4,015	492
3	(1971)	4,622	1,125	212	799	476	1,412	46	4,070	552
4	(1972)	4,738	1,125	212	785	476	1,483	47	4,128	610
5	(1973)	4,877	1,125	212	771	476	1,557	49	4,190	687
6	(1974)	5,000	1,125	212	757	476	1,635	50	4,255	745
7	(1975)	5,300	1,125	212	743	476	1,717	53	4,326	974
8	(1976)	5,500	1,125	212	729	476	1,802	55	4,399	1,101
9	(1977)	5,700	1,125	212	715	476	1,892	57	4,477	1,223
10	(1978)	5,900	1,125	212	701	476	1,987	59	4,560	1,340
11–22	(1979–1989)	5,900	1,125	212	629*	476	1,987	59	4,488	1,412
23–46	(1990–2014)	5,900	675	212	314*	476	1,987	59	3,723	2,177
Column Number		1	2	3	4	5	6	7	8	9

Columns:

1. Gross Rent increments are based on lease expiration schedule. See Schedule III for backup. No increments are projected beyond 1979. 2. Life Insurance Company owns land and building. Lease runs to December 31, 2014. Rental is fixed at $1,125,000 through 1989; $675,000 thereafter. 3. First mortgage of $3,000,000 (Savings Bank) matures 2/1/79. Prepayment possible as of 2/1/74. Analysis assumes mortgage is not refinanced until maturity. 4. Second mortgage of $9,000,000 matures 12/31/2014; carries a 7% interest rate; fixed amortization of $196,000 (approximately 2%) brings cash yield up to 9%. Mortgage is secured by leasehold. 5. Most present leases have full tax escalation provision and expect to sign all future leases on this basis also. 6. Projected annual increase of 5% for operating and maintenance expenses. Most of expense increases will be absorbed by tenants. 7. Supervisory fee. ABC Realty Company receive 1% of gross revenues. 8. Equals total of columns 2 through 7. 9. Equals total of columns 1 through 8.

* Average annual amount for period.

DATE

100 MAIN STREET
(000's)

Lease Expiration and
Incremental Income from Renegotiated Leases

Year	Annual Rental	Sq Ft	Current Gross	Proj. Rate	New Gross	Increment +	Increment {Existing Lease / Escalations} =	Total Increment
1970	$4.42	79,000	$349M	$5.25	$ 415	$ 66	$76	$142
1971	5.00	80,000	400M	5.51	441	41	74	115
1972	5.15	102,000	525M	5.78	589	64	52	116
1973	5.38	156,000	845M	6.07	947	102	37	139
1974	5.40	126,000	680M	6.37	803	123		123
1975	5.09	188,000	957M	6.69	1,257	300		300
TOTAL		731,000	$3,756*		$4,452			

* This represents 86% of 1969 gross income.

Further Readings and References

Eisen, Albert. "Officeonics—Highrise," *Journal of Property Management*, September–October, 1969, 198–205.

Fisher, Robert Moore. "The Boom in Office Buildings: An Economic Study of the Past Two Decades," *U. L. I. Technical Bulletin No. 58*. Washington, D. C.: Urban Land Institute, 1967.

Herd, John J. "A Broker's Observation on Office Buildings," *The Appraisal Journal*, July, 1961, 328–332.

Jennings, Christopher R. "Predicting Demand for Office Space," *The Appraisal Journal*, July, 1965, 377–382.

Parker, King, Jr. "Commercial and Small Office Building Investments," *Developing, Selling and Syndicating Real Estate Investment Property*. Los Angeles: California Real Estate Association, 1964.

Seligman, Daniel. "The Future of the Office Building Boom," *Fortune*, March, 1963, 84–88, 214+.

Smith, Robert H. "Developing Office Buildings to Stand the Test of Time," *Journal of Property Management*, July–August, 1969, 154–158.

Thomsen, Charles. "How High to Rise?," *The Appraisal Journal*, October, 1966, 585–591.

13

Residential Property

Investment in residential property is primarily in the form of apartment houses, especially large-scale complexes involving several hundred units along with various amenities, such as swimming pools and other recreational facilities. The major portion of this chapter is devoted to the apartment complex.

Investor interest is strong and rapidly growing in the mobile home park as well as in the condominium form of ownership. Attention will be given in this chapter to the detached-house condominium, while the mobile home park will be the subject of the following chapter.

Some investors have found the single-family house to be an attractive investment outlet, although this form of residential property is predominantly associated with owner–occupancy-type use. Points to consider in analyzing an investment of this type are presented in this chapter.

APARTMENTS

A well-located, well-designed, realistically financed, and properly maintained apartment building or project can be a sound investment. The overall

215

demand for apartments from the viewpoint of the consumer is supported by a number of factors in the economy:

1. Demographic or population composition favors apartment living. Large segments of the population, for a variety of reasons, prefer apartment living: young singles and marrieds, and older and retired people whose families are grown.
2. There is an increased mobility of the population. More people are on the move each year, and apartments frequently meet the housing needs of these people better than single-family residences.
3. Increased costs of home ownership may cause people to postpone home purchases or to sell their homes and move into more economical apartments. As land values rise, construction costs increase, and maintenance costs jump, the prices of homes increase, down payments increase, and monthly mortgage payments may reach a level where the consumer indicates a strong preference for apartment living.
4. The modern apartment building and unit itself offers attractive amenities for the tenant's convenience, comfort, and enjoyment. Total environmental planning may be found in soundly conceived apartment projects, including good architecture and land planning and social and recreational benefits—swimming pools, putting greens, recreation rooms, sauna baths, gymnasiums, health clubs, and spectacular scenic views in many instances. Apartment living has become a popular way of living.

From the viewpoint of the developer and investor, the apartment project or venture is attractive for several reasons in addition to the basic general market demand forces discussed above. Among these other attractions are the following:

1. *Availability of financing offering good leverage and good yield possibilities.* A sound apartment project, either proposed or existing, is usually attractive to lenders, and developers are frequently able to accomplish the objective of building with little or none of their own cash in a project. Even in periods of tight money, funds are frequently available for good apartment projects, whereas they may not be for single-family residences. The lender is able to obtain a higher return from the apartment project.
2. *Good income tax benefits.* Depreciation deductions can be substantial, since the depreciable building portion of the property is usually a large percentage of the total value. These deductions, along with mortgage interest deductions, are usually sufficient to generate an

income tax loss in the early years of the investment. Also, refinancing possibilities and capital gain benefits are further attractions for the investor in apartments.

3. *The high cost of suburban land in most growing locations.* This has forced developers to seek to maximize the return on their land; more housing units must be placed on a given tract to create sufficient income to justify the project. Apartments will produce a greater income than, say, single-family residential development.

MARKET WEAKNESSES

As with any investment, there are areas of caution which the prudent real estate investor will keep in mind before making an apartment house investment decision. The development and construction of an apartment project can be a tricky business. Consider these factors:

1. Consumer tastes can change quickly, and so can neighborhoods. Shifts in either can adversely affect demand for a given apartment project between the time of its inception and its completion.

2. The apartment house construction and capital lending markets lack a unifying force. The apartment house construction field is relatively easy to enter; it is made up of thousands of builders—some professionals and some amateurs. The easy financing usually available means that builders need little capital to enter the market. Funds are available from a variety of sources, many of them relatively small and sometimes inexperienced in apartment lending.

3. There are no key or anchor tenants in apartment buildings such as are found in office buildings and shopping centers. Such tenants would serve the very useful function of guaranteeing advance rental of apartment units, thereby giving a project some assured income immediately upon completion.

FEASIBILITY STUDY

The attractiveness of a proposed apartment project to an investor depends upon whether it is economically feasible. An excellent discussion of this concept and the essential steps involved is given by James E. Gibbons, M. A. I., in his article "Apartment Feasibility Studies," *The Appraisal Journal,* July, 1968, 325–332.

Apartment Feasibility Studies

by James E. Gibbons

In the appraisal field today the term, feasibility study, is used with increasing frequency. This term is relatively new, and there seems to be a misapprehension on the part of some practitioners that an entirely new procedure or operation is involved. A brief examination of the problem, however, reveals that any carefully prepared appraisal is truly a feasibility study.

To support this contention it is necessary to review basic economic principles upon which rests the entire appraisal science. First, it is clear that the value of real property represents the appraiser's estimate of the present worth of future benefits a property owner will enjoy. His acquisition of real estate is not based on what it produced in the past, but rather on what he expects from it in the future. The past is useful to an investor only to the extent that it helps him make realistic forecasts. Valuation, therefore, is a discounting process through which future expectations are translated to present worths.

Next, the principle of highest and best (most profitable) use should be considered. In the simplest description of this appraisal principle, highest and best use of a property is that which produces the best rate of earnings to land. In this connection one should recall that there are four agents in production:

1. *Labor*: wages and salaries
2. *Coordination*: in real estate this is operating expenses
3. *Capital*: investment in building, equipment, etc.
4. *Land*

A property's net income must satisfy the requirements of these agents in the above order. In all cases, labor has first claim on income. The next demand to be met is operating expenses, which must be paid for the property to produce any income. Next are the demands of capital invested in the building, equipment, etc. Appraisers recognize that the investor requires an attractive, competitive rate of earnings on outstanding capital,

James E. Gibbons, M.A.I., is Executive Vice President of Sackman–Gilliland Corporation of Brooklyn, New York, and a national vice president (Central Atlantic Region) of the A.I.R.E.A., for which he served as chairman of the Division of Publications in 1967, and as a member of the Division of Courses. He is a former vice president of the East New York Savings Bank (Brooklyn).

Reprinted with permission of the American Institute of Real Estate Appraisers from the July, 1968, issue of *The Appraisal Journal*.

and he also demands provision for recapturing such funds. After meeting requirements of the foregoing three agents, whatever income remains is available to the fourth agent, land. An economically feasible property improvement program exists if there is sufficient residual income to show an appropriate rate of earnings on the cost of land acquisition. On the other hand, lack of feasibility is indicated if such income is inadequate to provide a competitive rate.

Nature of Appraising

Consider the nature of a typical appraisal assignment: the appraiser is asked to estimate a property's market value. He carefully analyzes all market data, from which he projects future benefits accruing to an owner of the property. He then discounts these expectations to present worth, using an appropriate capitalization method. Selecting the proper rate of discount is a critical element in the procedure. It is also important for him to be aware of the goals and ambitions of investors, because the rate he selects must provide best prospects for realizing such aspirations.

When the appraiser completes his discounting process, he has an indicated value. A comparison between this figure and the cost to create the property, or its asking price, measures feasibility of the cost or asking price.

Apartment Project Feasibility

An apartment project is economically feasible when its projected future net income affords an investor an appropriate rate of earnings on capital, and provides for its recapture. In other words, he must be satisfied with the carefully forecasted "bottom line." In each case, what constitutes a satisfactory rate of earnings is a question the appraiser resolves after intensively studying many factors, including attendant risks, forecasts of local and general economic conditions, earnings, prices of comparable properties, and yields available from competitive investment opportunities. The feasibility study is generally one of two types. The problem might be to examine prepared plans of an apartment project and judge its ability to show attractive earnings and adequately recapture capital. Or he may have to determine an improvement program which represents highest and best use of a particular parcel.

The Market

To this point, it is clearly indicated that the market is the source of all data from which the appraiser draws his conclusions. Hence, a logical first consideration should be the nature of the real estate market in which the proposed apartment project will be situated. One must, therefore, first determine the boundaries of the area from which the operation is likely to draw its support and competition. Once this area has been delineated, attention is directed to its population. People constitute the market, and they make value. Thus, the number of people residing in the section is important; and since valuation is concerned with futures, population trends have even greater significance. The values of apartment projects are functions of rental incomes they produce, and such incomes are limited by people's capacity to pay. Thus, appraisers are concerned with population not only because of density but also because of its earning abilities. The appraiser must consider the economy in areas where construction is proposed.

People will remain where there are good job opportunities, which generally draw additional people to such areas. It is therefore necessary to study the volume of industry and business in and around the apartment property's location. Since value is tied into futures, industrial diversity is of particular importance because it generally assures future employment stability, whereas single industry locations involve substantial hazards. The appraiser must then examine wage levels, as prevailing pay scales will quickly reveal rent paying abilities. Also, type and quality of projected apartments must be closely related to incomes of prospective tenants.

The current and forecasted size of families is also a significant consideration. Obviously one should not plan to build numerous efficiency apartments in areas where tenant families are expected to average four to five people.

Apartment project layouts should be designed (as best as possible) to suit the tastes and desires of likely users. Where substantial capital is to be invested in an apartment building, it is wise to analyze (statistically, by random sample) tenant attitudes toward layouts, locality, room sizes, closet space, recreational facilities, appliances, air conditioning, parking facilities, utilities, etc. With this information a developer could handle project design with assurance of customer acceptance.

Statistical analysis is now perfected to the point where it is clearly recognized as one of industry's most valuable tools for appraising markets. Since real estate is an asset which comprises the largest segment of the nation's wealth, its marketing demands as much or more care and study as any other commodity, necessitating statistical analysis for optimum results. This field is probably beyond the scope of an average appraiser's experience and knowledge, but this situation does not justify its omission. It simply indicates the appraiser's clear obligation to employ competent consultants who can render the required services. Such expert assistance should be contemplated in setting an appraisal fee, a small but critically necessary item when millions of dollars are to be invested in real estate. In such cases proper and adequate appraisals should contain complete market interpretation.

In market analysis, competition is of prime importance. Supply–demand relationships are critical considerations in planning to market any commodity, and apartments are no exception. Current competition is not the major concern if one accepts the thesis that value is the present worth of future benefits. Instead, the appraiser must research probable future competition and its effect on supply–demand conditions. The apartment market consists of standing units, as well as units nearing completion which are being offered for lease. Investigation will quickly reveal current utilization and, consequently, the vacancy factor. But this information alone is insufficient for the type of conclusions generally sought in feasibility studies; the appraiser must also forecast future additions to the apartment supply. Such predictions are not too difficult. He must carefully examine existing construction trends and then after studying all economic factors thoroughly, project such trends into the future, giving attention to both magnitude and direction.

To summarize, a feasibility study's necessary conclusions are developed by analyzing all material obtained through the following three steps. First, weigh competition by evaluating the standing stock of apartments. Other pertinent considerations are apartment utilization, effective demand, and market breakdown into rent level categories. Second, explore population trends in relation to expanding or contracting demand, thus assessing future apartment construction, a prerequisite to forecasting anticipated wage levels, which indicate rent paying ability. Third, estimate probable future apartment construction, a prerequisite to forecasting anticipated supply factors. Properly executed market analyses should enable the appraiser to project apartment demand by volume, size and type; desired facilities, equipment and aesthetics; and the market's rent paying capabilities.

Capital Investment

After determining present and future apartment demand along with expected rent levels, the appraiser must consider the capital investment required to create the desired facilities. Too many developers treat this subject superficially and suffer serious damage. The purpose of this article is not to extensively consider cost estimating procedures, but rather to focus on the critical importance of capital investment. However, if a successful investment provides attractive earnings on invested capital along with adequate recapture, one must know how much capital is required since this estimate serves as the base against which to measure anticipated net monetary returns.

Capital Availability

After estimating how much capital is required, a more important consideration is its availability. Investors generally seek large mortgage and thin equity financing to gain leverage in equity earnings rate. To achieve their objectives, these sources of capital must be at hand. The project is unfeasible without capital available at proper cost, regardless of its favorable prospects.

In the following example, the appraiser finds adequate support at required rent levels after researching and analyzing the market. Capital requirements to create the project are accurately assessed, and net income producing ability is properly estimated. The overall earnings rate is the ratio of net income to cost. For feasibility, this rate must equal the weighted average of costs to acquire the segments of capital which comprise the investment. For example, the study may show a probable overall earnings rate of 9.5%. Further, 75% of the purchase capital can be acquired as a mortgage loan at 7% interest for 20 years, with an annual 9.3% rate for monthly interest and amortization payments. The 25% balance will be equity contributions, and this capital requires a 10% annual cash flow dividend. The weighted average of these costs is:

$$75\% \text{ mortgage at } 0.093 = \qquad \begin{array}{r} 0.06975 \\ 0.02500 \\ \hline 0.09475 \end{array}$$

25% equity at dividend rate of 0.10 =

Rounded to 0.095

Such analyses demonstrate the project's economic feasibility. The money market is a variable which changes rapidly and frequently. The cost and availability of various types of capital fluctuate in response to local, national and international economic conditions, and average money market conditions over the past ten years are of no interest to an investor. Only today's situation is applicable to his activity, because mortgage money is not always readily obtainable. At such moments, meritorious projects simply cannot get off the ground. Hence, a feasibility study is inadequate and probably misleading unless capital availability receives proper attention.

In estimating cost to create apartment projects, standard techniques should be followed. Buildings are designed for maximum plot utilization, optimum use of building space, and for satisfying the renting public's demand for facilities. After preparing plans and specifications, a quantity survey cost analysis might be procured or, as an alternative, the required investment might be assessed by a "trade breakdown" of costs. Only the best qualified researcher should be employed for such studies, and appraisers should have the integrity to consult an expert if their knowledge of costs is insufficient for the task. Observation indicates, however, that capable cost estimators are often concerned only with a project's major physical characteristics, failing to consider fully the many economic factors involved.

Several features of apartment projects may not be overlooked, in addition to direct and indirect construction costs. One must also consider these costs: land financing, feasibility studies and interim construction financing, including such closing expenses as attorney, title search, brokerage, origination fees, etc. After completing physical construction a rental program must be pursued. It may require considerable expense to promote the apartments, bring them to public attention, and secure interested potential tenants. Then, too, the rental period might begin at a time of temporary oversupply, although every indication points to future desirable occupancy. The problem is getting the project off the ground and achieving at least a break-even between income and operating expenses, and debt service. To reach this condition in reasonable time it is often necessary to provide expensive tenant incentives and concessions. In the matter of cost, one might also overlook the demand for initial operating capital. When first tenants occupy the building after construction, occupancy is not adequate to provide required operating funds. Owners must be prepared to supply any deficiency until the project is self-sustaining. Many well-conceived apartment projects have been distressed by lack of initial operating capital.

The appraiser considering feasibility must therefore realistically examine capital investment requirements. He should not conclude his study with usual direct and indirect cost estimates, but is obligated instead to assess carefully the problems of promotion expense, rental concessions and incentives, and initial operating capital requirements. He must forecast these items and add them to his customary cost estimates, thereby accurately portraying the required volume of capital investment. Net income must be weighed against this realistically computed total cost to judge the probable rate of capital earnings.

Capitalization Considerations

A project is considered economically feasible if anticipated net monetary earnings provide adequate recapture and an attractive rate of return on capital. After deciding type and quality of building improvements to be erected, estimating total capital requirements and forecasting net earnings through market analysis, the appraiser must determine whether such earnings are acceptable in relation to the investment. The project is economically feasible if investors are interested in buying the right to receive the property's net income, and are willing to pay a price at least equal to capital investment. In fact, the developer hopes the investor is willing to pay something in excess of total costs, providing attractive profit margin.

It is critically important to estimate operating expenses carefully. Since the appraiser is always working from forecasts of net income, the accuracy of any projection will depend on his ability to deal with the expense item. Again, one must remember that value is the present worth of anticipated future benefits. Such benefits in apartments are "bottom line" returns, and they are vitally affected by the expected magnitude of expenses. While history generally shows a pattern of increasing expenses (forming a basis for predictions), one or two items may move more rapidly than the average. A notable example is real estate tax. The locality's demands for various improvements, the rate of future growth and other items, all indicate the probable growth of tax burdens. Since the appraiser is forecasting futures, consideration of taxes is germane to valuation and feasibility studies.

The appraiser must process his estimate of net income to express capital value. By comparing such value with cost he then formulates feasibility conclusions. To plan capital recapture, the practitioner who customarily relies on the straight line capitalization method would probably concern himself first with estimating the apartment building's remaining economic life. This concept embraces so many diverse and complicated factors that the appraiser is appalled at the immensity of making the estimate. But the method requires it.

With this forecast completed, the appraiser next selects the proper interest rate to discount anticipated earnings, one which would probably attract investment capital. The projected net income figure is then processed by first subtracting the amount which provides the required interest earnings on invested capital and, on a straight line basis, the amount which provides for recapturing such capital over the building's remaining economic life. Any residual income would be allocated to land, and discounting it at an appropriate interest rate, the result should indicate land value. If this figure is less than the land acquisition cost, the proposed apartment improvements lack economic feasibility. On the other hand, if the land value estimate is equal to or above acquisition cost, economic feasibility is demonstrated.

While many appraisers use straight line capitalization, there is growing dissatisfaction with the technique. Many now believe that property should not be considered "free and clear," but should be studied in view of the necessary financing. They recognize that the typical apartment investor borrows as much of the purchase price as possible in the form of mortgage capital and then adds the balance as equity, hoping it will be quite thin. He then regards the property's anticipated net income as a composite of debt service (interest and amortization of mortgage debt) and of cash flow profits or dividends. He expects to keep the investment as long as the mortgage amortization is sheltered by the income tax depreciation deduction on building improvements. After that he is well advised to either change investments or refinance the mortgage. Thus it is clear that cash flow dividends are not his sole profit expectation. Instead, the extent to which mortgage amortization exceeds property value depreciation over an ownership period is recognized as additional equity profit. The yield on equity investment is therefore a composite of cash flow dividends and equity growth resulting from the difference between property value depreciation and mortgage amortization.

It is thus apparent that the proper overall rate at which the appraiser should discount future benefits is a weighted average of debt service and the dividend rate necessary to attract equity capital. (In other words, it is an average of costs to acquire the two segments of capital used to create the apartment investment.) For example, if an apartment investment normally comprises 75% mortgage capital and 25% equity, one must examine the costs of such capital. Mortgage money may be available typically with monthly payments of 8% on a constant annual basis, at 6% interest. The market may also reveal that a minimum cash flow dividend of 10% is required to attract equity capital. If these conditions prevail the proper overall rate is indicated by the following band of investment:

75% first mortgage at 8% (interest and amortization) = 0.06
25% equity at 10% (dividend)   = 0.025
                                                      ‾‾‾‾‾
                                     Overall rate   0.085

The overall rate selected by a band of investment, averaging the costs of mortgage and equity capital, can be used to process income by this formula:

$$\frac{d}{R} = V$$

where d = net income
       R = overall rate
       V = value

If resulting value at least equals capital investment requirements, the project is economically feasible; if value falls below investment, it is not.

To further support the overall rate (R) utilized to test the project's feasibility, the appraiser can analyze the rate and by so doing make an investment analysis of the property. The material in *Ellwood Tables for Real Estate Appraising and Financing*, second edition, sets forth full details. For simple and quick results one can refer to the table entitled "75% Mortgage, Analysis of Selected Capitalization Rates" commencing on Page 327. Returning to the example of 75% mortgage at 8% debt service with 6% interest and 25% equity at 10% dividend rate, the indicated overall rate is 8.5%. Page 334 indicates that for an expected ten-year ownership with full mortgage amortization in approximately 20 years, the property can lose 23% of its value in ten years and still show an equity yield of 9%. It also indicates that if the property loses 10% of its value in ten years the equity yield will be 12%. Thus, if an appraiser believes the property will lose no more than 20% value in ten years and probably no less than 10%, he would estimate equity yield as at least 9% and most likely 10% to 11%. This would lend strength and plausibility to the rate he selected for testing the project's economic feasibility.

It is apparent that economic feasibility studies do not differ essentially from appraisals. Value is the present worth of future benefits. To estimate value one must formulate a "rate" at which futures are to be discounted. The feasibility study should commence logically with a market analysis. This will indicate the nature and strength of the market, its ability to pay, its tastes, and its anticipated future trends. On the basis of such information the appraiser will either judge the market acceptability of a proposed apartment project or, where no plan has been prepared, will advise which project will most likely meet the renting public's approval. Next, he must carefully estimate the amount of capital required to create the facilities. In this connection, the appraiser must be certain he has included all costs, direct and indirect. Finally, anticipated net monetary benefits from the property must be discounted to present worth. The discount rate should logically be a weighted average of the costs to acquire the investment capital; that is, a weighted average of debt service and equity dividend. For an indication of feasibility, the resulting value must at least equal capital investment requirements.

APARTMENT RESEARCH REPORT

The Research Committee of the Florida Association of Realtors made a study of apartment dwellers in ten selected communities throughout the state. The Summary from this study is presented below; it should be informative to apartment developers, lenders, and investors.

A Study of Florida Apartment Dwellers As Tenants and Owners
Florida Association of Realtors
Real Estate Research Project No. 7
(1968)
Clayton C. Curtis, Ph.D., *Project Director*
University of Florida

Summary

Each of the individual cities in the selected group of 10 Florida communities has been analyzed in considerable detail in terms of the answers provided to the questions posed. This summary, therefore, is not intended to repeat answers which can be checked by reference to the appropriate chapter. Instead, this summary will point out similarities and differences and draw some general conclusions from the information gathered.

The cities included in this survey span the entire state. The diversity of people in terms of age and the other factors is also very wide. Despite this diversity, one of the most striking results indicated by answers to the survey questions is the great similarity of many responses to the basic queries. For example, when respondents were asked what they liked most about apartment living, in all 10 cities the top choices were lack of maintenance worries, location of units, greater ease in houskeeping; freedom to travel, and availability of good recreational facilities. There were some differences among the cities in the ranking importance of these factors, but differences were not large.

Location An Important Factor

The factor of location appears first in the "most-liked" question and then again in answering why apartment living was selected over other alternatives. The location factor also appears in responses to the question of selection of this particular apartment, and is implied in answers to the query about factors desirable in a neighborhood. In all of these questions, location was considered important in all cities and by all the groups represented. The degree of importance varied somewhat among age groups and among cities, but location was one of the more important factors cited in all cases. This underlines the validity of the appraisers' belief that location makes value.

A more precise meaning of location—as far as survey respondents are concerned—can be gleaned from their comments and from answers to other questions. For example, while location does not appear as such in the possible replies to the question about attractive neighborhood characteristics, answers given describe, in effect, the kind of locational attributes meant in the other answers.

Apartment dwellers in all cities surveyed placed a suburban residential character at or near the top of desired neighborhood characteristics. Nearness to shopping was ranked high by apartment dwellers in most communities, particularly by older groups in cities of substantial size, and nearness to work ranked high with younger groups in several cities. A prestige reputation was considered important by both groups in a high proportion of the areas surveyed.

Neighborhood Characteristics Reviewed

Shopping proximity was important to older groups who apparently consider shopping as recreation, in part. The distance which people will walk to shopping—and this is related to location—is a maximum of three blocks as a median for the bulk of people in all cities surveyed. The range and number of people who would walk farther than the median three blocks is higher in the larger cities and with older age groups.

In the field of unattractive neighborhood characteristics, there was a high degree of agreement among the cities and the groups that the least liked aspect was a poor neighborhood physically. Next in line came street noise, traffic, and proximity to commerce. These factors in many cities are linked closely together.

In many cities, it would be difficult to find an area where a suburban residential character could be matched with proximity to other desirable factors. A matching of the more important attractive features, accompanied by a minimum of the most unattractive, should result in the best chance of success.

Complaints About Apartment Living

Features of apartment living found unattractive by apartment dwellers are agreed upon to about the same degree as attractive features. The outstanding complaint about apartment living centers around the lack of room. Because a large proportion of apartment dwellers surveyed came from single-family homes, the comparison in terms of space is with a one-family house.

The average house usually contains more space than the average apartment, but the same complaint about lack of room is heard in Naples, for example, where average apartment size was well above the national average size for single-family dwellings. Apartments in Naples are generally expensive and presumably the tenants came from similarly expensive homes, so it can be said that the size issue is a relative one. This knowledge can be important in terms of a prospective apartment relative to the type of house the prospect occupied before.

Storage Space Mentioned

Another major complaint is the matter of insufficient storage space. This factor also ranks high as a "demand" feature in apartment living. The inadequate storage space complaint probably derives, as does the feeling about general room space, from conditioning received by living in a single-family dwelling. Storage space is a problem the apartment developer could solve with a little ingenuity at no great increase in cost.

Noise was another complaint ranking high among apartment dwellers, and noise appeared earlier as a disturbing factor in relation to location. In that context, the complaint was about external street noises, while noise as a least-liked factor means internal noise generated by people living in the apartments. This is reinforced by the unpopularity of the nearness-to-the-others factor, which would seem to be associated with noise as well as proximity. This is a problem which can be solved or minimized by current technology.

There were several other factors important enough to merit attention, especially in relation to specific cities, but one response among the top four unattractive features in most cities was the lack of outdoor living. This factor spanned the age groups, but it is a lack which developers can meet, although it might influence the height of structures, as high-rise apartments usually make outdoor living facilities more difficult.

Parking Is Desirable

In the area of amenities people would like to have in their apartments, as apart from comforts they demand, covered parking rated in the top four in all cities except Daytona Beach. In more than half the cities it was the number one item. Covered parking can be added at some extra cost, but where it is so clearly desired the expense could be partly offset by an additional charge to tenants. Additional auto storage space or parking also ranked high in all cities covered, but here the developer often runs into two problems. The first is the high cost of land, especially in the developed areas of a city, and the second is pressure from insurance companies to maximize the number of units on the land—this requirement often precludes additional parking areas.

From evidence gathered in this survey and from other investigations, it seems that when apartment construction reaches a saturation point, or when overbuilding occurs, the units containing the most desirable features will be the units that weather the storm the best. This should be pointed out to the insurance companies, for factors which they apparently believe increase loan safety may in the long run actually reduce it.

Security Guard Important

Large numbers of apartment dwellers in 8 of the 10 cities surveyed would like to have a security guard added to their apartment features. Only in the smaller communities of Ocala and Naples was this considered relatively unimportant. Desire for a security guard tended to be more important to apartment dwellers as the size of the city increased. A guard was not more important to the older age groups; in fact, the younger groups in the larger cities were more concerned about a guard than the older groups. In other cities there was not much difference in attitude as related to age or location.

Two other desirable features did not receive as much endorsement as parking or security guard, but deserve mention as important in several cities to several groups and these are a combination recreation and community room and more attractive yards. The room is somewhat more attractive to respondents than the yards, and a recreation/community room is more important to the older groups, but this is not universal among the cities surveyed.

Heat And Air Are Essential

Central heat and air conditioning is the number one feature which apartment dwellers consider essential and hence demand. Other items considered essential do not display the same high degree of unanimity among cities as do answers to some other questions, except for laundry facilities, which is in the top 4 in 9 of the 10 cities. Ample storage is high in several cities, and in some areas carpeting is high on the list, as are built-in appliances. The relationship of age to these essentials varies, and reference is made to the discussion of findings by individual cities. Answers were more diverse than usual to the question of why tenants picked the particular apartment they occupied. Location received a high rating, and availability was important in several areas, but this should decline in importance as apartment building continues. The rental charge or cost was important in several areas, especially where older retired citizens were involved. The size of rooms was important in a good proportion of cases. . . .

INVESTMENT ANALYSIS

Four different condensed offerings of apartment projects are presented below to illustrate the investment or financial analysis of this type of property. While the arithmetic of the deal varies with each offering, there are certain basic apartment-value factors which are present in each one. These factors are clearly basic for the continued financial success of a project:

1. Proper location
2. High-quality construction
3. Professional property management
4. Good maintenance
5. Amenities desired by tenants in the market area of the apartment location
6. Attractive architecture and good land planning
7. Good interior layout
8. Properly selected market to which to appeal
9. Competent and reputable developer and owner
10. Sufficient cash from the project to cover operating costs and debt service
11. Careful analysis and verification of income and expense figures of the project and determination of their reasonableness in light of recognized standards

---

OFFERING NO. 1

A preferred one-half interest in 514 modern garden apartments (5 projects), with the remaining one-half put up as security for the guaranteed income. The deal in brief is as follows:

Cash equity price for preferred one-half interest $ 750,000

One-half of existing mortgage
balances of $5,153,181 $2,576,590
                                               ──────────

Total purchase price for preferred
half-interest $3,326,590

1. The firm sale price of the preferred one-half interest is $750,-
   000, and the investor will receive a guaranteed net, net return
   of $90,000 per year (12% net return on $750,000 cash invested).
2. The seller will pledge his remaining one-half of the property
   as collateral for the faithful payment of the guaranteed net
   return. This gives the investor approximately $750,000 in
   property as security.
3. To provide protection against inflation, the investor will receive 20% of all gross apartment rental collections over $1,100-
   000 after first allowing for all real estate tax increases.
4. This transaction will be set up so that the investor is the
   limited partner and the XYZ Corporation is the general partner. The investor, through mutual agreement, will receive the
   benefit of all the depreciation on all properties (the bottom
   line on the partnership tax return). This will produce double
   the usual tax shelter.
5. In the event of a refinancing or sale, the proceeds will be divided 50–50.
6. The XYZ Corporation is one of the nation's finest development
   and management companies and will be completely responsible
   for all management and maintenance of the property.

PROJECTED INCOME AND EXPENSES
FOR THE 5 PROJECTS

INCOME:

Project A	(118 units)	$ 243,457	
Project B	(136 units)	243,082	
Project C	(140 units)	325,588	
Project D	(48 units)	90,991	
Project E	(72 units)	151,360	
Total	514 units	$1,054,478	$1,054,478

EXPENSES:

Project A	$ 75,224
Project B	72,932
Project C	97,060

Project D	$ 33,160	
Project E	57,800	
Total Expenses	$ 336,176	$ 336,176
Operating Net Total		$ 718,302

MORGAGE PAYMENTS:

Project A	$ 107,095	
Project B	112,296	
Project C	137,511	
Project D*	26,781	
Project E	61,608	
Second	44,004	
	$ 489,295	489,295

Projected cash flow for the five projects	$ 229,007
Less: Long-range maintenance and replacement	
reserve at $100 per apartment per year	51,400

PROJECTED TOTAL CASH FLOW AFTER ALLOWANCE
FOR LONG-RANGE MAINTENANCE RESERVE OF $100
PER APARTMENT PER YEAR $ 177,607

* The Project D Mortgage payment until August, 1970 is $38,009 yearly. Thereafter, yearly payment shall be $26,781.

INDIVIDUAL PROJECT STATEMENT
OF INCOME AND EXPENSE

Included in the offering brochure is an income and expense statement for each of the five projects. The format of each is similar and only two are shown here for illustration purposes.

Project A

Annual

INCOME:

8—3-BR Luxury —2-bath	@	$254.00	$24,384.00
32—3-BR Executive—1½-bath	@	209.00	80,256.00
16—2-BR Executive—1-bath	@	179.00	34,368.00
8—2-BR Executive—1½-bath	@	189.00	18,144.00
32—2-BR Standard —1-bath	@	149.00	57,216.00
22—1-BR Standard —1-bath	@	134.00	35,376.00

Audit by Accounting		Projected Gross	
Firm	$230,568.00	Income	$249,744.00 (1)
Add: 5 Vacancies	$9,660.00	5% Vacancy Allow.	12,487.00
Actual Gross *	$240,228.00		
		Adjusted Income	$237,257.00
		Miscellaneous Income	6,200.00
		Total Net Income	$243,457.00

EXPENSES: (Actual)

Advertising & Promotion	$2,701.00
Insurance	3,360.00
Legal & Accounting	1,823.00
Custodial Incl. Apartment, Salary, Payroll Taxes)	11,991.00**
Repairs & Maintenance	9,098.00
Real Estate Taxes	16,410,00 **30**%
Public Utilities	20,564.00 3 0 9 pt. 35,500
Vehicle Expense (Courtesy Car)	2,070.00
Management	7,207.00 **5**%

Total Expenses	$ 75,224.00
Available for Debt Service	$168,233.00
Annual Mtg. Pymt.	107,095.00
Cash Flow	$ 61,138.00

** Includes company management training costs.

Note: The debt service of $107,095 does not include the second mortgage. Details on this mortgage are shown in the "Mortgage Schedule," p. 235.

Project C

Annual

INCOME:

    16—3-Bedroom Luxury   @ $249.50 per month
    72—3-Bedroom Executive @   209.50 per month
    32—2-Bedroom Executive @   189.50 per month

12—2-Bedroom Standard @   149.50 per month
8—1-Bedroom Standard @   137.50 per month

Gross Income	$336,408.00
5% Vacancy Allowance	16,820.00
Adjusted Net Income	$319,588.00
Miscellaneous Income	6,000.00
Total Net Income	$325,588.00

EXPENSES:

Management	$16,000.00	
Advertising & Promotion	3,000.00	
Insurance	3,360.00	
Legal & Accounting	400.00	
Maintenance	9,600.00	
Supervision & Custodian with Suites	14,400.00	
Utilities	20,200.00	
Landscaping & Snow Removal	1,000.00	
Real Estate Taxes	26,200.00	
Telephone	600.00	
Trash Removal	2,300.00	
Total Expenses		97,060.00
Amount Left for Mtg. Service and Cash Flow		$228,528.00
Annual Mortgage Payment		137,511.00
Cash Flow		$ 91,017.00

POSSIBLE 10-YEAR REFINANCING BENEFITS

During the 10 years between 1969 and 1979 (exact dates omitted in this condensed illustration), the mortgages on the 514 apartments will be reduced to:

Property	Original Balance	Balance 1968	Balance 1978
Project A I	$ 645,000	$ 603,342	$ 421,185
Project A II	650,000	624,508	479,050
Project B I	410,000	397,902	290,690
Project B II	460,000	431,589	274,620

MORTGAGE SCHEDULE

Property	Developer Personal Liability	Original Mortgage Amount	Perm. Effec.	Monthly Payment	Current Interest Rate	Maturity Date	Prepayment Penalty	Mtg. Bal. Date
Project A Phase I	None	$ 645,000	March, 1966	$ 4,355.09	6½%	Feb., 1991	None	$ 603,342
Project A Phase II	None	$ 650,000	Aug., 1967	$ 4,569.50	6¾%	July, 1992	None	$ 624,508
Project B Phase I	None	$ 410,000	July, 1967	$ 2,772.00	6½%	June, 1992	Closed 5 Years	$ 397,902
Project B Phase II	Full	$ 460,000	Nov., 1966	$ 3,255.00	6½%	May, 1989	Maximum of 20% any one year	$ 431,589
Project B Phase III	Full	$ 300,000	Nov., 1967	$ 3,331.00	6%	Oct., 1977	None	$ 257,317
Project C	None	$1,605,000	April, 1969	$11,459.32	7%	May, 1993	Closed 10 yr, 3–2–1% after	$1,605,000
Project D	None	$ 375,000	Sept., 1965	$ 2,231.80 ($3,167.47 until August, 1970)	6%	Sept., 1987	Maximum of 10% any one yr, 6 yr— 3% declining	$ 303,604
Project E	Only to $600,000 or end of 6th yr	$ 720,000	March, 1967	$ 5,134.00	6½%	April, 1989	None	$ 679,919
Second Mortgage covering Projects A & B	None	$ 250,000	June, 1969	$ 3,667.00(1)	12½%	June, 1974*	Closed 1 yr, 2nd yr 5%, pay. pen. every yr after 4, 3, 2, & 1	$ 250,000
TOTALS		$5,415,000		$40,774.71				$5,153,181

* 5-year maturity with payments based on 10-year amortization. After 5 years, lender will work out new amortization schedule.

235

Project B III	$ 300,000	$ 257,317	$ -0-
Project C	1,605,000	1,605,000	1,227,820
Project D	375,000	303,604	169,310
Project E	720,000	679,919	467,280
	$5,165,000	$4,903,181	$3,329,955

The above figures excluded the $250,000 second mortgage. If the investor chooses, he may make an additional investment of $250,000 on July 1, 1970, and this mortgage will be completely paid off. The investor will receive an additional $30,000 per year guaranteed income if he chooses to do this.

This additional investment is purely optional, for XYZ Corporation will agree to pay off the second mortgage from the cash flow of the property during the period from June, 1974 to June, 1979.

The above figures show that if the mortgages (excluding second) are refinanced back to their original amounts after the investor has owned the property for 10 years, there will be a recapture of amortization as follows:

Original mortgage principal	$5,165,000
Balance 1979	3,329,995
Refinancing proceeds	$1,835,005
50% of refinancing proceeds to go to investor	$ 917,503

Based on the above figures, the investor may receive a tax-free amount after 10 years of $917,503, which represents an additional 122% return on his original $750,000 cash invested.

BENEFITS TO PURCHASER

The Realty Company handling this offering has analyzed the 514 apartments. The potential benefits according to their analysis are as follows:

1. *Strong income flow:* Income and expense projection shows this property should have a gross income of $1,054,470 per year based on a 5% vacancy allowance. After allowing for operating expenses plus principal and interest on the mortgages (plus a long-range maintenance and replacement allowance of $100 per apartment per year), there is a projected cash flow of $177,607. From this cash flow, the investor will receive a guaranteed net leaseback return of $90,000 per year. This makes a 12% return on $750,000 cash invested.
2. *Mortgage refinancing benefits:* The original mortgage balances were $5,165,000. The growth of the area and the pressure of

inflation should enable the buyer to refinance the mortgages in 10 years for a favorable amount. If the property is only refinanced back to the original balances, the investor should have the following in tax-free return:

Original mortgage balances	$5,165,000
1979, balances on mortgages	3,329,995
Refinancing proceeds	$1,835,005

Based on the above figures, the owner of a preferred half-interest should have $917,503 cash from the refinancing. This provides a tax-free return of 122% on the original $750,000 cash invested.

3. *Excellent tax-shelter benefits:* Although the investor is only purchasing a half-interest, by becoming the limited partner he can receive the benefit of *all* of the tax depreciation allowance on all of the 514 apartments.

4. *Future capital gain:* The excellent design of these apartments makes it likely that the growth of the areas plus the effects of the inflationary spiral of our economy will enable the buyer to have an excellent future capital gain when he sells the property.

5. *Great security with freedom from management:* The builder–developer has agreed to put up the remaining one-half of the property as security for the faithful payment of the guaranteed net income.

RECOMMENDATIONS

The five projects have been personally inspected by a representative of the Management Department of the Realty Company. The apartments are well located in active rental markets, they are well constructed and maintained, and their occupancy record is excellent. The caliber of the XYZ Corporation is excellent and the firm is professionally competent and operationally conscientious. The properties should be a trouble-free leaseback to an investor who is seeking excellent leverage, high-depreciation benefits, good cash flow return, and excellent future capital gain.

When the investor purchases a half-interest in the 514 properties and becomes a limited partner (with the XYZ Corporation functioning as the general partner), the IRS regulations provide that the partners may, by agreement, allocate different proportions of the benefits along the lines other than the 50–50 basis on which the property is owned; in other words, by agreement, it may be decided that one partner gets the benefit of all of the depreciation. This is fully set forth in Section 704 of the Internal Revenue Code of 1954 under the subsection entitled "Partners' Distributive Share."

After careful analysis, Realty Company highly recommends this package of 514 diversified garden apartments.

OFFERING NO. 2: INCOME AND EXPENSE ANALYSIS

	1st	2nd	*Years Following Closing* 3rd	4th	5th
INCOME					
Rental Income	$154,260	$158,850	$163,440	$168,030	$172,620
Vacancy	6,170	6,354	6,537	6,721	6,905
Net Effective Rental	$148,090	$152,496	$156,903	$161,309	$165,715
Miscellaneous Income	2,060	2,121	2,185	2,251	2,318
Total Income	$150,150	$154,617	$159,088	$163,560	$168,033
Operating Expenses	38,181	41,588	42,687	43,803	44,936
Operating Income	$111,969	$113,029	$116,401	$119,757	$123,097
FINANCIAL EXPENSE					
Interest	$ 59,760	$ 58,080	$ 57,600	$ 55,760	$ 55,200
Depreciation	63,000	59,220	55,650	52,290	49,140
Total Financial Expense	$122,760	$117,300	$113,250	$108,050	$104,340
Pretax Income (Loss)	$(10,791)	$ (4,271)	$ 3,151	$ 11,707	$ 18,757
Income Tax	0	0	0	0	4,082
Net Operating Loss Carryover		10,791	15,062	11,911	204
Net Income (Loss)	(10,791)	(4,271)	3,151	11,707	14,675
Less: Mortgage Amortization	13,840	15,520	16,000	17,840	18,400
Plus: Depreciation	63,000	59,220	55,650	52,290	49,140
NET CASH GAIN	$ 38,369	$ 39,429	$ 42,801	$ 46,157	$ 45,415
TOTAL GAIN	$ 52,209	$ 54,949	$ 58,801	$ 63,997	$ 63,815
Including Amortization					

OFFERING NO. 2: FINANCIAL ANALYSIS

INVESTMENT

Cash Investment	$ 306,000.00
First-mortgage Debt	800,000.00
Total Investment	$1,106,000.00

ANNUAL CASH GAINS (from Income & Expense Analysis)

Years Following Purchase

	1	2	3	4	5
Amount Cash Gain	$38,369	$39,429	$42,801	$46,157	$45,415
As Percentage of Total Cash Investment	12.5%	12.9%	14.0%	15.1%	14.8%

TOTAL INVESTMENT INCOME

	Amortization of Mortgage Debt	Cash Gain	Total Investment Income	As % of Total Cash Investment
First Year	$13,840	$38,369	$52,209	17.06
Second Year	15,520	39,429	54,949	17.96
Third Year	16,000	42,801	58,801	19.21
Fourth Year	17,840	46,157	63,997	20.91
Fifth Year	18,400	45,415	63,815	20.85
Total Five Years			$293,771	
Five-year Average				19.198

OFFERING NO. 2

This is an offering of garden apartments consisting of two 3-story residential buildings well located in a metropolitan area. These buildings were completed in 1970 (exact dates are omitted in this condensed illustration). Architectural design, interior layout, and construction all conform to the highest standards. The property consists of 72 apartments as follows:

    51—1-Bedroom Apartments
    18—2-Bedroom Apartments
     3—Efficiency Apartments

Three efficiency apartments, 17 one-bedroom apartments, and 11 two-bedroom apartments are fully furnished. All apartments are fully equipped with major appliances. All bathrooms have vanities and the best-quality bathroom fixtures and hardware. All floors are concrete; baths are tiled with ceramic tile; all kitchens have vinyl floor covering and Formica-top cabinets; the rest of the floor area is fully carpeted with heavy nylon carpeting over foam-rubber padding. All of the apartments are fully draped and equipped with traverse rods.

Construction is considered AAA, all floors and roofs being concrete. The buildings contain two self-operating, fully automatic electric elevators, and two large swimming pools having completely automatic filtering systems. The grounds are beautifully landscaped, and paved parking is provided in the excess of one space per apartment.

Each bedroom apartment is equipped with thermostatically controlled individual central air-conditioning and heating units, and all apartments are provided hot water by two fully automatic gas-fired boilers.

OFFERING NO. 3

The offering is for 201 new apartments with unusually fine recreational facilities.

Cash Investment Required	$510,000
Cash Flow Return on Investment	13.4%
Depreciation Tax Shelter (1st 10 years)	$847,200
Capital Gain if Resold (After 10 years)	$451,000

THE CITY:

Metropolitan area.

THE LAND:

The apartments occupy approximately 13 acres, an unusually large tract for 201 apartments. There is, therefore, plenty of open area around each building, an advantage possessed by very few garden-type apartments. The land value is estimated to be $20,000 per acre or $260,000.

There are 3 lots, approximately 100 × 140 ft each, on which single-family homes could be built without seriously affecting the apartment project. It is estimated that these lots could be sold to builders for at least $5,000 each. At that time, an attractive fence would need to be built across the back of the lots.

THE LOCATION:

Approximately 7 miles (20 minutes' driving time) from downtown of major city. Neighborhood shopping centers are close at hand, and larger complete shopping areas are within a few minutes' drive. The project is within walking distance of the elementary and high schools. The location is excellent.

THE BUILDINGS:

The 13 buildings contain 94—2-bedroom, 2-bath apartments and 107—3-bedroom, 2-bath apartments. The project was completed in 1968 (exact dates omitted in this condensed illustration).

Construction is wood frame with brick and Clodex board veneer. Sliding aluminum windows. Doors to individual apartments are metal and entrance doors to the buildings are glass framed with aluminum. Second- and third-floor apartments have balconies.

Kitchens in the ground-floor apartments have vinyl tile floors. Those on the second and third floors are carpeted. Sinks are stainless steel.

Kitchen equipment—refrigerators, electric ranges with exhaust fans and charcoal-filter hoods, dishwashers and disposals are of Frigidaire make.

The laundry rooms have a total of 18 washers and 8 dryers—owned by the project. Many projects lease this equipment and receive only 35–40% of the income from the coin-operated machines. The project pays only $500.00 per year to service the machines and the income from them is running in excess of $13,000 per year.

There are approximately 380 parking spaces for tenant cars—1.9 spaces per apartment.

The rental area of the apartments is approximately 202,000 sq ft. We estimate that it would cost $12.00 per sq ft to build and equip this project today. Replacement cost, therefore, is estimated at $2,424,000.

RECREATION FACILITIES:

One of the most attractive features of this project is its large clubhouse with its indoor pool, two sauna baths, and second-floor party room. It is the only apartment project in the area with an indoor pool—an important advantage in this area.

The project also has a tennis court, a basketball court, a putting green, and a playground for children. These facilities are seldom available in apartment projects and should be an important factor in keeping the buildings occupied by happy tenants.

APARTMENT SIZES AND RENTALS:

The apartment floor plans vary slightly, but the 2-bedroom units contain approximately 860 sq ft and the 3-bedroom units approximately 1,150 sq ft.

Existing rentals range from $160 to $190 per month for 2 bedrooms and $200 to $230 per month for 3 bedrooms. Some of these apartments were rented last year at the lower figures at a time when the developer was seeking to build up occupancy to meet the terms of his mortgage commitment.

The present rental schedule is as follows:

Two Bedrooms
Ground Floor—facing court	$180.00
" " —facing front	$175.00
Second Floor —facing court	$190.00
" " —facing front	$185.00
Third Floor —facing court	$185.00
" " —facing front	$180.00

Three Bedrooms
Ground Floor	$200.00
Second Floor	$230.00
Third Floor	$225.00

The owner has apparently encountered little difficulty in renting the apartments at the higher rates. Ten of the 3-bedrooms have been leased for $230 and 7 for $225. Eight of the 2-bedrooms have been leased for $190 or more and 10 have been leased for $185. When all of the units have been leased at the present rates, the gross rental income at 100% occupancy should be close to $490,000.

FURNISHED APARTMENTS:

Twenty-two of the 201 units are furnished at the present time. The furniture rental ranges from $40 to $55 a month on the 2-bedroom apartments and $63 to $70 a month on the 3-bedroom units. Since the furniture cost was only $800–850 per unit for 2 bedrooms and $900 to $1,000 per unit for 3 bedrooms, the additional rental pays for the furniture in less than 2 years.

The owner has accepted deposits on ten 3-bedroom apartments and one 2-bedroom unit from a group of University students for occupancy September 1. These apartments are to be furnished by the new owner at an estimated total cost of $10,000, but the tenants will be paying the full unfurnished rate plus the furniture rental rate plus $10 per month for each student in excess of 2 in the apartments.

Ordinarily, we prefer to rent apartments unfurnished, as this reduces the tenant turnover. With a total of 33 of the 201 apartments furnished, this ratio is not objectionable, and the additional income will add considerably to the net income.

PRESENT MANAGEMENT:

The owner of the project is primarily a home builder with practically no experience in managing apartment projects. He is operating the property with a Resident Manager, who receives only $125 per month plus her apartment. He has not shown prudence in selecting his tenants and has had to evict several tenants because they were undesirable. His tenant turnover has been above normal for a project of this character.

This property is not being properly maintained at the present time. The lawns need attention which they are not receiving.

These deficiencies can be quickly corrected by competent agency management. We would plan to place the management in the hands of a capable Certified Property Manager who is currently managing some 1,800 apartment units in the area. This man has a well-trained staff equipped to handle leasing and maintenance in an efficient and economical manner.

THE GROUND LEASE:

The project is built on a very favorable 99-year ground lease, renewable forever at a net rental of $16,000 per year. This lease commenced on July 1, 1966. The lessee has $16,000 on deposit with the lessors, but the lease provides that this deposit will be credited against the lease rental at the rate of $666.66 per month ($8,000 per year) starting June 1, 1972.

The ground lease provides that the lessee may purchase the land for $200,000 during the 2-year period commencing June 16, 1973.

This ground lease is a very favorable plus factor in this investment. The option price of $200,000 is very reasonable. By refinancing the mortgage, the purchase of the fee could easily be accomplished without the investor having to provide additional funds.

If inflation continues at its present pace, the $16,000 fixed income will quite probably diminish in its purchasing power to the point where the owner of the fee will be anxious to sell it for much less than the $200,000 option price.

At the closing, this $16,000 deposit will have to be paid to the seller in addition to the purchase price.

INSURANCE:

Seller is currently carrying a 3-year blanket policy written (date) at an annual cost of $9,236. Coverage is:

Fire & Extended Coverage on Building	$2,500,000
Fire & Extended Coverage on Contents	25,000
General Liability $1,000,000 Limits	
Rental Value	344,250
Burglary	10,000
Personal Injury $1,000,000 Limits	

With Workman's Compensation, the estimated total annual insurance cost is $10,000.

FIRST MORTGAGE:

XYZ Life Insurance Company holds the first mortgage, original amount $2,100,000; balance as of June 1 approximately $2,075,000, 7½% interest. Monthly payments of $15,575 ($186,900 per year) pay off the loan completely by June, 1993. Original date of mortgage—September 1, 1968.

Insurance companies are prohibited from lending more than 75% of their appraised value of the property. The loan would indicate that the insurance company appraisers valued the property at not less than $2,800,000.

PREPAYMENT:

The privilege is reserved on prepaying the full balance of principal on any installment due date after 12 years subject to giving not less than 30 nor more than 90 days' prior written notice and to payment of a premium of 5% if prepaid during the first 12 months after this privilege is operative, said premium to reduce at the rate of 1% for each additional 12-month period thereafter, any such premium to be computed upon the balance of principal then outstanding.

ADVANTAGEOUS MORTGAGE INTEREST:

Mortgage financing in today's market would command an interest rate of 8½ to 9% for this property, and probably participate in the earnings as well. The existing mortgage adds value to the investment because of its low-interest (7½%) note.

ESTIMATED INCOME & EXPENSES

INCOME:

Present Rental Income—100% Occupancy		$478,060
Furniture Rental—Actual		12,565
		$490,625
Less: 6% Vacancy Reserve		29,435
Laundry Income—Jan.–March Annualized	$13,095	
Vending Machine Income	360	
Pool Table Revenue—Jan.–March annualized	930	$ 14,385
		$475,575

EXPENSES:

Payroll—Manager	$ 3,600 plus apt.	
—Assistant Manager	— apt. only	
—Maintenance Man	6,500 plus apt.	
—2 Porters @ $3,300	6,600	
	$ 16,700	
Payroll Taxes	1,550	
Staff Apartments (3)	7,380	
Gas & Electricity	63,000	
Water	8,200	
Real Estate Taxes	37,000	
RCA Antenna Service	3,000	
Insurance	10,000	
Advertising	2,400	
Pest Control	540	
Washers & Dryers Service Contract	500	
Maintenance, Repair, & Replacement @ $130 unit	26,130	
Management—5%	23,780	
Land Lease Rental	16,000	216,180

ESTIMATED NET INCOME: $259,395

Less Mortgage Payments:		
1st Mortgage	$186,900	
2nd Mortgage	4,200	$191,100
	$191,100	

CASH FLOW: $ 68,295

PURCHASE PRICE & TERMS:

The owner of the project will sell his equity for $534,000 payable as follows:

Cash	$ 494,000
10-Year 2nd Mortgage at 6%	
Interest (9% constant)	47,000
	$ 541,000
1st Mortgage Balance—approximately	2,075,000
Total Purchase Price	$2,616,000

CASH REQUIRED TO PURCHASE:

To purchase this property outright will require $520,000 cash:

Cash for Equity	$494,000
Refund of $16,000 Deposit on	
99-Year Lease	16,000
	$510,000

As pointed out previously, the $16,000 deposit will be returned to the lessee in a 2-year period starting June 16, 1973.

ANALYSIS OF PRICE:

The price of $2,616,000 for these 201 units computes to $13,014 per unit. Due to the rapid increase in building costs since this property was constructed, today's costs would be considerably higher. Yet the buildings are practically new and partly furnished.

ALLOCATION OF PURCHASE PRICE—$2,616,000:

Land	$ 260,000
Building	2,211,000
Equipment	145,000
TOTAL	$2,616,000

ESTIMATED DEPRECIATION ALLOWANCES:

Comment: Your accountant should be consulted regarding the depreciation method; however, you may want to consider the approach which follows:

Building	$2,211,000—40 years, 150% declining balance
Furniture & Equipment	145,000—10 years, straight-line

DEPRECIATION SCHEDULE

Year	Building	Furniture & Equipment	Total
1	$ 82,900	$ 14,500	$ 97,400
2	79,800	14,500	94,300
3	76,800	14,500	91,300
4	73,900	14,500	88,400
5	71,200	14,500	85,700
6	68,500	14,500	83,000
7	65,900	14,500	80,400
8	63,400	14,500	77,900
9	61,000	14,500	75,500
10	58,800	14,500	73,300
Total	$702,200	$145,000	$847,200

Thus, based on the above depreciation schedule, the investor will have $847,200 of deductions for depreciation during the first 10 years of ownership.

ESTIMATED CAPITAL GAIN WHEN PROPERTY IS SOLD:

After 10 years of ownership, the liberal depreciation allowances which the investor can use to offset income taxes are usually reduced to the point where it will be to the investor's advantage to sell the property and reinvest the proceeds. At that time, the first and second mortgage will have been reduced to about $1,671,000.

Income-producing real estate historically appreciates in value. The steadily increasing demand for prime properties, rising costs of construction, and the inflationary trends which produce higher rents very often make it possible to sell the property after 10 years for a price substantially higher than the investor has paid.

If present inflationary trends continue, the property should be producing more net income at the end of 10 years than it is producing today.

In estimating the resale price, it is assumed that the net income 10 years hence will be the same as it is today, and that the property will be sold, at that time, at the same price paid for it today.

On this very conservative assumption, the client should receive a capital gains profit on resale of the leasehold as follows:

Selling Price of Property	$2,616,000
Mortgages at End of 10 Years	1,671,000
Proceeds from Sale	$ 945,000

Deduct Cash Invested ($510,000 — 16,000) $ 494,000

Estimated Capital Gain on Resale $ 451,000

This estimated profit equals 88.4% on the cash invested, and is in addition to the estimated average annual cash return. The combined yield—cash annually plus annual capital gains profit—is an excellent overall return on the investment.

RECOMMENDATION:

The Realty Company recommends the purchase of this apartment project for the following reasons:

1. The apartments have an excellent location. Their indoor swimming pool with its sauna baths provide recreational features not usually found in garden-type apartments. This should enable the property to maintain a high level of occupancy. The present rentals are very reasonable and under efficient management can be expected to increase.
2. The ground rent of $16,000 per year is only 8% of the $200,-000 recapture price, and this lease can be renewed indefinitely.
3. A stable gross income of $490,625 is projected. Expenses (exclusive of ground rent) are 40.8% of the gross potential income, and cash flow of $68,295 after mortgage payments, provides a return of 13.4% per year.
4. $16,000 of capital will be returned during the 2-year period June, 1973–June, 1975 by reduced ground rent payments.
5. Approximately $847,200 of income and amortization will be sheltered from income taxes because of depreciation allowances.
6. A minimum capital gains profit of $451,000 may be realized if the property is sold after 10 years.
7. The Realty Company's team of investment analysts and Certified Property Managers has carefully inspected this property and have assisted in estimating the operating expenses.

OFFERING NO. 4

This offering is for a combination apartment and office space complex. Essential financial data is as follows:

INCOME:

45 one-bedroom apartments   furnished at $140.00–$195.00 per month
18 one-bedroom apartments unfurnished at $125.00–$160.00 per month
 3 two-bedroom apartments   furnished at $170.00–$200.00 per month
—
66 apartments are now averaging, from owner's latest
        report, $11,000.00 per month $132,000.00

OFFICE SPACE ON GROUND FLOOR LEASED AS FOLLOWS:

Cocktail Lounge	$ 400.00 per month (+ escalator)	
Travel Agency	200.00 per month	
Insurance Co.	145.00 per month	
Building Corp.	135.00 per month	
Doctor	75.00 per month	
Jones 3 Units	130.00 per month	
Smith South Wing	519.00 per month	

$1,604.00 per month   19,248.00

Annual Gross $151,248.00
5% Vacancy & Replacement Allow.   7,562.40

Balance $143,685.60
Miscellaneous Income   1,500.00

GROSS TOTAL $145,185.60

EXPENSES:

Taxes—City and County	$15,553.00
Personal Property Tax	1,369.00
Insurance	1,413.00
Water	1,600.00
Electricity	3,000.00
Pool Service	600.00
Exterminator	400.00
License and Fees	516.00
Garbage Collection	948.00
Air-conditioning Contract	1,050.00
Elevator Contract	330.00
Repairs, Maintenance, & Supplies	4,500.00
Resident Manager	4,800.00 *

* The resident manager expense includes an apartment and salary of $250.00 per month.

Advertising	$ 750.00
Parking Lot Rental	1,200.00
Miscellaneous	1,000.00

Total Expenses	$ 39,029.00

Income Before Debt Service	$106,156.60

EXISTING MORTGAGES:

1st mortgage in approximate balance of $460,000.00 payable $3,618.00 per month including 6% interest until paid (no pre-payment penalty)	$43,416.00
2nd mortgage in approximate balance of $90,000.00 payable $10,000.00 per year including 6% interest until paid ($10,000.00 additional payment required in 10th year of mortgage; no prepayment penalty)	10,000.00
Existing mortgage in approximate balance of $75,000.00 payable $1,000.00 per month including 8% interest until paid (no pre-payment penalty)	12,000.00
Proposed purchase-money mortgage in the approximate amount of $175,000.00 payable $1,531.25 per month including interest at 8%	18,375.00

Debt Service	83,791.00

NET, NET, Cash Flow	$ 22,365.00

PURCHASE PRICE: $950,000.00

Assume 1st Mortgage	$460,000.00
Assume 2nd Mortgage	90,000.00
Assume 3rd Mortgage	75,000.00
Purchase-money Mortgage	175,000.00

Less: Mortgages	800,000.00

Cash Required	$150,000.00

RETURN ON CASH INVESTED OF $150,000.00

$$\frac{22,365.00}{\$150,000.00} = 14.9\%$$

EQUITY ACCUMULATION—1st Year of Purchase:

Amortization	Interest	Principal	Annual Debt Service
1st Mortgage	$26,000.00	$17,416.00	$43,416.00
2nd Mortgage	5,400.00	4,600.00	10,000.00
3rd Mortgage	6,000.00	6,000.00	12,000.00
Purchase-money Mortgage	14,000.00	4,375.00	18,375.00
	$51,400.00	$32,391.00	$83,791.00

$$\frac{32,391.00}{150,000.00} = 21.5\%$$

RETURN FIRST YEAR   36.4%
(Cash Plus Equity Accumulation)

PROPERTY PROJECTIONS

Projection of: _____
Prepared for: _____

DEPRECIATION COMPUTATION

Allocation of Basis $ 950,000.00

	%	Allocation	Life	Method	First Year
Land	6	57,000.00			
Improvements	79	750,000.00	25	150%(6%)	45,030.00
Personal Property	15	142,500.00	5	150%(30%)	42,750.00
First-year Depreciation					$ 87,780.00

TAXABLE INCOME

Maximum Gross Annual Receipts		$152,748.00
Less: Vacancy Allowance—5%		7,562.00
Income Before Operating Expenses		145,186.00
Less: Operating Expenses		39,029.00
Net Operating Income		106,157.00
Less: Interest	$51,400.00	
Depreciation	87,780.00	139,180.00
Taxable Income (Loss)		$(33,023.00)

NET SPENDABLE INCOME

Net Operating Income	$106,156.00
Less: Principal and Interest Payments	83,791.00
Spendable Income Before Tax LESS: Federal Income Tax or Saving	22,365.00
Taxable Income (Loss) ($33,023.00) Tax Saving @ 50 % Bracket	16,511.00
Net Spendable Income	$ 38,876.00

RETURN ON INVESTMENT

Net Spendable Income	$ 38,876.00
PLUS: Principal Payment	32,391.00
Return on Investment	$ 71,267.00
Percentage Return on $ 150,000.00 Investment	47.5%

GUIDELINES FOR DEPRECIATION

LAND IMPROVEMENTS:

20 years—5%.

LAND IMPROVEMENTS INCLUDE:

Paved surfaces, sidewalks, canals, drainage facilities and sewers, bridges, fences, landscaping, shrubbery.

BUILDINGS:

Includes the structural shell of the building and all integral parts thereof; includes equipment which services normal heating, plumbing, air conditioning, fire-prevention and power requirements, and equipment such as elevators and escalators.

Type of Building	Life Years	Percentage
Apartments	40	2.5 %
Banks	50	2.0
Dwellings	45	2.222
Factories	45	2.222
Garages	45	2.222

Grain Elevators	60	1.667
Hotels	40	2.5
Loft Buildings	50	2.0
Machine Shops	45	2.222
Office Buildings	45	2.222
Stores	50	2.0
Theaters	40	2.5
Warehouses	60	1.667

COMPOSITE METHOD

Under this method, the depreciation rate used each year represents the average rate that the entire improvement is wasting. Although the foundation, roof, painting, electrical and plumbing systems all wear out at different rates, one average rate is estimated.

If an apartment building was valued at $100,000.00 for the improvements and straight-line (S/L) depreciation is used, under the composite method, taking an average life of the building to be 25 years, the depreciation rate would be 4% per year, or $4,000.00 the first year.

COMPONENT METHOD

Sometimes, you may be able to justify higher depreciation allowances by using components rather than the entire asset considered as a unit.

As an example:

Item	Cost	Life	S/L %	S/L Depr.
Shell of Building	$ 40,000.00	40 years	2½	$1,000.00
Roof	5,000.00	10	10	500.00
Elevator	10,000.00	12½	8	800.00
Plumbing	15,000.00	12½	8	1,200.00
Electrical	15,000.00	10	10	1,500.00
Heating	7,500.00	10	10	750.00
Air Conditioning	7,500.00	12½	8	600.00
	$100,000.00			$6,350.00

GARDEN APARTMENTS
PROPOSED JOINT VENTURE

Assume developers have purchased 35 acres of land at a good location and propose to build 406 garden apartments in two phases. The first phase will include 192 apartments on 17 acres as follows:

102 One-Br. (700 sq ft) @ $145.00 per month
38 Two-Br. 2-bath Gardens (1,020 sq ft) @ $195.00 per month
52 Two-Br. 1½-bath Townhouses (1,120 sq ft) @ $220.00 per month

Construction costs for the first phase are estimated as follows:

Apartment Building:	166,736 sq ft	
	@ $9.50/sq ft	$1,584,000
Clubhouse:	4,000 sq ft	
	@ $8.00/sq ft	32,000
Site Preparation and Landscaping		125,000
Paving		28,000
Pool and Tennis Courts		22,125
Interest during Construction, Legal and		
Closing Fees		140,000
		$1,931,125
Land		218,875
Total		$2,150,000

The financing approach is for a life insurance company to make a loan of 100% of cost, $2,150,000, for one-half of the equity. This would require funding the initial land purchase of $218,875 at the front end with the remaining $1,931,125 paid out on completion in 18 months. The developers are general contractors and are entitled to 5% construction overhead but no development fees.

The remaining 18 acres are covered by a purchase-money mortgage of $200,000, at 8% interest, payable at $2,166 per month for 12 years. This debt is subordinated and could be paid off or left to amortize when the second stage is developed.

It is proposed that the life insurance company make a loan of $2,150,000 at 8½% interest for a term of 25 years. The life insurance company would receive one-half of the equity at the front end. It is anticipated that cash flows will increase the yield to the life insurance company to 9½% the first year plus equity build-up plus tax shelter. Title should be taken in a form which will permit cash flows and tax benefits to flow directly to the venturers.

A pro forma income and expense statement for the venture might appear as follows:

INCOME: 102 1-Br. 1-Bath Units @ $145.00/mo $177,480
38 2-Br. 2-Bath Units @ $195.00/mo   88,920
52 2-Br. Townhouse Units @ $220.00/mo 137,280

Gross Income		$403,680
Less: Vacancy Allowance (5%)		20,190
Gross Dependable Income		$383,490
EXPENSES: Taxes	$35,520	
Insurance	5,400	
Management Fee (6%)	23,010	
Repairs & Maintenance	6,130	
Electric (Public Space)	4,600	
Water	4,400	
Janitor	10,000	
Painting & Decorating	12,225	
Replacement Reserve	12,960	
Carpeting Reserve	11,700	
Miscellaneous	6,000	131,945
NET INCOME:		$251,545
DEBT SERVICE: $2,150,000 @ 8½%, 25 Years		
(9.67 annual constant)		207,905
CASH FLOW:		$ 43,640

THE DETACHED-HOUSE CONDOMINIUM *

An increasingly popular housing concept in Florida is the single-family, detached-house condominium. It is a departure from the typical residential condominiums—namely, low-rise and high-rise apartments and townhouses. The new development involves the construction of free-standing private residences which are clustered or scattered around a common lawn and which are marketed under the condominium form of ownership (Figure 1). The one-family variation is relatively new, and its origin is generally attributed to a Sarasota builder who has enjoyed tremendous sales success with it since 1966. Numerous builders in Florida are now using the concept, primarily for the retirement market, and it is likely that the idea is already being used in other states.

Condominium itself, as a form of legal ownership of real property, is not new. It is complete ownership of an individual living unit, such as an apartment or a townhouse, and fractional ownership with other persons in the project of the common areas or elements of the project.

* This section originally appeared as an article in Economic Leaflets, Vol. XXVI, No. 12 (Gainesville, Florida: Bureau of Economic and Business Research, University of Florida, 1967).

Common areas and facilities are set forth in the legal instruments establishing the condominium and these items may vary among projects.

Specific statutory provision for condominium ownership in Florida is given in the Florida Condominium Act, Florida Statutes, Chapter 711 (1963). Actually, condominiums created by contract existed in Florida before the passage of the Condominium Act, and these projects were satisfactorily financed and sold, even though no state statute specifically authorizing such form of ownership existed. Widespread practical acceptance of the concept by developers, lenders, and title insurance companies, however, required a state law which would give statutory recognition to the condominium form of ownership of real property. The Condominium Act was passed by the legislature and now provides the legal basis for this form of ownership. Where the term "statute" is used elsewhere in this [discussion], it refers to the Florida Condominium Act unless otherwise noted.

Instruments Needed to Establish

Even though the condominium form of ownership is receiving increasingly widespread use, there is no such thing as a typically routine condominium transaction. Therefore, the specific documents must be prepared individually to fit each project. Further, the condominium is a detailed and technical legal arrangement, with individual states having their own condominium statutes which set forth differing requirements. It is essential that the developer seek competent legal counsel and other professional assistance in the early stages of a proposed project. Attorneys, surveyors, architects, financial institutions, property insurance companies, and title insurance companies may be involved in the transaction, so it is highly desirable that all possible parties be consulted in advance in order to avoid later delays and difficulties.

The three basic instruments generally used in a condominium are: the declaration of condominium, the bylaws, and the deeds to the individual units. The declaration of condominium describes the project in detail and may be said to be the heart of the project. This instrument is discussed further in the following section. The bylaws provide for the government of the condominium and set out rules of operation for the property. Members' meetings, directors and officers, fiscal management, voting rights, and matters of procedure are typical items which might be found in the bylaws. Owners receive fee titles to their respective units and an undivided interest in the common areas by means of warranty deeds.

Declaration of Condominium

As mentioned above, the declaration of condominium is the basic legal instrument which describes the project in detail. While the declaration must be individually tailored for each project, the Florida statute sets forth a procedure for the creation of condominiums and specifies certain minimal requirements which must be met. These minimum provisions are designed to protect unit owners against the possible omission of essential items from the condominium instruments. They are also designed to give definite and clear authority for the powers and duties of the legal entity operating the condominium—that is, the association.

Essentially, the statute provides that the declaration must: be properly executed; contain a statement submitting the condominium property to condominium ownership; properly identify the property by name, legal description of the land, identification of the units, and include a survey, plot plan, and a graphic description of improvements (permanent structures and betterments) so that all aspects of the property may be tied together; set forth the undivided shares, stated as percentages or fractions, in the common elements which are appurtenant to each of the units; set forth the proportions or percentages and manner of sharing common expenses and owning common surplus; and set forth the name of the association and whether or not it is incorporated. Further provisions may be included in the declaration so long as they are not inconsistent with the statute.

A discussion of several important typical provisions of a declaration follows. . . .

PHYSICAL UNIT. An exact description of what constitutes a physical unit is essential. This term apparently may refer to any part of the condominium property which is to be subject to private ownership. A description might provide, for example, that the unit consist of the space bounded by the surface of the outside finished walls, and from the peak of the roof and include the roof overhang, eaves, windowsill, porches, stoops, all projecting, integral parts of the structure, the attached carport, and the portion of any enclosed courtyard lying within the boundaries of the unit extended. The physical unit is further identified by a survey and plot plan attached to the declaration which locates the improvements and identifies each unit and the common elements and their relative locations and approximate dimensions.

COMMON ELEMENTS. The illustrative declaration provides that a condominium unit automatically carries with it an undivided share of the common elements and the right to use the common elements in conjunction with the owners of the other units. Common elements set forth include: the easements through condominium units for conduits, ducts, plumbing, wiring, and other facilities for furnishing the utilities services to the various condominium units and the condominium elements; any utility room and all utility services which are available to more than one unit; any and all recreational devices and areas; all lawn and planting areas, private streets, driveways, and sidewalks, excluding enclosed courtyards, and all other land and improvements not included within the definition of a unit as set forth in the declaration.

Reference should be made to the statute for an enumeration of certain common elements. This listing, however, does not prohibit the declaration from setting forth other parts as common elements. It is possible that some common elements may be designated as "limited" if they are to be reserved for the use of a particular unit or units to the exclusion of other units. Garden plots or use of certain vehicle parking areas, for example, might be limited to particular units. Such limited common elements should, of course, be clearly designated as such in the declaration.

PERCENTAGE OF OWNERSHIP AND COMMON EXPENSES. The percentage of ownership and the individual shares of the respective condominium units in the common elements, and the manner of sharing common expenses and owning common surplus may be prorated on two bases. One plan is to prorate according to the value of the individual unit and its relation to the total value of the project. Another plan is to prorate on a unit basis. If there are twelve similar units in a project, for example, then each unit's ownership and share of common expenses is one-twelfth. Such arbitrary assignment of equal shares to units is usually acceptable to buyers when there is a high degree of similarity among units. Other variations and methods of determining the share in the common elements are possible. The statute does not set forth a method which must be used—only that some method must be given in the declaration. The method must be reasonable, of course, if it is to be saleable and accepted in the market.

Certain common expenses are listed in the statute but the list is not exclusive. The declaration or the bylaws may set forth any expense to be designated as common. Our illustrative declaration, for example, states common expenses to include: the cost of maintenance and repair of the common area; fire and liability insurance; costs of management of the condominium; administrative costs of the association responsible for the operation of the condominium; costs of water, electricity, and other utilities (not metered to specific condominium units) and supplies used in connection with the common elements; and any other costs duly incurred by the association to operate, protect, manage, and conserve the condominium property.

ASSOCIATION. An association is established to be responsible for the operation of the condominium. The association is recognized by statute as a legal entity, either profit or nonprofit, and may be incorporated or unincorporated. Unit owners must be members of the association regardless of its form of organization, and the declaration for any project usually has a provision to the effect that all persons owning a vested present interest in the fee title to any of the condominium units shall automatically be members of the association.

The powers and duties of the association are usually set forth in the declaration and bylaws. Certain stated powers are also available under statute, unless these are not desired, in which case they may be expressly prohibited by the declaration or bylaws. Generally, the association, through its board of directors, exclusively controls all of the affairs and property of the condominium. The board of directors is usually elected annually by the association members with each unit owner having one vote. Typically, the board consists of not less than three nor more than five members.

The developer of a condominium will usually want to maintain his right to the management of the affairs of the condominium and to all decisions of the association until all of the contemplated improvements are completed and the sales of all units have been closed, or until a specified date, or until the developer elects to terminate his control. Such rights of the developer may be assured by specification in the declaration and bylaws. Also, effective assurance may be had simply by naming the first board of directors and then deferring for a reasonable time the first election of directors.

The maintenance of the common areas is by statute the responsibility of the association. Considerable experience with such associations of home owners and their handling of the maintenance of common areas has been accumulated. Several factors have become generally accepted as being essential for the success of these associations:

1. some form of prorata assessment of unit owners for costs, with the association having the power to adjust the assessments as needed as well as having the power to enforce the assessments by means of a lien on individual units;
2. the association's definite responsibility for maintenance, taxes, and liability insurance on the common elements;
3. perpetual restrictions on the open space;
4. mandatory membership in the association for each unit purchaser and his successors; and
5. the creation and existence of the association prior to the sale of any units. All of these considerations are usually provided for either in the statute, declaration, bylaws, and deeds to individual units or in all of these sources.

MAINTENANCE AND REPAIRS. The respective responsibilities of unit owners and of the association for maintenance and repairs of units and common elements are, of course, of primary importance. The statute places the responsibility for maintenance of the common elements on the association. The illustrative declaration provides that each unit owner must maintain everything within the confines of his unit in good condition and repair. All plumbing, electrical, heating and air-conditioning, appliance, masonry, carpentry, exterior wall, and roof repairs, and repair or replacement of windows, screens, or doors with respect to an individual unit are made by the unit owner. All repairs and replacements which are visible from the exterior of the unit must be identical to the original items so as to maintain a harmonious appearance with the remaining improvements in the condominium.

No owner is permitted to paint any exterior wall, door, window, patio, or any exterior surface, or plant any planting, or erect any exterior lights, or erect or attach any structures or fixtures within the common elements, or to make any structural additions or alterations to any unit or to the common elements, without the prior written consent of the association.

If an owner fails to maintain or repair his condominium unit properly, the association, at its discretion, may make the necessary repairs and assess the cost against the defaulting unit owner. The association has a lien against any unit for the cost of any repairs it makes to the unit plus interest and a reasonable attorney's fee incurred in the collection of the costs.

Each unit owner in the illustrative condominium pays for all utilities which are separately metered to his unit. This, of course, could vary among different projects.

The association is responsible for the maintenance and repair of all the common elements, including all driveways, and for painting of the exterior walls and roof surfaces of the units. It also determines the landscaping, exterior color scheme and decoration, and exterior lighting of all buildings and improvements. The association must maintain the landscaping and exterior appearances of all of the condominium property in first-class condition. To accomplish its maintenance responsibilities, it may employ part-time or full-time agents or contractors.

ASSESSMENTS AND LIABILITY. The expenses of maintaining the common elements are provided for by assessing the unit owners. The assessments are made in proportions or percentages of shared common expenses provided for in the declaration.

The statute sets forth certain provisions concerning the personal liability of unit owners for assessments. The entire question of liability, however, is quite technical and complicated and requires competent legal counsel. Such questions as the following illustrate liability issues which may arise: When does liability for an assessment begin? What is the liability of a mortgagee or other purchaser of a unit at a legal foreclosure sale for unpaid assessments? What is the liability of a decedent's estate for assessments unpaid at death? What is the effect of recording and the priority of claims? How may claims against the association and individual unit owners be collected? These are obviously matters which address themselves to attorneys and are presented here to illustrate and emphasize the necessity for such counsel in the establishment of a condominium.

INTEREST LIABILITY. The statute establishes a liability for interest on assessments that are not paid when due. The interest rate is set forth in the declaration. It, of course, must not exceed the legal rate of interest in the state.

DESTRUCTION, RECONSTRUCTION, AND INSURANCE. A declaration might provide that each unit owner must maintain fire and extended coverage insurance upon all of the insurable improvements included in his respective unit for its full replacement value. The coverage must be with a responsible insurance company satisfactory to the association. The association is named as loss payee of the policy. In the event an owner fails to maintain such insurance, the association may insure the unit and assess the cost thereof against the defaulting owner.

Further, the association must maintain fire and extended coverage insurance upon all insurable improvements in the common elements, and the premium for such coverage is assessed against the unit owners as part of the common expenses. The association has authority to compromise and settle all claims against its insurance carrier. The original policy of insurance covering the common elements is held by the association and the institutional first mortgagees are furnished mortgagee endorsements covering their respective interest.

The declaration will usually further specify that in the event of a destruction or casualty loss to any of the improvements, all insurance proceeds payable under the respective unit owner's policies or the association's policies are collected by the association treasurer and immediately paid over to the designated banking corporation of the association in the county of the subject property. The proceeds are held by such bank in trust to be used for the immediate repair and reconstruction of the damaged improvements.

In the event of the substantial destruction of more than one-half of the condominium improvements, the improvements are to be restored with the insurance proceeds, unless two-thirds of the membership of the association vote to terminate the condominium. In the event the condominium is terminated, all owners of units must convey their right, title, and interest to their respective units to the bank trustee to be held in trust. The trustee then collects all insurance proceeds payable as a result of such destruction, collects all assets of the association which may remain after the association pays its liabilities, and effects a sale of the condominium property, by whatever means it deems best, for the highest and best price consistent with market conditions.

After payment of reasonable trustee's fees and costs reasonably incurred, the trustee apportions the remaining funds in its hands among the unit owners in accordance with their respective percentage of ownership. Holders of mortgages and other liens encumbering any unit are first to receive a distribution of each owner's share of the funds.

The above illustration of typical and rather detailed provisions in a declaration concerning insurance and the handling of insurance proceeds in case of loss points out the necessity for specific instructions on these matters. There are simply too many items for possible disagreement for the matter to be left to voluntary discretion, although even with the best of instructions decisions must often be a matter of judgment. All units must be insured so that adequate funds will be available in case of loss. Further, such funds must be definitely available if any reconstruction after a loss is to proceed. It is only appropriate, therefore, that all policies be made payable to the insurance trustee and held for the benefit of the unit owners, the lenders, and the association.

RESTRICTIONS, EASEMENTS, AND APPURTENANCES. Certain restrictions may apply to the condominium and each condominium unit, some obviously tailored to particular owner populations. Typical provisions may provide that: only one-family residences are permitted on the premises; no children may reside in a unit for longer than 30 days in any calendar year; nothing may be done by a unit owner which would increase his insurance rates; each owner has a perpetual easement for ingress and egress to and from his unit over steps, terraces, walkways, lawns, driveways, and other common elements from and to the public or private roadways bounding the condominium property; no unit owner or occupant may in any way obstruct way of ingress or egress to the other units or to the common elements; consent of the association is required for such things as pets, signs, exterior clothes lines, antennas, wires, garbage receptacles, and the subdivision or structural alteration of a condominium unit; and no noises or odors are permissible which are objectional or obnoxious.

SALE, TRANSFER, LEASE, OR OCCUPATION OF UNIT. The association must approve all sales, transfers, leases, or occupation of a unit in advance of the transfer. A lessee may not assign his lease or sublet his unit without prior approval of the association. Such restriction on the transfer of units is deemed desirable in order to maintain a community of congenial residents who are financially responsible and to protect the value of the units and of the project. The manner of handling the sale of a unit as prescribed in one declaration is offered as an example. Patterns may differ, of course, for other declarations.

First, the unit owner gives the association notice of intent to sell which cites the name and address of the intended buyer and other reasonable information desired by the association. The owner may also include a demand that the association furnish a purchaser if it does not approve the proposed purchaser. Approval or disapproval by the association must be given within 30 days after receipt of notice. A certificate is issued which will be recorded if approval is granted.

If the association disapproves a transfer of ownership of a unit, it must deliver to the owner within 30 days an agreement to purchase the unit which is signed by a purchaser approved by the association. The unit owner must sell to this purchaser upon certain specified terms as set forth in the declaration. If the association fails to provide a purchaser, or if a purchaser provided by the association defaults in his agreement to purchase, the association is then deemed to have given approval to the original transfer of ownership and must issue a certificate of approval. If the proposed transaction is a lease, the unit owner is advised in writing of the association's disapproval and the lease is not completed.

RIGHT OF INSTITUTIONAL FIRST MORTGAGES. Institutional lenders which hold first mortgages upon any units, such as savings-and-loan associations, banks, and insurance companies, usually require that their written consent be obtained before the condominium performs certain actions. Typical actions might be: (1) the subdivision of any condominium unit; (2)

any change in the percentage of ownership of the common elements or of the common surplus; (3) any change in the percentage of participation of the common expenses or assessments; (4) any amendments to the declaration or to the bylaws; or (5) termination of the condominium.

TERMINATION. Our illustrative declaration provides that the property may be removed from the provisions of the declaration at any time by the vote of two-thirds of the units and unanimous consent of all of the institutional holders of first mortgages. Other forms of declarations may, of course, specify other procedures for termination. The termination instruments must be properly drawn, executed, and recorded. After termination, the owners possess the condominium property as tenants in common in undivided shares that are the same as the undivided shares of the owners in the common elements prior to the termination.

AMENDMENTS. A declaration must provide a method for its amendment. A typical method provides for amendment at any time by an affirmative vote of a given percentage (one declaration required a 66 percent vote, while another required an 85 percent vote) of all the condominium units. There are, of course, appropriate limitations on the amendment power, as in the following declaration: "No amendment shall discriminate against any unit owner or owners without their consent; no amendment shall change any unit nor its share in the common elements, nor increase the owner's share of the common expenses, unless the owner and the mortgage holder on the unit or units join in the execution of the amendment; and, record owners of all mortgages upon the condominium must join in the execution of any amendment which changes the provisions pertaining to insurance coverage and the handling of insurance proceeds, reconstruction, and repair after casualty." One declaration also prohibited the amendment at any time of certain easements necessary to the overall utilization of the project, such as paved roads and driveways, utility easements, and drainage areas. In addition, unanimous vote of all units is necessary to change the voting rights of the unit owners.

Saleable Features

The single-family, detached-house condominium offers numerous attractive features to the developer, the investor, the lender, and the occupant. Many of these attractions are not necessarily limited to this particular use of the concept but may be characteristic of the condominium form of ownership in general. Nor are all of these features necessarily an "advantage" of this form of housing over other forms of housing, since the latter can have some of the same features. The points which follow are simply an enumeration of the features of the single-family, detached-house condominium which have been found attractive either to the developer, the investor, the lender, the occupant, or all of these groups, and have thereby become saleable items. There is no ranking of importance of individual items in relation to each other.

Ease of maintenance is an especially attractive feature; maintenance and yard work are not a personal problem. Common areas—landscaping, lawn, gardens, patio, and pool—are all maintained for a monthly fee, as are the exteriors of the building. The common maintenance also involves less work with a resulting lower cost. It is more economical to use one professional maintenance service to handle all of the units than to use one man for each unit.

The single-family, detached-house condominium may take the form of a duplex or quadruplex with the units arranged in a cluster pattern rather than in a row pattern. The cluster arrangement permits the grouping of the houses in a rather close semicircle around a common green or recreation area. Builders are able to open up large common greens for recreation facilities (whose upkeep and maintenance does not fall individually on the buyers) and at the same time offer lower land costs per unit. The condominium and cluster development results in a maximum utilization of the land with corresponding costs reduction to all parties.

The single-family, detached-house condominium units are taxed separately, and each is entitled, in Florida, to the full $5,000 homestead exemption. Because each unit receives its own property tax bill, these ad valorem taxes are, of course, allowable income tax deductions. Also, since each unit is taxed individually, the default of one taxpayer does not have potentially so serious a consequence as if the tax bill were simply on the entire property, as in the case of a stock cooperative project. A high vacancy rate in the latter, for example, could cause the remaining owners to lose their units because of their inability to meet the entire tax bill on the building as a whole.

Better locations are possible with the condominium because of the possibility of a more efficient land use; more expensive land can be purchased and developed and an attractive rate of return may still be maintained. In fact, most developers seek out the better tracts of land for their projects, even though the initial cost is greater. The better location usually results in a more saleable project.

The condominium may offer the buyer amenities and luxuries which might otherwise be beyond his means, such as a golf course, a view of the ocean or a lake, a swimming pool, or an attractive recreation area. In addition, he may receive more housing for his money, since the percentage of land cost in relation to the total cost of the unit tends to be less than the percentage for a single-family dwelling. A residential lot, for example, might represent 20 to 25 percent of the total cost of an average property, whereas in a condominium it usually would tend to be less, perhaps around 10 to 15 percent.

The single-family, detached-house condominium gives its owners many of the usually claimed advantages of home ownership. In addition to the homestead exemption, such features would include the possibility of building up an equity, the possibility of appreciation, a hedge against inflation, and the possibility of lower cost of ownership as compared with renting.

There is also the possibility that an owner can custom-design his own unit, thus adding to the usual intangible factor of satisfaction that comes from owning one's own property.

There are financial advantages of condominium ownership both to the lender and to the unit owner. Excellent long-term financing is usually available to purchasers, which reflects the favorable acceptance by lending institutions of the condominium concept. Conventional financing up to approximately 80 percent of the purchase price for a 24-year period at the current market rate of interest is usually available. The availability of numerous financial arrangements and loan sources gives the unit owner a degree of flexibility in financing his initial purchase as well as in any resale, since the condominium can be refinanced. The condominium loan is also usually attractive to lenders. Each unit carries its own mortgage and promissory note. While the mortgage risk is concentrated in one area, it is nevertheless spread over many borrowers, each of whom is personally liable for his own debt. Each homeowner has the usual pride of ownership and would hesitate to lose his unit through foreclosure; the "moral risk" is generally good.

Individual condominium loans naturally result in increased cost, paper work, and time for the lender as contrasted, say, with a single loan on an entire property. However, once the lender has spent considerable time and expense with a developer on the initial package of condominium papers for a given project, it is highly probable that the developer will stay with the lender not only for the construction money but for the permanent financing on the individual units. The increased cost may be offset with a service charge which the borrower will pay as an item of closing costs for his loan. Further, the lender stands to gain from possible refinancing opportunities as ownership of the individual units changes in future years.

Possible Limitations

The condominium concept is essentially sound and has been generally accepted in the market by buyers as well as by lenders. The possible limitations to the concept are largely technical in nature and are of primary concern to lawyers, title insurance companies, real estate appraisers, and institutional lenders. This is not to say that they are not also of great importance to owners and potential buyers.

It is possible that the matter of maintenance could be a source of disagreement in a condominium project. There may be a question concerning the extent to which an association can legally enforce a set of maintenance regulations on all of the unit owners. In addition, there could be disagreement among the unit owners as to the desirable degree of needed maintenance. If some owners did not participate in the common maintenance, the marketability of the entire project could be impaired.

Possible solutions to these problems, however, will no doubt be developed as operating experience is accumulated and as the courts render decisions in individual cases. Lenders have expressed some concern about the possibility of common areas falling into disrepair. No individual unit owner can by himself proceed to prevent neglect of the common areas. The lender, of course, can declare the mortgage in default due to lack of maintenance, but this does not appear to be a practical solution and may not be an enforceable solution.

The condominium units may have utilities metered separately to each unit. It is possible that such an arrangement would be more expensive as contrasted with the bulk-rate cost available for a single meter to an entire project.

Experience has shown that one condominium project may be accepted by the market while another only a short distance away may be rejected. The failure lies not in the concept of condominium but in its application. A condominium is like any other real estate development with respect to the importance of certain vital features. The location must be right or the project will fail. A proper location, tied in with the proper price and proper benefits, should attract purchasers. Amenities and "extras" may occasionally minimize the market consequences of a poor location but seldom will entirely overcome it.

A project competes with local rental units and existing single-family homes and, therefore, must offer good value to the buyers. The condominium concept will not sell if the project is inferior. It should offer the latest in amenities. Something new may well convince the apartment dweller to quit renting or may lure the owner out of his present home. The developer should be well established, experienced, and should have enough equity to carry the project through to completion. Further, he should know how to conduct an effective sales program. He must know his local market and the product which will satisfy the demand.

The cluster idea is basically sound and has the potential to be successful. Layout standards generally have been high, but it is questionable whether such quality will continue to predominate as an increasing number of developers utilize the concept. Cluster, of course, achieves higher density on a given site than conventional row or gridiron patterns; this is the primary attraction to developers who are faced with continually rising land costs. The open space of the surrounding area creates the setting for the clustered housing units. A proper balance between density and open space is essential for a pleasant living environment. Developers who tend to create unreasonable density on a site by reducing the size of the open area defeat the benefits of the cluster idea. The "open space" becomes a cramped enclosure.

Also, as cluster developers increasingly utilize the detached house on relatively small sites, there is a tendency toward standardization of unit design and layout (although a variety of interior floor plans is usually offered). The objective, of course, is to create a uniform and harmonious appearance of the cluster. There is a danger, however, that as these standardized units and layouts multiply and as the volume use by imitators leads to lesser quality, a uniform monotony will be created as unattractive as some of the gridiron patterns which presently dot the landscape. Exterior design and the relationship of one unit to another in the cluster are very important considerations which require imaginative and expert planning.

Prices and Promotion

The single-family, detached-house condominium is available in a wide range of prices from approximately $11,000 upwards to $90,000 and more. The majority of the single-family, detached-house condominiums built thus far in Florida, however, have been for the retirement market and range in price from around $11,000 to $20,000.

One typical project, for example, offers a choice of five house plans whose relative size may be estimated from the number of bedrooms and baths:

Plan A	one bedroom, one bath	$15,450
Plan B	two bedrooms, one bath	17,950
Plan B-2	two bedrooms, two baths	18,750
Plan C	two bedrooms, two baths	19,450
Plan D	two bedrooms, two baths	19,250

These prices include landscaping, walks, driveways, yard lighting, undivided interest in pool, patio furniture and equipment, and, of course, a fee title to the property plus an undivided interest in the area used in common, such as the gardens, ramada, and pool. Kitchens are equipped with oven, range, counter, and sinks. All units in this project have garbage disposals and plumbing and have installed the wiring for dishwasher, washer, dryer, and refrigerator. These latter appliances are not included in the price nor are carpet, draperies, and furniture. Practice may vary among projects, of course, as to what equipment is included in the price.

Long-term, conventional financing is available to unit purchasers in this project. Approximately 80 percent of the purchase price may be financed for a 24-year period. The financing schedule is as follows:

Plan	Down Payment	Loan Amount	Monthly Payment
A	$3,150	$12,300	$ 82.57
B	3,650	14,300	95.99
B-2	3,750	15,000	100.68
C	3,950	15,500	104.04
D	3,850	15,400	103.37

Each owner pays his own real estate taxes on his individual unit and property and may receive a homestead exemption if he qualifies by making Florida his legal residence. Assuming the presence of homestead exemption, the estimated taxes in this project are:

Plan A	$14.00 per month
Plan B	17.50 per month
Plan B-2	18.50 per month
Plan C	19.00 per month
Plan D	18.75 per month

The owners' association of the project is responsible for negotiating a maintenance contract with a management company which provides professional management and is responsible for a single, all-inclusive maintenance to owners. This maintenance is intended to insure to owners the full and active use of the roads, streets, sidewalks, swimming pool, grounds, and utilities, and to keep deterioration to the lowest level possible which is consistent with good maintenance practices.

The monthly maintenance fee of $45 per unit includes the following services: cleaning and maintaining the swimming pool; maintaining and fertilizing the lawn; trimming, pruning, and spraying trees, and watering and replacing plants as needed; daily service of outside lighting, grounds, sidewalks, roads, and so forth; pest control on outside of buildings; the cost of all electric and water bills for the exterior lights, of water for pool and landscaping; liability insurance for common areas; painting of outside of buildings on a periodic basis; spray cleaning roofs of buildings on a periodic basis; and trash and garbage collection.

Promotion of projects usually stresses the numerous amenities or factors which contribute to enjoyable living—the pleasant atmosphere of open space and carefree living. Excellence of design and location and the uniform high quality of the maintenance of grounds and buildings are pointed out as factors which guarantee property values for the future and make for a secure investment. Social and recreational benefits are emphasized. The significance of detached units is emphasized as enabling custom design, privacy, low noise transmission, and an unobstructed view of the gardens and recreation area where the cluster concept is employed.

The cluster concept itself is often promoted through several appeals to the buyer in addition to the idea of condominium. Cluster is cited as being the "modern" kind of housing—the new way of living to which everyone should aspire. The group living—friendly neighbors and a self-governing association of unit owners—is stressed. The combining of privacy with togetherness is an attempt to gather the advantages of two opposite consumer wants. Also pointed out is the safety of the protected recreational opportunities in the common area and the absence of heavily traveled streets.

Promotional media for projects almost always includes an illustrated brochure. In the case of the lower-priced projects designed primarily for the retirement market, the brochure will stress, in addition to the above features, the following items: practicability of group costing with the added benefits of mass manufacturing and planning; all-inclusive care; recreational facilities on premises or adjacent to such facilities; master television and FM antennas; central air conditioning and heating; guest parking; separate storage; and proximity to shopping areas.

The promotional brochure of an illustrative upper-price project stresses the "definite appeal to conservative and discriminating people." Reasons given to support this appeal include the following: congenial people of compatible taste and culture; a location that is immune from encroachment and only a short distance from local shopping and other facilities; privacy; membership in an exclusive, private club on the premises; care-free living through year-round maintenance service and regular inspection when unit owner is not in residence; availability of ocean beach; underground utilities for greater safety and preservation of natural beauty of the landscape; availability of golf cottages and club suites; lakes and waterways which are navigable by large yachts; a complete turnkey architectural and building service; and the appeal of an existing established community which is available for inspection.

The Outlook

The single-family, detached-house condominium is basically a new marketing idea for an existing ownership concept that has already been generally accepted by the buying public. The single-family twist to the condominium concept is rapidly spreading in Florida and is no doubt being developed in other states. The majority of detached houses built thus far in Florida have been for the retirement market, but the concept is capable of being used to tap the market of younger families with children. Projects which are soundly conceived, soundly financed, and properly marketed should find ready market acceptance for the foreseeable future.

The adaptation of the condominium concept to the detached single-family house represents another forward step in the ever-growing number of ways of using the concept to meet the housing needs of our increasing population.

THE SINGLE-FAMILY HOUSE

Acquisition of a single-family house for investment purposes may take one of several or a combination of forms: (1) purchase for holding and rental and possible eventual resale, even though rental income is the primary objective; (2) speculative purchase for immediate resale at a profit, usually after a minimum of necessary rehabilitation and perhaps some modernization; or (3) purchase of older houses for extensive rehabilitation, remodeling, and modernization, and their resale at a profit.

RISK REDUCTION FACTORS

The single-family house is generally considered to be an undesirable investment, although some investors have been quite successful with it. It is a speculative and specialized activity, and while there are no set rules to follow, the factors listed below will tend to reduce the risks and help to insure success:

1. The investor should know something about construction and repair work on houses and be able to hire subcontractors and supervise all work on the house. Contracting out repair work can be expensive, and considerable money can be saved if the investor is handy with tools and enjoys such work.
2. Be prepared to spend time and give attention to the property or be willing and able to hire a professional management firm to perform this function. Tenants must be carefully selected, and prompt attention should be given to their service requests. Constant supervision is necessary for preventive maintenance.
3. Rehabilitation and remodeling costs must be accurately estimated as well as the market value of the house after the work is completed. The market must be able to absorb the renovated house at a price profitable to the investor. Costs and value estimations require experience and good judgment.
4. Know the market. Along with costs, know locations, neighborhoods (need not be the best, but at least a fairly good one which has declined somewhat), values (prices on new and existing houses), rentals (competitive rentals, especially in new apartment houses which will compete with the single-family house), type of housing in demand, and appreciation potential.
5. Know financing sources and plans and how to apply them advantageously. Federal agency programs, such as FHA, offer a variety of loan programs dealing with residential and rental property. Also, for the experienced investor, bank credit and supplier credit is available.
6. Keep within reason on rehabilitation, remodeling, and modernization;

do not overdo it, and avoid frills. Make the house livable and presentable and within reason for the area. Costs of an overimprovement are seldom recovered.

7. Before buying, check out such things as property taxes, availability and costs of hazard insurance, and local government safety, health, and zoning regulations as they apply to rental property. Be careful about buying a house which has serious limitations as to what can be done with it because of governmental limitations or because governmental regulations will require too great of an expense in preparing the property for rental or sale.

8. Some successful investors in single-family houses recommend that it takes several houses at a time to really make the activity profitable. It is also suggested that the investor deal mainly with relatively low-priced houses where the market is wider and maintenance requirements are not as exacting or as costly.

Limitations

Perhaps the most serious limitation to this form of investment is that the loss of the tenant in a house means a 100 per cent vacancy rate—and a 100 per cent decrease in income from the property. Expenses on the house continue—property taxes, insurance, mortgage charges, and maintenance. Maintenance can become an expensive factor, since an unoccupied house can decline quickly as well as be attractive for vandalism.

Less serious limitations, but nevertheless ones the investor should consider before embarking upon single-family house investments, are the possibilities of insufficient numbers of suitable houses available for investment at the right price, and of prohibitive financing costs. The latter situation can easily prevail in periods of tight money. As for the scarcity of suitable houses, while the supply of older houses is generally plentiful, careful selection must be made for investment purposes. Not every older deteriorated house is a potential investment—at least not a potentially profitable investment.

Favorable Factors

Several factors lend support to the investor in single-family houses. In some areas there may be a strong demand for larger older houses because of the extra space they provide. Even smaller older houses may be in demand because of their locations close to town or because of their generally lower property taxes or favorable locations near schools and parks.

It is possible that small houses or cottages at lake or seashore resort locations can be attractive investments. These houses can usually command high in-season rentals, which can cover the property taxes and other costs as well as maintenance for the slack seasons and still show a good return to the investor.

The acquisition of old houses in historical areas can be a profitable venture for the prudent and well-informed investor. The investor should leave such houses "as is" and sell them for a purchaser–owner to restore. The restoration opportunity is one, if not the primary, attraction of these old houses in many designated historical areas. Restoration must follow guidelines established by local historical commissions in many locations.

Another factor supporting the investor in single-family houses is inflation and the rise in money and construction costs. Appreciation on a good older house in a good area can be as much as $1,000 to $2,000 or more per year. Where an adjoining extra lot may also be acquired with the house, the lot may be held as an investment, or construction of a house on it may be feasible. Generally, however, the construction of a single-family house for rental or sale is not feasible unless the investor is also a builder and can do the work himself with his own labor crews as well as buy materials at builder's prices.

There are profit making opportunities in single-family houses for the prudent investor, and this form of investment can be attractive, particularly to the small investor with limited capital. The risks can be substantial, but for the investor who knows the field, these risks can be reduced through sound judgment.

Further Readings and References

American Institute of Real Estate Appraisers. *Case Studies in Apartment House Valuation*. Second Edition. Chicago: American Institute of Real Estate Appraisers of the National Association of Real Estate Boards, 1969.

Clark, Louis M. "The Real Estate Condominium: Its Tax Problems and Implications," *The Appraisal Journal*, October, 1967, 475–492.

Clurman, David, and Edna L. Hebard. *Condominiums and Cooperatives*. New York: Wiley–Interscience, 1970.

"Do Single Family Homes Pay Their Way?," *Urban Land*, Vol. 27, No. 8, September, 1968. Washington, D. C.: Urban Land Institute, 1968.

Glenn, James D., Jr. "Apartment House Investments," *Developing, Selling and Syndicating Real Estate Investment Property*. Los Angeles: California Real Estate Association, 1964.

Norcross, Carl, and John Hyson. "Apartment Communities—The Next Big

Market." *U. L. I. Technical Bulletin No. 61.* Washington, D. C.: Urban Land Institute, 1968.

Schraub, Edgar D. *How to Invest in Residential Property.* Englewood Cliffs, N. J.: Prentice-Hall, Inc., 1968.

Wary, Albert M. (ed.). *Apartment Houses.* Los Angeles: California Real Estate Association, 1968.

14

Mobile Home Parks

The soundly conceived and properly developed modern mobile home park offers an excellent investment opportunity in many areas of the country. The mobile home industry has experienced substantial growth, and the product competes successfully with conventional housing in many locations, particularly housing in the lower price range. Demand for the mobile home comes from a variety of persons: young married couples, retired couples, military personnel, construction workers, students, economy-minded couples, second-home vacationers, seasonal employees in resort areas, building contractors who need immediate on-site housing, developers of new industries needing instant housing, and even some doctors, lawyers, and millionaires.

MOBILE HOME ATTRACTIONS

The mobile home can offer several advantages over the conventional house, depending upon the owner's objectives and personal situation.

274

Among the factors attracting people to mobile homes are the following:

1. Reasonable total monthly housing costs may be lower than rent or a mortgage payment and other costs on a conventional house with comparable accommodations.

2. Frequently, the initial costs (down payment plus closing costs) are lower on a mobile home than on comparable conventional housing.

3. Economy is not always a deciding factor in the purchase of a mobile home. Increased sizes of units and luxury interior accommodations are attractive features for many buyers.

4. There has been a tremendous improvement in layout and architectural standards of mobile home parks. The mobile home unit itself has undergone and continues to undergo design changes.

5. In most areas where the mobile home is very popular, there is an active resale market for the units.

6. The mobile home may be purchased completely furnished, including kitchen appliances, at a cost which may be lower than unfurnished conventional housing. In areas where the cost of conventional housing has increased substantially, the mobile home is an attractive buy for many families. Mobile home housing has tended to dominate the market in some areas where builders have found it impossible to build lower-priced housing at a profit.

7. In areas where apartments are in short supply, the mobile home is providing an increasing share of the housing. Also, where apartment rentals are high, the mobile home with its lower costs may attract persons unwilling or unable to pay the rents in luxury apartments.

8. A shortage of real estate mortgage funds in an area can seriously reduce the ability of conventional home buyers to acquire a home. The mobile home, on the other hand, is not totally dependent upon real estate mortgage money, but rather can be financed through dealers or through commercial bank consumer loans.

9. The mobile home loan may be attractive to lenders. These loans usually carry higher interest rates and payments and are of shorter term than are conventional real estate mortgages. Typically, there is less paperwork and servicing involved in these loans.

10. Buyers also find the mobile home attractive because of its mobility, its compactness, and the reduced maintenance needed as contrasted with conventional housing.

THE MARKET

The general market for the mobile home is growing and park development has generally not kept pace with the production of units. Nevertheless, the market must be carefully analyzed by the investor and a number of factors kept in mind in making an investment decision. Some of these factors are as follows:

1. A park is not a small undertaking, either in terms of investment capital outlay or of planning and development. The trend is toward large (100 to 500 to 1,000 or more spaces) and elaborate parks, each of which can be a community in itself.

2. A park must be planned for long-term (15–25 years) use and expansion without excessive obsolescence occurring. Provision must be made for the future; flexibility is essential. Availability of land for expansion is highly desirable.

3. Abundant expert advice is available for mobile home park planning and development; it should be used. The field is well covered by its trade association, private studios, publications, and real estate counselors.

4. Complete packaged parks are offered through franchise operations. Included in such license arrangements are complete services on land selection, development, financings, and marketing as well as guidance in the actual operations of the park—accounting, personnel training, rules for park operation, and so on.

5. General guidelines and rules-of-thumb are available in the development and operation of mobile home parks. However, for each potential park the facts must be gathered and analyzed in light of the market in that particular locality. Among factors to be determined in a given area are the following: size of park; number of spaces per acre; space rentals; recreational facilities; ratio of cost of land to total development cost; estimated annual return on investment; and the investment per mobile home space, excluding land and buildings.

6. The value of the land in a mobile home park space is usually higher than the value of the improvements, and there is a possibility of residual value in the improvements after the park has ceased operation. A park may later be redeveloped for another use, such as a shopping center or a conventional residential subdivision. In fact, an investor may acquire land in advance of the growth pattern of the area and lease or develop it and operate it as a mobile home park until the site is ready for another and more profitable use, such as commercial usage.

7. The investor should not overlook the fact that the mobile home park may be an excellent use for land located between two areas of different land uses, such as land between residential and commercial neighborhoods. Such land often does not develop rapidly, and the mobile home park may be a desirable buffer-type utilization.

8. The mobile home is not looked upon with favor in all communities or by all planning and zoning bodies. Further, property taxation of the mobile home unit is a controversial and unsettled matter in some locations. The developer and investor must thoroughly investigate these factors as a part of his market study.

ECONOMICS OF DEVELOPMENT

The development of a mobile home park can be a profitable undertaking. An excellent illustration of the potential in such development was presented by an authority on the subject at a symposium on the mobile home industry who reported as follows:

Our studies show us that, excluding the value of appreciation of property, investors in some MHP's have enjoyed a return on equity invested of about 25% on the average. If we include in this equation the added value of appreciation of land this return rises to about 45%. In both instances it is assumed that depreciation is permitted on a 15 year schedule. In order to realize this kind of return the average charge for a space which costs $2,500 to buy and develop is a rental equivalent of about $45 per month.

In order to illustrate how this type of return evolves let us look at the following proposal for a property to be developed in Texas. The original proposition called for the use of 32 acres at a cost of approximately $96,000. It was proposed that 270 spaces would be provided or about 8 spaces per acre. This represents a generous land allocation per unit. The cost of preparing each space is approximately $1,700 for a total cost of $572,000 (including the price of the land). (Also included in the cost of space development was an aggregate charge of about $16,000 to provide for working capital during the period of development.) Let us assume that mortgage financing could be obtained at 8% interest for 75% of the cost and that the remaining 25% would necessarily reflect equity. (As you will see, these are very conservative assumptions.) This results in a mortgage of about $430,000 and an investment of $150,000. Annual operating costs were estimated at about $38,000 per year; interest expense ($34,000) and depreciation ($23,000) brought total annual expenses up to approximately $95,000. At a rental of $37.50 per lot per month and assuming a 5% vacancy, total revenues per year were slightly more than $115,000. Thus pretax income came down to about $20,000 with as much again available in cash flow from depreciation. In this particular instance the pretax earnings represent a return of well over 15% on the $150,000 investment. But actually the property valuation exceeded $690,000. The 75% mortgage obtainable on this would have been approximately $515,000 or about 90% of the total cost of the developed property. Approximately a $50,000 investment would have been required on this basis and after slightly larger interest charges pretax income would have been about $13,000 which would represent a return of about 25% before taxes. As I mentioned, allowable depreciation in both cases represented a tax shelter for another $23,000 worth of cash flow. Obviously this is a desirable investment. Now if one cares to look into future years we must include the affect of appreciating property values. As I said on a $2,000 cost site this may add up to $500 in a 5 year period which substantially adds to the park owner's equity without accruing commensurate taxes since it would be subject to a capital gains tax when realized. And of course we all know the value of depreciation.[1]

Another authority on the subject, Mr. Paul D. Shlensky of Mobile Home Management Corporation, Northbrook, Illinois, reports on the economics of a mobile home park development in an issue of *Real Estate Investment Ideas*. The illustration below, from Mr. Shlensky's article, shows the profitability of a properly located, planned, developed, and managed park:

HOW THE DOLLARS AND CENTS OF A 300-SPACE MOBILE HOME PARK WORK OUT

[The following cost, cash flow, and tax-shelter analysis given by Mr. Shlensky assumes a 50-acre park costing $3,000 per acre, containing 6 spaces per acre, and costing $2,500 per space to develop.]

How Your Investment and Financing Requirements Shape Up: Mr. Shlensky says that the average rental price per space has been about $40 a month. With increasing interest rates and construction costs, the range today runs between $40 and $60 per month per space. The $60 figure used by Mr. Shlensky, as well as the other figures used in his calculations, are for a "deluxe" park with "country club" services and atmosphere.

Original Cost		$150,000
Development Costs Per Acre:		
Engineering and design	$ 200	
Grading and extension of off-site utilities	200	
Paving streets, curbs, walks, sites, drives and gutters	500	
Water supply (municipal), fire hydrants	200	
Sanitary sewers (municipal)	160	
Electrical, telephone, street lighting, underground services	250	

[1] Leslie Jones, Mobile Home Manufacturers Association, "The Mobile Home Industry," a special report of the Symposium sponsored by Kohlmeyer & Co., Investment Securities, New York, August, 1969, pp. 10–11.

Recreational facilities, administration and laundry buildings	300
Landscaping	100
Interim construction finance costs	250
Fences	50
Storage facilities	200
Miscellaneous	90
Total	$2,500

Total Development Cost for Park (300 spaces)	750,000
Total Investment in Property	$900,000
Less Equity Requirement	225,000
Development Loan Guarantee Commitment	$675,000

How You Get a Cash Flow of 16% of Your Investment After All Expenses and Debt Service But Before Depreciation Deductions: The following cash flow analysis assumes a rental of $60 per month per space, a 5% vacancy factor and an annual operating cost coming to 40% of effective gross income.

Gross Annual Income (100% of rental of 300 spaces at $60 per month per space)	$216,000 ($18,000/month)
5% Vacancy Factor	− 10,800
Effective Annual Gross Income	$205,200
Annual Operating Costs (40% of effective gross income)	− 82,000
Cash Flow Before Debt Service	$123,200
Debt Service (loan of $675,000— 75% loan) @ 10% interest for 15-year term (12.90% constant)	− 87,075
Cash Flow (after debt service and expenses but before depreciation deductions)	$ 36,125

How You Come Out with Tax-Free Income Plus Additional Tax Shelter to Boot: The following analysis assumes a 15-year useful life of improvements and depreciation at one and one-half times straight line:

Improvement Costs	$750,000	
Depreciation Deduction		$75,000
Reduction of principal amount of loan in one year	20,925	
Cash flow after debt service	36,125	
Tax-free Income		57,050
Additional Tax Shelter		$17,950

Of course, during your early years of operation, your tax shelter will be very high and, as the years go on, the tax shelter will become smaller and smaller.

How Your Depreciation Deductions Break Down: Mr. Shlensky says that the 15-year-life 150% declining balance method of depreciation is, at present, the normal method of depreciation for mobile home parks. Where the park developer feels that he can get greater depreciation benefits by itemizing his deductions, the following schedule of improvements with estimated useful life may be employed:

	Years
Landscaping	5
Grading	15
Service roads, etc.	7
Underground utilities	8
Meter boxes	2
Park equipment	5
Swimming pool	15
Recreational equipment	3
Laundry equipment	4
Fences	7
Recreation building	15
Utility building	15
Furniture in recreation building	5
Office equipment	10
Neon sign	8
Plumbing and heating in buildings	10
Storage cabinets	5
Engineering and design	15
Concrete work	10

Source: Paul D. Shlensky, "How the Dollars and Cents of a 300-Space Mobile Home Park Work Out," *Real Estate Investment Ideas*, October 28, 1969, pp. 2–4. Reprinted with permission of the publisher, Institute for Business Planning, Inc., 2 West Thirteenth Street, New York, New York 10011.

PROPOSAL FOR DEVELOPMENT
OF A MOBILE HOME PARK

The following proposal is from a Realty Company offering to develop mobile home parks in the form of joint ventures and syndications. The Company has carefully analyzed the local market and determined there is a definite need for first-class parks.

Plans call for complete recreational facilities, including swimming pools, badminton courts, large recreation halls with full fireplace and kitchen, billiard rooms and game tables. Wide, spacious streets, curbs and gutters, good off-street parking, and large lots are proposed. There will be playgrounds and scenic landscaping.

In developing mobile home parks, a prime consideration is location— not only for natural beauty, favorable topography, and availability of utilities—but for easy accessibility to schools, churches, shopping, etc. Land for parks in the local area will range from $2,500 to $10,000 per acre. Monthly rental per space is generally in direct ratio to land cost. Current rentals range from $40 per month to as much as $100 for prime locations with good waiting lists. Additional income to park managers and developers is also derived from: coin-operated equipment, including washers and dryers; sales of utilities (electricity and gas); club facilities; and sale of mobile homes and related equipment, such as awnings, skirts, and carports.

A cost analysis of a typical 100-space mobile home park development is presented below. Also shown is an income-and-expense analysis of a 100-space park at varying acreage costs and rental rates. The data is based upon local sources, and represents conservative results from the experience of the Realty Company.

DEVELOPMENT COST ANALYSIS OF A TYPICAL MOBILE HOME PARK

	100-Space Park	Cost per Space	Percentage of Total
RECREATIONAL			
Clubhouse, Office, Laundry	$ 32,000	$ 320	16%
Swimming Pool, Playground	8,000	80	4
	$ 40,000	$ 400	20%

GENERAL

Engineering, Grading, Utilities	$ 10,000	$ 100	5%
Temporary Utilities & Facilities	2,000	20	1
Supervision & Planning	8,000	80	4
Water Meter	1,000	10	½
Permits, Insurance, Bond	2,000	20	1
Overhead & Contractors Profit	12,000	120	6
Indirect Costs	11,000	110	5½
	$ 46,000	$ 460	23%

INDIVIDUAL SPACES

Land Preparation	$ 4,000	$ 40	2%
Landscaping, Sprinklers	6,000	60	3
Signs, Fence	8,000	80	4
Electrical, incl. Street Lights & Phone Conn.	30,000	300	15
Plumbing, Sewer Lines	36,000	360	18
Material for Patio Blocks, Street, Walks	30,000	300	15
	$114,000	$1,140	57%
	$200,000	$2,000	100%

INCOME–EXPENSE ANALYSIS OF 100-SPACE PARK

Land Cost per Acre	$ 2,500	$ 5,000	$ 7,500	$ 10,000
Total Cost—10 Acres	25,000	50,000	75,000	100,000
Plus: Construction Cost	200,000	200,000	200,000	200,000
TOTAL	$225,000	$250,000	$275,000	$300,000
Less: 70% Loan	157,500	175,000	192,500	210,000
INVESTMENT	$ 67,500	$ 75,000	$ 82,500	$ 90,000
Schedule—Income per Space	$ 40	$ 50	$ 60	$ 70
Schedule—Income per Month	4,000	5,000	6,000	7,000
Schedule—Income per Year	48,000	60,000	72,000	84,000
Less: 3% Vacancy Allowance	1,440	1,800	2,160	2,520
Stabilized Gross Income (84%)	$ 46,560	$ 58,200	$ 69,840	$ 81,480
Plus: Other Income				
Utilities Sales (12%)	6,652	8,314	9,977	11,640
Vending Machine & Laundry (4%)	2,217	2,772	3,326	3,880
Gross Operating Income (100%)	$ 55,429	$ 69,286	$ 83,143	$ 97,000
Less: Operating Expenses				
Salaries (5%)	3,464			
Maintenance & Repairs (5%)	3,464			
Supplies (1%)	693			
Advertising (2%)	1,386			
Office & Miscellaneous (1%)	693			
Insurance (1%)	693			

Taxes	(6%)		4,157		
Utilities	(9%)		6,236		
Replacement Reserve	(5%)		3,464		
TOTAL	(35%)	$ 19,400	$ 24,250	$ 29,100	$ 33,950
Net Operating Income		36,029	45,036	54,043	63,050
Capitalization Rate		16.0%	18.0%	19.7%	21.0%
Less: Debt Service (8½%, 15 years)		18,617	20,680	22,754	24,822
CASH FLOW		$ 17,412	$ 24,356	$ 31,289	$ 38,228
Yield on Investment		25.8%	32.5%	37.9%	42.5%
Break-even Occupancy (50% expenses)		65.2%	57.9%	53.1%	49.6%

Further Readings and References

Borstein, Alan S. "The Boom in Mobile Home Parks," *Journal of Property Management*, May–June, 1970, 120–124.

Flickinger, Lowell D. "Trends in the Mobile Home Park Industry," *The Appraisal Journal*, July, 1965, 344–346.

Free, John E. "Creative Management, Market Analysis Save Obsolescent Trailer Park," *Journal of Property Management*, November–December, 1969, 278–279.

Gade, George. "Economics of Operating a Mobile Home Park," *The Appraisal Journal*, July, 1965, 351–356.

Jacobson, Charles E. "The Development of a Mobile Home Park," *The Appraisal Journal*, July, 1965, 347–350.

Randall, William J. "Mobile Home Subdivisions," *The Appraisal Journal*, July, 1967, 360–373.

"Trailers and Mobile Homes in Use Have Doubled in the Past 10 Years," *The Real Estate Analyst, Housing Bulletin*, March 9, 1970, 89–96. St. Louis: Roy Wenzlick Research Corp., 1970.

1	Years:	Original	1	2	3	4
2	Land (at 12.5% Growth Rate)	$ 50,000	$ 56,250	$ 63,281	$ 71,191	$ 80,090
3	Improvements (@ 15-year S/L depr.)	200,000	188,000	176,000	164,000	152,000
4	*Property Value*	250,000	244,250	239,281	235,191	232,090
5	Less: Loan Balance	175,000	168,964	162,394	155,244	147,461
6	*Equity*	75,000	75,286	76,887	79,947	84,629
7	Average Rental per Space	50.00				
8	Gross Operating Income	69,286	70,672	72,085	73,527	
9	Less: Expenses (35%)	24,250	24,735	25,230	25,734	
10	*Net Operating Income*	45,036	45,937	46,856	47,793	
11	Capitalization Rate	18.4%	19.2%	19.9%	20.6%	
12	Net Operating Income	45,036	45,937	46,856	47,793	
13	Less: Interest	14,643	14,110	13,529	12,897	
14	Less: Depreciation	12,000	12,000	12,000	12,000	
15	*Net Taxable Income*	18,393	19,827	21,327	22,896	
16	Income Tax (50%)	9,197	9,914	10,664	11,448	
17	Net Operating Income	45,036	45,937	46,856	47,793	
18	Less: Debt Service	20,680	20,680	20,680	20,680	
19	*Cash Flow*	24,356	25,257	26,176	27,113	
20	Less: Income Tax	9,197	9,914	10,664	11,448	
21	Net After-tax Income	15,159	15,343	15,512	15,665	
22	Cash Flow Yield on Investment	32.5%	33.7%	34.9%	36.2%	
23	Net After-tax Yield on Investment	20.2%				

15-YEAR PROJECTION FOR A MOBILE HOME PARK

5	6	7	8	9	10	11
$ 90,102	$101,364	$114,035	$128,289	$144,325	$162,366	$182,662
140,000	128,000	116,000	104,000	92,000	80,000	68,000
230,102	229,364	230,035	232,289	236,325	242,366	250,662
138,991	129,772	119,738	108,817	96,931	83,994	69,914
91,111	99,592	110,297	123,472	139,394	158,372	180,748

Net Operating Income

5	6	7	8	9	10	11
54.12					59.75	
74,997	76,497	78,027	79,588	81,180	82,803	84,459
26,249	26,774	27,309	27,856	28,413	28,981	29,561
48,748	49,723	50,718	51,732	52,767	53,822	54,898
21.2%	21.7%	22.0%	22.3%	22.3%	22.2%	21.9%

Net Taxable Income

5	6	7	8	9	10	11
48,748	49,723	50,718	51,732	52,767	53,822	54,898
12,209	11,461	10,646	9,759	8,793	7,743	6,599
12,000	12,000	12,000	12,000	12,000	12,000	12,000
24,539	26,262	28,072	29,973	31,974	34,079	36,299
12,269	13,131	14,036	14,987	15,987	17,040	18,150

Cash Flow & Net After-tax Income

5	6	7	8	9	10	11
48,748	49,723	50,718	51,732	52,767	53,822	54,898
20,680	20,680	20,680	20,680	20,680	20,680	20,680
28,068	29,043	30,038	31,052	32,087	33,142	34,218
12,269	13,131	14,036	14,987	15,987	17,040	18,150
15,799	15,912	16,002	16,065	16,100	16,102	16,068
37.4%	38.7%	40.1%	41.4%	42.8%	44.2%	45.6%
21.1%					21.5%	

Notes:

Line 2—Based upon a population growth rate of over 5% per year for the area. Also, the 12½% growth rate projection is a typical projection based upon the fact that real estate values generally increase at the rate of about four times population growth in more populous areas.

Lines 3, 14—Depreciation is straight-line method over 15 years with 10% salvage remaining.

Lines 7, 8—Increase of 2% per year to offset inflation.

Line 11—Capitalization rate is net operating income expressed as a percentage of property value.

Line 16—Assumes 50% average income tax bracket of owner.

15-YEAR PROJECTION FOR A MOBILE HOME PARK—(Continued)

1	Years:	12	13	14	15
2	Land (at 12.5% Growth Rate)	$205,495	$231,181	$260,079	$292,589
3	Improvements				
	(@ 15-year S/L depr.)	56,000	44,000	32,000	20,000
4	*Property Value*	261,495	275,181	292,079	312,589
5	Less: Loan Balance	54,589	37,910	19,756	0
6	*Equity*	206,906	237,271	272,323	312,589
7	Average Rental per Space				65.97
8	Gross Operating Income	86,148	87,871	89,629	91,421
9	Less: Expenses (35%)	30,152	30,775	31,370	31,997
10	*Net Operating Income*	55,996	57,116	58,259	59,424
11	Capitalization Rate	21.4%	20.8%	19.9%	19.0%
12	Net Operating Income	55,996	57,116	58,259	59,424
13	Less: Interest	5,355	4,000	2,526	921
14	Less: Depreciation	12,000	12,000	12,000	12,000
15	*Net Taxable Income*	38,641	41,116	44,003	46,503
16	Income Tax (50%)	19,321	20,558	22,002	23,252
17	Net Operating Income	55,996	57,116	58,259	59,424
18	Less: Debt Service	20,680	20,680	20,680	20,680
19	*Cash Flow*	25,316	36,436	37,579	38,744
20	Less: Income Tax	19,321	20,558	22,002	23,252
21	Net After-tax Income	15,995	15,878	15,577	15,492
22	Cash Flow Yield on Investment	47.1%	48.9%	50.1%	51.7%
23	Net After-tax Yield on Investment				20.7%

Notes:

Line 2—Based upon a population growth rate of over 5% per year for the area. Also, the 12½% growth rate projection is a typical projection based upon the fact that real estate values generally increase at the rate of about four times population growth in more populous areas.

Lines 3, 14—Depreciation is straight-line method over 15 years with 10% salvage remaining.

Lines 7, 8—Increase of 2% per year to offset inflation.

Line 11—Capitalization rate is net operating income expressed as a percentage of property value.

Line 16—Assumes 50% average income tax bracket of owner.

EFFECT OF RAPID-DEPRECIATION METHOD AND PROPOSED SALE IN 5 YEARS

Basis for Depreciation:

	Allocation	Unit Value	Total	Economic Life	Method
Land	20%	$ 500	$ 50,000	—	—
Improvements	75	1,900	190,000	15 years	200%
Equipment	5	100	10,000	5 years	S/L
	100%	$2,500	$250,000		

Year	200%	S/L	Total	Straight-line
1	$25,327	$ 2,000	$ 27,327	$12,000
2	21,964	2,000	23,964	12,000
3	19,019	2,000	21,019	12,000
4	16,492	2,000	18,492	12,000
5	14,307	2,000	16,492	12,000
	$97,109	$10,000	$107,109	$60,000

Years	1	2	3	4	5
Net Operating Income	$45,036	$45,937	$46,856	$47,793	$48,748
Less: Interest	14,643	14,110	13,529	12,897	12,209
Less: Depreciation	27,327	23,964	21,019	18,492	16,492
Net Taxable Income	$ 3,066	$ 7,863	$12,308	$16,404	$20,047
Income Tax (50%)	1,533	3,932	6,154	8,202	10,024
Net After-tax Income (Cash Flow less Income Tax)	22,823	21,325	20,022	18,911	18,044

Total 5-year Tax-free Income = $101,125

This projection is for an owner in a 50% tax bracket, using rapid depreciation over a 5-year period. Sales price in the early life of a mobile home park may range from 5 to 8 times gross income, and later on from $1,500 to $4,000 per space.

Original Cost	$250,000
Less: Depreciation Taken	107,109
Adjusted Cost Basis (Book Value)	$142,891
Excess Depreciation over S/L	82,891
% Recapture = 100 — (60 — 20)	60%
Amount Subject to Recapture	49,735
Sale Price (6 × Gross Income)	$449,982
6 × $74,997	142,891
Less: Adjusted Cost Basis	
Less: Cost of Sale, 6%	27,000
Recognized Gain	$280,091
Less: 25% Capital Gains Tax	70,023
Less: Depreciation Recapture, 50%	24,868
NET GAIN ON SALE	$185,200
Plus: 5 Years Tax-free Income	101,125
Total Net Benefits	$286,325
or Investment of $75,000 Returned Plus	281.77%

Index

Index

E

D

F

Y

Yield
  analysis and projection, 125–32
  appreciation, 10

Yield (*cont.*)
  high, 15
  income tax saving, 10
  mortgage amortization, 10
  sources, 9–10
  traditional, 9